Pg 130 NIH
140 State of the Art
174 Inc - Cost Pricing
177 Multistage Pricing
184 Total Dist Cost Concept

MARKETING
FOR MANAGERS

FREDERICK E. WEBSTER, Jr.

Professor of Business Administration
The Amos Tuck School of Business Administration
Dartmouth College

Marketing for Managers

HARPER & ROW, PUBLISHERS
New York   Evanston   San Francisco   London

Sponsoring Editor: John Greenman
Project Editor: Carol E. W. Edwards
Designer: June Negrycz
Production Supervisor: Stefania J. Taflinska

MARKETING FOR MANAGERS

Library of Congress Cataloging in Publication Data

Webster, Frederick E
    Marketing for managers.

    Bibliography: p.
    1. Marketing management.   2. Marketing.   I. Title.
HF5415.13.W37   658.8   74–11180
ISBN 0–06–046971–4

For
Lynn, Mark, and Lisa

CONTENTS

PREFACE

The idea for this book grew from my experiences teaching and working with practicing managers who wished to know more about marketing. I had tried to use a variety of the available marketing textbooks to fill this need, but none had been entirely satisfactory. From the manager's viewpoint, the typical marketing text is often too descriptive and relies too heavily on consumer marketing practice. It can lack focus on the real issues of managerial strategic planning and tend to be overly theoretical. Here, I have tried to stress ideas and problems of interest and usefulness for **practicing** marketing managers, in a variety of industrial and multinational contexts.

This book has been written for four somewhat different audiences with similar interests: experienced managers participating in management development programs; young managers enrolled in marketing courses in evening or extension courses at universities; students in full-time university programs enrolled in marketing courses with a strategic planning emphasis; and the practicing businessman wishing to become familiar with current marketing management issues and practice.

We academicians often write books primarily for one another. Footnotes are used extensively, not only to show that we are *au courant*, but also to give credit to our colleagues where credit is due. Therefore, I must now apologize to several colleagues whose ideas have been used here for the fact that I have tried to minimize the number of footnotes and thus to reduce the clutter that often occurs. Footnotes were used only when the alternative was copyright infringement or plagiarism.

Marketing is an interesting and important activity, not just for marketing managers, but for all managers in both business and non-business organizations. It also has tremendous importance from a societal standpoint. This book is intended for **all** managers interested in marketing. Many of the ideas presented here have been shared with reasonably enthusiastic listeners not only in the traditional management education forums of North America and Western Europe, but with managers in the Soviet Union and other Socialist countries, in developing African nations, and with managers from such diverse institutions as hospitals, the Boy Scouts, and the Burmese Air Force. A major cause of my interest in demystifying the presentation of marketing ideas has been the lessons that I have learned from trying to communicate with managers from very diverse backgrounds.

The book was written while I was serving as Faculty Member at Centre d'Etudes Industrielles in Geneva, Switzerland, an excellent and and truly international institute devoted to the single purpose of continuing management education. I wish to publicly thank the Director, Bohdan Hawrylyshyn, and his able Associate Director, Jeremiah J. O'Connell, not only for supporting my writing activities (most chapters first appeared as CEI lectures), but also for making possible the contact with several hundred managers from many different parts of the world who contributed to, and helped to refine, the ideas presented here.

I wish to express a special note of thanks to my very able and charming secretary, Bathilda Vogel, who helped to make my stay in Switzerland both productive and enjoyable.

Frederick E. Webster, Jr.

MARKETING MANAGEMENT AND CORPORATE STRATEGY

Marketing is the function by which the firm responds to changes in its environment. This is a definition of marketing quite different from that found in most marketing textbooks, where marketing is defined as all activities involved in managing the flow of goods from producer to consumer. Another definition is also found frequently: all activities involved in the determination and satisfaction of customer needs at a profit.

Our definition of marketing is intended specifically to focus attention on the relationship between marketing and other parts of the business, especially as these come together in the development of corporate strategy. The analysis will begin by looking at the relationship between the business firm and its environment in a framework that leads to an understanding of the role of corporate strategy. Next we will consider the several components of the business firm as these determine its ability to respond to its environment. In this way we can develop a good understanding not only of the relationship of marketing to the rest of the organization but also of the determinants of effectiveness in the marketing management function itself.

THE FIRM AS A SYSTEM OF LOGISTICS AND MANAGEMENT

The business firm is a unique creation designed to deliver goods and services determined to have value in the marketplace. To accomplish this purpose, the firm must organize a collection of inputs (including raw materials, personnel, financing, plant, and equipment), develop a production process to turn these inputs into products and services, distribute these outputs to the marketplace, and conduct the transactions with buyers necessary to recover expenditures and investment, hopefully creating some surplus value ("profit"). *Management* can be defined as those activities involved in the planning, organizing, and controlling of the combination of inputs to produce the desired mix of outputs.

A very useful view of the firm as an organized system of business action has been proposed by H. Igor Ansoff.[1] According to this view, the firm is a goal-seeking, purposive organization that achieves its goals through two processes—the logistic process and the management process. The *logistic* process involves transfering and converting resources (labor, materials, capital, and information) obtained from the environment into products and services offered back to the market. The logistic process is designed and guided (that is, planned, organized, implemented, and controlled) by the *management* process, which handles information. The inputs to the management system are perceived needs for modification of the logistics process, and the outputs from the management process are action instructions to redirect or change the logistics process. This is diagramed in Figure 1-1.

Management as a process involves three distinct types of action and decision areas—strategic, administrative, and operating decisions. *Strategic* decisions establish the relationship between the firm and its environment, and are concerned primarily with developing and maintaining a viable mix of goods and services to be offered in the marketplace (which involves decisions about raw materials, production process, product design, distribution, etc., not just "product policy" decisions, narrowly defined). *Administrative* decisions establish the shape and structure of the firm, including not only formal organization structure but also communication, status, evaluation, and reward

See above

---

[1] H. Igor Ansoff, "Toward a Strategic Theory of the Firm," in H. Igor Ansoff, ed., *Business Strategy* (Harmondsworth, Middlesex, England: Penguin Books, 1971), pp. 11–40.

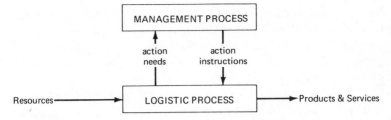

FIGURE 1-1
Relationship between logistic process and management process.

Source: From H. Igor Ansoff, "Toward a Strategic Theory of the Firm," in H. I. Ansoff, ed., Business Strategy (Harmondsworth, Middlesex, England: Penguin Books, 1971), p. 14.

systems. Finally, *operating* decisions are concerned with selecting the "operating levels" of the firm—that is, the specific values of each of the input variables.

The concept of value

Economic value is created in the operation of a market mechanism bringing together a willing and informed buyer and a willing seller. In the process of exchange both give up something and both gain something in return; for both there is an individual gain measured by the difference between the value of the thing given up and the value of the thing received. This surplus value is called *profit*. Profit is at once both the stimulus to economic activity and the reward. It is also the fuel that feeds the economic process in that surplus value must be created if there is to be growth. The individual producer must have profit to reinvest in capital equipment, plant, research and development, and other uses of funds necessary to develop inputs for future production. For the buyer the difference between the value of the purchased product or service and the value of the thing given up (usually money earned in exchange for work) is measured by a gain in individual satisfaction, or "utility" in the economist's vocabulary. Thus, the free-market system works to create consumer satisfaction by offering profit opportunities to those who are willing to take the risks required to invest in the means of production. Profit is the reward for delivering customer satisfaction.

Derived demand

Except for retailing, there are relatively few firms actually involved in serving consumer markets compared with the large number serving so-called industrial markets—manufacturers, nonprofit institutions, transportation companies, banks, distributing companies, and so on. Industrial markets consist of organizations that produce goods and services, as opposed to individual consumers. Industrial markets operate just like consumer markets, with the exchange process creating value measured in terms of profit for the seller and satisfaction for the buyer. But industrial markets have the important distinction that the ultimate demand for the industrial customer's products and services is a determinant of the demand for the seller's goods and services. In other words, all industrial-market demand is ultimately derived from consumer demand. It therefore follows that the ultimate criterion of industrial marketing effectiveness is the extent to which the seller's goods and services help the industrial customer produce its goods and services. If the industrial customer is profit-motivated, then the purchased goods and services should help him earn a profit. If the customer is not profit-oriented, the criterion for marketing effectiveness is probably simply the mirror image of profitability—the extent to which the seller helps the customer meet a cost or budget constraint.

There may very well be a long chain of transactions between the industrial marketer and the ultimate consumer market, say from iron ore producer to steel maker to automobile manufacturer to automobile dealer to consumer. Each transaction along the way involves the bringing together of a willing buyer and a willing seller, the exchange of things valued and the creation of surplus value, and the satisfaction of a customer.

Relationship to the environment

The business firm does not exist independent of the environment but in interdependence with political, economic, social, legal, technological, and cultural forces that define the resources, opportunities, and threats available to and facing the firm. Obviously, all of the input factors to the production process must come from the external environment. The marketplace also exists in the external environment, where a variety of factors beyond the control of the firm are shaping the nature of customer demand. As these forces continue to develop and change, they determine new requirements for the effectiveness of the firm. The three main forces operating to create the need for new responses from the firm are (1) changing consumer preferences and tastes, (2) developing technology, and (3) competition.

Growth and obsolescence

Two forces motivate the healthy firm to grow: (1) the need to create new opportunities for owners and employees in the form of new earnings, higher returns on investment, enhanced and more rewarding responsibilities, and the challenge of new problems; (2) the need to adjust to changing market conditions (customer preferences, new competition, and new technology). Because the environment is changing, the healthy firm has no choice but to continue to change with it or face the inevitable consequences of obsolescence—lower profitability, sales, and return on investment; higher operating costs; the need to remove personnel from the payroll; and eventually bankruptcy or liquidation. Preservation of the status quo is simply not a feasible objective for the firm. It must change if it is to survive, and it must grow if it is to meet the expectations of owners and employees, and their needs for personal growth and advancement.

So the question is not whether to change but how to change. Change can be planned or unplanned. It can be guided by some shared vision of common purpose by those who are responsible for the life of the firm, or it can be an essentially random set of responses to environmental changes as they occur. Change can occur in anticipation of changes in the environment based on the best possible view of the future, or it can occur after the environment has changed. Some firms are much better than others in adjusting to changes in the environment. A principal determinant of the quality of the firm's response is the extent to which it has a well-developed *strategy*, which can be defined as a pattern of planned responses to changes in the environment and in anticipation of those changes.

CORPORATE STRATEGY

A strategy is "a pattern of purposes and policies which are unique to the firm."[2] More formally, a strategy is a planned course of action in pursuit of clearly stated objectives in the face of limited resources, a changing environment, and intelligent competition. This more formal definition is broad enough to include strategy in poker, business, or war. Going back to Ansoff's view of the firm, strategic decisions establish the relationship between the firm and its environment, especially with respect to the goods and services to be offered to the market. Ansoff stresses the importance of strategic decisions in these words:

In many ways strategic decisions are the basic determinants of the success of the firm for, unless the firm's products are addressed to market areas in which demand exists and in which the competitive climate is favorable, even the very best organizational form, or the most brilliant control of operations, will fail to produce profit.[3]

[2] Kenneth R. Andrews, "New Horizons in Corporate Strategy," *McKinsey Quarterly* (Winter 1971): 34–43.
[3] Ansoff, op. cit., p. 15.

Someone once defined strategic decisions as those concerned with "doing the right things," as contrasted with operating decisions, which are concerned with "doing things right."

Short horizons

Unfortunately, it is a natural management tendency to focus attention, interest, and time on operating decisions. In the competition among strategic, administrative, and operating decisions for management attention, there is a kind of Gresham's Law of planning in which the problems with the shortest time horizon tend to win. There are several reasons for this:

- *They are routine and repetitive.*
- *They are routinely brought to management's attention by lower level managers and by management reporting systems.*
- *They occur frequently and in large volume.*
- *Many managers find these operating problems familiar and even comforting to deal with, due to previous training and experience at lower levels of the organization where operating decisions are the sole concern.*[4]

In the firm that does not devote sufficient time to strategic decision making, changes in the environment are perceived indirectly through the impact they have on the logistic process. Demand for products and services deteriorates; major problems develop with existing channels of distribution or with existing sources of supply; price competition develops because competitors have benefited from adopting new production techniques; and so on. When changes in the environment are perceived in this indirect fashion, however, the response of the firm is made less effective by its tardiness. The response is likely to be incomplete or even wrong, since the world has continued to change while the firm was perceiving the first set of changes and slowly responding to them.

In attempting to diagnose the reasons for problems in the logistic process, the management with the short time horizon will look first at problems in the area of operating decisions. It may very well find problems in this area, and corrective action will therefore be taken. The original problem may not be solved, however, and a further time lag may occur before the management realizes that it has only been dealing with symptoms rather than basic causes. Realizing that the problem goes deeper than the operating level, management is likely to turn next to the area of administrative decision making. Here the emphasis will be on organization, personnel, procedures, information flows, and so on. Again, some problems will be defined and some corrections and improvements made; but the basic strategic problems are

[4] Ibid., pp. 15–17.

still not defined and solved, and further time is lost in response as management temporarily assumes that the administrative solutions will solve the basic problems. Only as a last resort does management diagnosis shift to the area of strategic decision making. By this time, very important time lags have occurred and major opportunities have been lost.

Ansoff characterizes this as a sequential approach to management problem solving—from operating to administrative to strategic analysis and decision making, as diagramed in Figure 1–2. In place of this he advocates a parallel approach, in which operating, administrative, and strategic levels of decision making are considered simultaneously and management time is allocated accordingly. The parallel approach is illustrated in Figure 1–3.

Planned responses

When changes in the environment are observed indirectly through the effect they have on the logistic process, management response must inevitably be lagged. But if procedures and systems are established for continuous surveillance of the environment, it is possible to

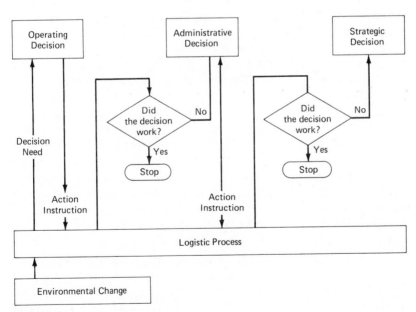

FIGURE 1-2
Sequential decision making in response to environmental change.

Source: Adapted from H. Igor Ansoff, "Toward a Strategic Theory of the Firm," in H. I. Ansoff, ed., Business Strategy (Harmondsworth, Middlesex, England: Penguin Books, 1971), p. 17.

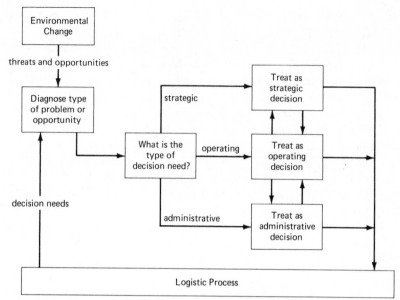

FIGURE 1-3
Parallel decision making in response to environmental change.

implement changes at the operating, administrative, and strategic levels in anticipation of changes in the environment, creating the possibility of competitive advantage and increased efficiency. Another kind of planned response is characterized by Ansoff as "self-triggered" in that attention to strategy is independent of changes in operations because the firm is continually searching for new opportunities for growth and expansion.

It is the fact of environmental change that makes it necessary to have a strategy, a planned pattern of responses to environmental change. It follows that the need for strategic planning is directly related to the rate at which the environment of the firm changes—including customer preferences, technology, and competition. For example, an iron ore company exists in a much more stable environment than an electronics firm and therefore can devote less attention to the task of strategic planning. Its strategic plan will require less frequent adjustments. Nonetheless, it is still essential that the iron ore company have a strategic plan that will create an orderly pattern of responses to such environmental changes as changing labor conditions, the depletion of ore deposits, changing customer needs and preferences with respect to ore quality and characteristics, new competition from other metals and other materials, and so on. No firm is free of the need for attention to strategic decisions, but management in firms in relatively stable environments can spend relatively more time on operating and administrative decision making than their counterparts in firms whose environments are changing more rapidly.

Strategic planning based on informed assessment of changes occurring in the environment or likely to occur in the future gives the firm more control over its own development and destiny, and presents it with a broader choice of options. An analogy can be made to the operation of an automobile. A really careful and skillful driver keeps his attention considerably ahead of the vehicle and can drive both faster and more safely than the driver who does not look ahead. If the driver is devoting most of his time to appraising conditions immediately around the automobile, chatting with his passengers, or gazing around at the countryside without any particular purpose in mind, he must drive much more slowly and runs a larger risk of going off the road. At the ridiculous extreme, it is virtually impossible to drive forward if the operator has his vision focused on the rearview mirror. To mix metaphors, someone once said in stressing the need for strategic planning, "If you don't know where we are going, any road will take you there, but you won't know where you are when you get there."

THE ROLE OF MARKETING

The opening sentence in this book defined marketing as the function by which the firm responds to changes in its environment. That certainly sounds like a definition of the strategic planning function as well. The opening paragraph also offered two other definitions of marketing: as all activities involved in managing the flow of goods from the producer to consumer and as all activities involved in the determination and satisfaction of customer needs at a profit. The former definition implies that marketing is the part of the logistic function that occurs after the product leaves the factory door. The latter suggests that marketing includes the entire logistic function as well as strategic decision making, since it defines the product mix and the markets to be served. Most marketers would prefer this broader definition.

Quibbling over definitions has limited interest and value except that if not overdone, it helps to focus on basic concepts and to lend some historical perspective to dynamic phenomena. It is in this respect that a definition of marketing can help us grab hold of the basic ideas involved.

The traditional view

Until roughly the mid-1950s marketing was viewed essentially as the selling function of the business. Its major objective was to find customers and to maximize demand for the firm's productive resources in a profitable and efficient manner. Manufacturing produced goods and services, and marketing sold them. In fact, the chief marketing executive was usually the vice president of sales. Other supporting functions such as advertising and marketing research were usually seen as staff functions subordinate to sales. Contrasted with more recent conceptions of marketing, this view was product-oriented and short-term in nature, and emphasized larger sales volume (coupled with economies of scale and decreasing marginal costs of production and distribution) as the key to enhanced profitability.

The marketing concept

The traditional sales-oriented view of marketing became obsolete in the 1950s as the sellers' market of the postwar years gave way to a buyers' market of rising consumer incomes, increased competition as firms diversified and grew, and a resulting higher level of buyer choice and discretion. The old, short-term seller's view that "you need what I've got" would no longer suffice. Rather, increased consumer choice meant that the firm had to tailor its product and service offering to fit the needs of carefully defined segments of the market. The customer became the center of the progressive firm's planning activities.

As articulated by Peter Drucker,[5] J. B. McKitterick,[6] and others, "the marketing concept," as it came to be called, argued that the purpose of the business was to create a satisfied customer and that profit was not a meaningful objective by itself but rather the reward for delivering customer satisfaction. Thus, the marketing concept moved away from a relatively narrow, owner-oriented view of the business and moved toward a broader, customer-oriented view focusing on the public served with goods and services determined to have value in the marketplace. This view serves the useful, indeed essential, purpose, as explained earlier in the chapter, of orienting management thinking toward the ever-changing environment and the necessary challenge of strategic planning.

Under the marketing concept the focus of management attention shifts from short-term operating decisions (sales orientation) toward long-term strategic decisions (product and market orientation). The marketing concept recognizes that marketing is more than selling; it is the total business seen from the customer's viewpoint. It brings the customer's needs into all areas of business decision making as the major criterion of business action and effectiveness. It is based on a realiza-

---

[5] Peter F. Drucker, *The Practice of Management* (New York: Harper & Row, 1954), pp. 37–41.

[6] J. B. McKitterick, "What Is the Marketing Management Concept?" in *The Frontiers of Marketing Thought and Action* (Chicago: American Marketing Assoc., 1957), pp. 71–82.

tion that short-term sales volume objectives are most easily achieved when all other elements of the marketing mix have been integrated within a longer-term view of business purpose. In Ansoff's phraseology, the marketing concept takes the firm from lagged response to anticipatory or self-triggered responses to environmental change.

Relationship to strategic planning

Strategic change was earlier characterized as a shift in product and service mix offered by the firm and/or the markets to which it is offered.[7] It is the principal responsibility of the marketing executive to guide the firm in its choice of products and services to be offered and markets to be served. He is responsible for defining the marketing opportunities available to the firm and choosing among them. No decision is more critical to the future health and growth of the firm. But marketing is more than strategic planning, and strategic planning is more than marketing.

In addition to marketing inputs (primarily the identification of customer needs representing market opportunities), strategic planning requires a careful appraisal of other environmental forces (technological, economic, legal, political, social, and cultural) and of the strengths and weaknesses of the firm, including raw-materials availability, production capability, financial resources, management competence, patents, and the like. A variety of management competences in addition to marketing are clearly necessary to this task. The objective of strategic planning can be thought of as finding the best match between market opportunities and company resources, maximizing the impact of company strengths and minimizing the exposure of its weaknesses. A key idea in this calculus of matching resources to market opportunities is that of *market segmentation*, developed later.

Marketing management, like other management functions, has responsibility for operating and administrative decisions as well as strategic decisions. A common categorization of marketing responsibility defines four areas of decision—products, pricing, promotion (personal selling, advertising, and other forms of communication), and distribution decisions, including issues of dealer (wholesaler, retailer, etc.) relations and physical distribution (transportation, storage, inventories, and so on). The marketing executive must decide about such matters as advertising budgets, dealer margins, field sales supervision, package design, salesman recruiting and training, and a large variety of related operating and administrative problems. These decisions will be more effective to the extent that they are coordinated and integrated to achieve maximum synergy. This integration is more likely to occur if operating and administrative decisions are guided by a clearly stated

---

[7] Ansoff, op. cit., p. 21.

set of corporate and marketing objectives, a carefully developed appraisal of the market, and a thorough strategic plan.

Market segmentation strategy

No market is entirely homogeneous. Potential customers differ in size, rate of usage, needs and wants, ability to buy, willingness to innovate, and other characteristics. Each heterogeneous market can be divided into a set of smaller, more homogeneous segments, the number and nature of which depends on the purposes and imagination of the analyst. Just to illustrate, an industrial market might be segmented as follows:

1. by size of customer
   - large, medium, and small accounts in terms of purchases
   - number of employees, sales volume, or other measures of potential
2. by geographic area
3. by method of distribution
   - wholesale versus direct accounts
4. by SIC code
5. by amount of technical service required
6. by type of application
7. by reasons for buying and benefits derived from use
8. by nature of buying decision process and importance of various decision influences

Market segmentation has two benefits. First, it helps to define and choose among market opportunities in strategic planning. No firm can be all things to all potential customers. Choices must be made that recognize the firm's strengths and weaknesses vis-à-vis competition. The largest segments may not be the most profitable for the firm with specialized resources and operations. Smaller segments may offer less competition and a better opportunity to create a satisfied customer with a specialized product tailored to the unique needs of this segment.

Second, segmentation heightens marketing efficiency by assisting in operational planning. Specific pricing, promotion, and distribution tactics can be designed to recognize the differing response characteristics of each segment. This leads to *differentiated marketing*—tailoring marketing strategies (products, pricing, promotion, and distribution) to the unique requirements of heterogeneous segments. For the firm with limited resources, the optimal strategy may be *concentrated marketing*, focusing all attention on one segment. In both differentiated and concentrated marketing, rifle shots replace shotgun blasts at the market. Very rarely today is it possible for a firm to successfully follow an undifferentiated strategy of one product offered with one marketing mix to the total market. (Even Coca-Cola, the classic example of undifferentiated marketing, has added multiple products, package types, and package sizes.)

Market information

Accurate and up-to-date information about the total market and specific market segments is vital to the successful implementation of the marketing concept. The customer orientation of the marketing concept, the need for information as the basis for segmentation decisions, and the long-range strategic planning emphasis of the concept all demand market information, each for distinct and important reasons. One of the major indicators of the adoption of the marketing concept by industry has been the rapid growth in expenditures for market research. Questions of buyer needs, wants, preferences, attitudes, loyalties, uncertainties, buying patterns, and spending ability are central to the definition of market opportunities and competitive strengths and weaknesses.

Generic product concept

One last characteristic of the marketing concept central to understanding its usefulness in strategic planning is its focus on the benefits delivered by a product rather than its physical characteristics. A diamond drill tip is not a hard hunk of carbon but a durable and precise cutting tool that offers the user higher reliability and lower cost in use than alternative drills. Air freight is not an airplane but a high-speed, highly reliable transportation service offering benefits in the form of reduced breakage, loss, and handling expense; lower inventories; and more efficient customer service. As Professor E. Raymond Corey of the Harvard Business School has succinctly put it, "A product is what it does." Industrial buyers are buying profit-creating and cost-reducing products and services on the basis of estimates of supplier reliability, service, technical assistance, and so on as well as on the basis of personal satisfactions in terms of status, security, ego enhancement, and job satisfaction for the buyer. Housewives in a supermarket are buying not just nutrition but also convenience, affection, creativity, and social approval.

Definition of the generic product values to be offered in the market is a key step in strategic planning, one requiring a high degree of creativity and sophistication. The nature of the generic product concept defines competition. For example, what is the generic product concept in a video tape recorder? Is it an entertainment device competing with stereo radios and tape recorders, regular television sets, movies, and other forms of entertainment? Is it an educational device competing with books, correspondence courses, and formal education? Or is it a communication device competing with telephone, airline travel, sales conferences, and other means of bringing people together? From which areas will major competitive innovations come to eventually destroy the profitability of the video tape recorder? Obviously, different companies will answer this question differently—but not all answers will be equally useful to guide the company in its strategic planning.

A tendency to define the generic product concept—and thus the nature of the business—too narrowly is one of the major sources of weakness in strategic planning. This makes the firm blind not only to opportunities for product and market innovation but also to threats from unanticipated sources of competition. Theodore Levitt labeled this tendency "marketing myopia" and became famous for his observations about the railroads who defined their business as railroading rather than transportation and thus failed to anticipate and respond to increased truck and airline competition. He had similar observations about petroleum companies defining their business as discovering and refining oil rather than providing energy, only to be repeatedly saved from the consequences of their narrow-mindedness by developments occurring outside of their industry such as the internal-combustion engine, plastics, and petrochemicals.[8] No doubt Levitt's point is valid: A major strategic weakness is to define the business in terms of today's narrow products and technology rather than in terms of enduring and basic customer need satisfactions. The question, "What business are we in?" is central to all strategic thinking and can only be answered meaningfully by reference to the basic human satisfactions the firm ultimately provides in the marketplace.

To summarize, the pillars of the marketing concept are generic product definition, customer orientation, market information, market segmentation, integrated marketing, and a long-term viewpoint (Figure 1–4). The marketing concept has replaced the traditional sales emphasis of the marketing function and has brought marketing into a position of major visibility and responsibility in all forward-looking firms. While marketing is certainly not the only management function of the business, it "has priority of emphasis within the firm only by virtue of the fact that the market holds veto power over all the other activities carried on within the system."[9]

IMPLEMENTING THE MARKETING CONCEPT

Figure 1–5 presents a view of the several stages, occurring more or less chronologically, in developing a marketing strategy for the firm follow-

---

[8] Theodore Levitt, "Marketing Myopia," *Harvard Business Review* (July–August 1960): 45–56.

[9] T. A. Staudt, "Business Management as a Total System of Action," in T. C. Coram and R. W. Hill, eds., *New Ideas in Industrial Marketing* (London: Staples Press, 1970), pp. 1–9.

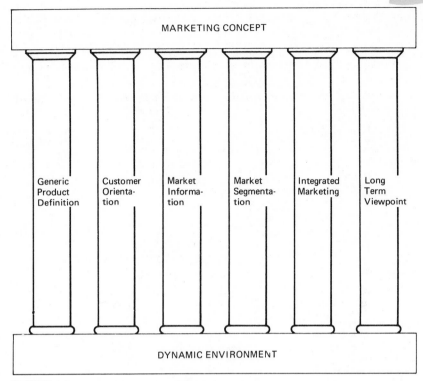

FIGURE 1-4
The pillars of the marketing concept.

ing the guidelines of the marketing concept. We have conceptualized the marketing planning process as having seven phases or stages:

1. Definition of the mission and objectives of the firm: "What do we want to be?" "What generic needs will we serve in the market?" This requires a systematic and honest appraisal of the firm's basic strengths and weaknesses.
2. Developing a market orientation: careful assessment of market trends to define specific profit opportunities, focusing always on customer needs.
3. Developing a strategy of differential advantage: a creative definition of the elements of unique strength that will make the firm more attractive to potential customers in selected market segments. Out of this vision of unique competence comes the statement of specific marketing objectives around which marketing resources will be organized.
4. Design of specific marketing policies and tactics for competing in the marketplace: development of the components of the marketing mix—goods and services, communications, and distribution—in light of the strategy of differential advantage, with the overriding objective of creating a satisfied customer at a profit.
5. Integration of marketing policies and tactics into a synergistic whole designed to produce maximum impact in the marketplace.

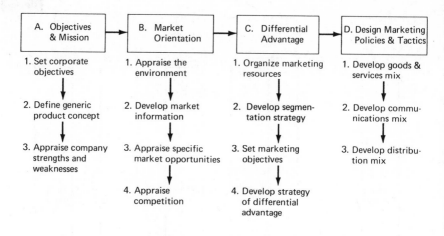

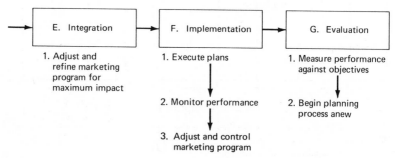

FIGURE 1-5
A schematic view of implementation of the marketing concept.

6. Implementation, including ongoing measurement and feedback of information with which to guide and adjust the marketing program.
7. Evaluation in the form of periodic, systematic measurement of program results to assess performance against specific standards and objectives, and to serve as input to the next round of marketing planning and corporate strategy planning.

The arrows in Figure 1-5 suggest an approximate sequence of events rather than a definite and unchanging regimen. Obviously there will often be a dropping back to refine statements of objectives, to reappraise opportunities, to gather more information, to redefine tactics, and so on. The sequence is not sacred, but each of the elements of the planning process is essential to its thoroughness and completeness.

In the initial stages of this process, the distinction between marketing strategy and corporate strategy is blurred. This is inevitable, since marketing strategy must grow from corporate strategy, and marketing factors, as we have seen, are essential—uniquely so—in the design of corporate strategy. Only in the fourth stage—design of marketing policies and tactics—does marketing strategy become free-standing, so to speak. In the previous stage—that of developing the strategy of differential advantage—equal emphasis is on the mustering of resources to achieve unique competence as well as on the definition of marketing objectives.

SUMMARY

Under the marketing concept the responsibilities of the marketing executive are expanded considerably beyond the traditional emphasis on sales volume. Marketing management and corporate strategy blend in a manner that substantially improves the ability of the firm to respond profitably to changes in the environment. Instead of reacting to these changes as they are perceived indirectly through problems occurring in the logistic process, management can more efficiently steer a course toward clearly defined market opportunities. Potential obstacles and barriers can be plotted and avoided long before a collision occurs, ensuring more efficient use of marketing resources. Profitability is enhanced because the firm does a better job of delivering value in the marketplace owing to its better understanding of customer needs and more effective and efficient response to them. That is the essential feature of marketing—it is the business function charged with responsibility for directing the firm's response to an ever-changing market environment and orienting all parts of the business toward the creation of a satisfied customer.

BUYER BEHAVIOR

The past few years have witnessed tremendous progress in developing a body of knowledge that can be called buyer behavior. This is a natural outgrowth of the increased acceptance of the marketing concept, with its emphasis on the customer as the basis of all marketing strategy decisions. It also reflects a basic shift in the study of marketing toward a "scientific" and rigorous approach to decision making and away from the intuitive and descriptive approach.

The place to start any discussion of buyer behavior is with a definition:

Buyer behavior—is all psychological, social, and physical behavior of potential customers as they become aware of, evaluate, purchase, consume, and tell other people about products and services.

Each element of this definition is important: It emphasizes that buyer behavior is both individual (psychological) processes and group (social) processes. It follows the buyer from awareness through to postpurchase evaluation. It includes communication, purchasing, and consumption behaviors. And it is broad enough to include both consumer (individual or household) and industrial (organizational) buyer behavior.

An understanding of buyer behavior in markets served is prerequisite to effective marketing planning. All strategic decision making involves prediction of buyer behavior in response to marketing actions. As the decision maker considers alternative courses of action, he evaluates them in terms of their expected influence on buyer behavior. A judgment about the effectiveness of alternative marketing actions therefore requires the use of some assumptions, or a model, of the cause-and-effect relationships beween marketing action and buyer response. The quality of the decision is thus partly a reflection of the adequacy of the model of buyer behavior being used by the decision maker. Some models are better than others in that they are complete, internally consistent, and accurate.

Another way to see this argument is with a simple diagram. In Figure 2–1 the consumer is seen as a "black box" into which we direct certain stimuli and from which we get certain responses. The objective of marketing strategy is to make potential customers behave in a manner that is consistent with our marketing objectives. While some might take issue with this rather manipulative definition of marketing strategy, that is really what it is all about.

Fortunately for both customers and marketers, the power in the buyer-seller relationship is largely on the side of the buyer. To get behaviors that are consistent with the firm's marketing objectives, therefore, the objectives must be made consistent with the buyer's self-interest. It is usually easier to modify marketing strategy to adapt to the consumer than it is to try to change the buyer very much. This is one way of looking at the essential argument of the marketing concept. It also provides a major argument for the study of buyer behavior. If the firm is to achieve its marketing objectives, it must understand its potential customers well enough to predict their responses and to adopt marketing strategies with the highest probability of obtaining behavior that is consistent with the firm's marketing objectives.

THE ROLE OF MODELS

A *model* is a simplified representation of some real-world system of variables and relationships among them. The purpose of modeling is to gain some additional understanding of the real-world system. Simplification is an important part of modeling because this makes it possible to focus on key variables and relationships without having to cope with the confusion of complexity. It is possible to manipulate the model in order to test alternative explanations, something that is not

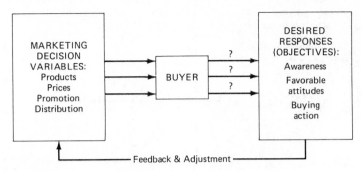

FIGURE 2-1
The buyer as a "black box."

possible in the real world. The simplest models are verbal models, simple descriptive statements of cause-and-effect relationships. Among the most complex models are computer-based, quantified models that can be explored in almost infinite variation using the powerful tools of simulation.

Models can be characterized in several ways, one common distinction being that between *descriptive* and *normative* models. Descriptive models describe a system, whereas normative models have prescriptive, decision recommendations. By definition, models of buyer behavior are descriptive models. However, every normative model in marketing has implicit in it a descriptive model of buyer behavior. In other words, every normative model in marketing requires a descriptive model. For example, it is impossible to develop an advertising budgeting model (normative) without also having a model of how sales (that is, buyer behavior) respond to changes in advertising effort.

Figure 2–2 presents a statement of the contribution of models of buyer behavior to the design of marketing research and marketing strategy. Models of the market and of buyer behavior are seen to provide guidelines for marketing research by suggesting what information is worth obtaining—the variables to be measured and the relationships to be explored. This research provides data that can be interpreted in light of the model to provide information on buyer behavior. Information obtained through research can also be used to update and improve the models of market and buyer behavior. Furthermore, the models of market and buyer behavior may also provide specific predictions that can be used in designing strategy. If the company is properly organized to analyze systematically marketing results, the data obtained from the market in response to marketing strategy—that is, data on company sales, profit margins, dealer inventory changes, and so on—can also be analyzed to further improve the models being used and to refine the decision makers' understanding of the markets.

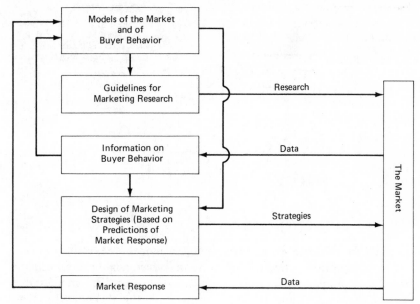

FIGURE 2-2
Use of models in designing marketing research and marketing strategy.

Source: From Frederick E. Webster, Jr., and Yoram Wind, *Organizational Buying Behavior*, © 1972, p. 4. Reprinted by permission of Prentice-Hall, Inc., Englewood Cliffs, N. J.

DETERMINANTS OF BUYER BEHAVIOR

A model of buyer behavior starts with an identification of the variables to be included in it. Among the forces operating to determine a buyer's response to marketing action, at least the following might be incorporated in our model:

- individual predispositions: memory, needs, goals, attitudes, values
- economic and physical reality (income, occupation, etc.)
- family
- friends and neighbors (face-to-face contacts)
- reference groups and social-class identifications
- subcultural influences—racial and ethnic identifications
- cultural influences
- other marketers' actions

These influences on the individual buyer can be grouped into individual factors, social factors, and cultural factors. Each group is the province of one of the behavioral sciences—psychology, social psychology, economics, sociology, and anthropology. The individual consumer can be thought of as imbedded in the center of a series of influences from other people—both those with whom he is in direct contact and the more subtle, noninteractive influences of social class, reference groups, and culture. Marketing actions, both our own and those of our competitors, must reach the individual through these filters that extend, modify, and in many cases nullify the original intent of the marketer. These ideas are illustrated and summarized in Figure 2–3.

Individual determinants

At the center of the buying behavior process is an individual decision maker who is motivated by certain needs and goals, who gathers information from the environment, and who responds to this information

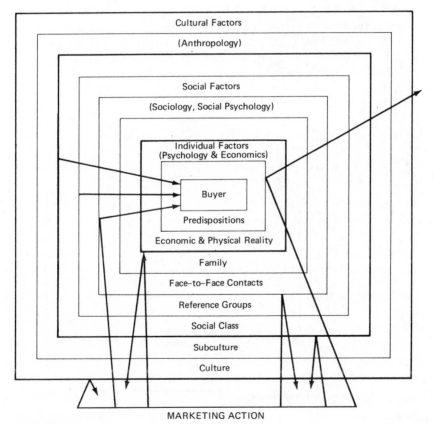

FIGURE 2-3
Determinants of buyer behavior.

according to his predispositions and the physical, economic, psychological, social, and cultural influences on him. This general view of
buyer behavior as a form of information processing and problem solving
applies to both consumer and industrial (or "organizational") buying
behavior. Figure 2–4 presents a simple model of individual buying
behavior that identifies three central mental processes—motivation,
cognition, and learning—and introduces the concept of "predispositions" as a central construct.

MOTIVATION   refers to the drive state of the individual—the needs,
goals, tensions, aspirations, and other forces impelling the individual
to take action. Needs range from the most basic physiological needs,
such as hunger, to complex social needs, to deep and pervasive intellectual and aesthetic needs. Goals are quite likely to reflect relationships
with other people as well as personal needs and objectives.

An individual in a "motivated" state can be thought of as ex-
periencing a kind of tension impelling action to change the individual's
situation. A hungry person searches for something to eat; boredom
leads to physical or intellectual activity; social deprivation leads to the
seeking of friendships; and so on. As the individual becomes aware of
needs or tensions, he begins to explore the environment for means of
satisfying his needs and reducing his tensions.

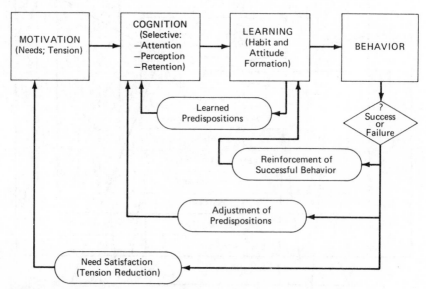

FIGURE 2-4
A simple model of individual behavior.

Source: From Frederick E. Webster, Jr., *Social Aspects of Marketing,* © 1974, p. 44.
Reprinted with permission of Prentice-Hall, Inc., Englewood Cliffs, N. J.

An important influence on individual needs, goals, and predispositions is represented by the physical and economic reality confronting the individual. In the past there has been some tendency in marketing analysis to focus on deep psychological and emotional factors in explaining buyer behavior without giving due recognition to the influence of such objective factors as income, occupation, place of residence, size of family, and the like. Take the case of automobile purchase, for example. The fact that an individual has no children living at home, lives in Manhattan, and earns less than $12,000 per year can explain why he owns a two-door sedan more than three years old. Personality variables may be relatively unimportant as explanations in this case. It is for this reason that a careful study of economic and demographic factors can be a critical starting point in analyzing any market and in identifying potentially valuable segmentations.

COGNITION is the mental process by which the individual attends to the environment, gathers information, and interprets it. The cognitive processes include attention, perception, and retention; these are called "selective" in Figure 2–4 because they are subjective in nature and reflect personal needs, previous experience, and other individual characteristics. Cognition refers to all activities that are usually called "intellectual" and to information processing, including memory and forgetting. People obviously have distinctly different cognitive styles. Some people are likely to oversimplify, for example, whereas others enjoy complicating a situation and consciously seek out more information.

The selective nature of cognitive processes deserves emphasis. At the attention stage, people actually pay attention to only a small part of the information impinging on their senses. For example, it has been estimated that the average person actually is aware of only a small portion (less than 100) of the 1000 or so advertising messages he is exposed to every day. Furthermore, people pay attention to information according to their predispositions; they are more likely to see information that is pleasant, favorable to their existing opinions, and otherwise consistent with their predispositions.

Selective perception, probably the best known of the selective processes, is the process by which the individual assigns meanings to the stimuli received from the environment. Perception is the interpretation of information to select responses. *Predispositions* can be thought of as categories of meaning stored in the individual's memory, based on previous experience, predisposing the individual to behave in a specific way toward a specific object in the environment. Viewed in this manner, perception involves a comparison process—comparing the stimulus to these categories of meaning in order to select a response to the stimulus. The concept of predisposition includes the more familiar concepts of attitudes, beliefs, goals, and values. Individuals are known to change their predispositions slowly; it is easier to get a response that is consistent with existing predispositions than it is to change those predispositions, especially if information is the only tool of persuasion. Thus, once a consumer has developed a brand preference, it is hard to change his attitude toward that brand and advertising for competing brands is, to a certain extent, "unbelievable" to him.

Through the working of selective perception, an individual may in fact distort reality in order to have information fit better with his predispositions. People misinterpret information by ignoring certain parts of it or by adding certain things to it, depending on what is required to make the information consistent with existing beliefs. Technically, these mental processes are called "leveling" and "sharpening," respectively. For example, when you see advertising for brands that you do not purchase, you may simply ignore some claims or dismiss them as "puffery" or even falsehood, whereas you are much more likely to accept the positive claims made for your favorite brands. Selective perception thus provides a powerful defense mechanism for existing predispositions. Of course, predispositions can change over time as information and experience accumulate showing that the predispositions are wrong, but this process is likely to be more in the nature of erosion than a sudden shift.

LEARNING is the process by which predispositions are formed over time. Learning has occurred when a response probability attached to a given environmental object or stimulus has changed. This notion of shifting response probabilities is a bit subtle, but it captures best the notion inherent in the learning process. In buyer behavior, learning is especially important in the development of brand loyalty and loyalty toward particular suppliers. Response probabilities change depending on whether the behavior (response) is successful in reducing the felt tension that motivated the behavior. The probability increases if the individual perceives that the behavior has satisfied his needs, and his predispositions will be adjusted accordingly.

We usually think of behavior change as a result of a change in predispositions. For example, we might assume that an individual will change product brands as a result of information that convinces him that the new brand is better than the old one. However, in many instances the behavior change may actually precede the change in predispositions, as when a special incentive is offered to try a new product (free offer, price discount, etc.); in this case the individual who is pleased with the new brand will shift his predispositions after having shifted his behavior. In Figure 2–4 it may be seen that adjustment of predispositions occurs after the behavior has been evaluated, just as predispositions also influence the cognitive process and determine initial response tendencies.

RETENTION is also a selective process. Pleasant incidents and information consistent with predispositions are retained much longer than unpleasant and contradictory information. This is further reason why repeated information may be necessary to shift predispositions. The viewpoints of a political candidate one does not intend to vote for are more quickly forgotten than those of the favored candidate (assuming that the opposing candidate was even listened to, which is unlikely). In other words, selective retention further serves to reinforce existing predispositions.

SOCIAL INFLUENCES Virtually all buyer behavior, both individual and industrial, is influenced to some extent by other people. Social influence takes two forms—provision of information and provision of standards of behavior against which to evaluate alternative buying behaviors.

At the most intimate level, the individual is influenced by members of his immediate family. The family defines purchase needs as well as providing the economic constraints within which the buyer must operate. In the family unit, different members occupy different buying roles—buyers, influencers, deciders, and users—depending on the product or service being purchased.

REFERENCE GROUPS are collections of individuals to which an individual refers for standards for his own behavior. He need not be a member of the group to have it exert an influence on him. Reference groups take many forms, including both positive and negative reference groups, anticipatory groups (those in which the individual aspires to membership in the future), and membership groups. The concept of reference group is quite similar to the concept of social role. For example, the following roles may provide reference group influences for an individual: father, Republican, husband, Protestant, football fan, lawyer, and Italian-American. Each role carries with it a certain set of expectations—of how people in that role should behave and how others should behave toward people who occupy that role. It should be stressed that reference group influence, like social role, influences buyer behavior by providing standards for behavior rather than by providing information.

PRIMARY GROUPS are groups in which there is interpersonal interaction among the members of the group. These groups influence both by providing information and by providing standards. Friends, neighbors, and colleagues all represent primary-group influences on the buyer, as do more formal groups such as social and service clubs, church groups, and so on. Some membership groups such as professional associations and political parties are not primary groups in that they do not influence the individual mainly through face-to-face contact. Some membership groups that are primary groups are fishing and hunting clubs, skiing clubs, discussion groups, and volunteer fire departments.

As we will see in a later chapter dealing with communication, word-of-mouth influence among potential customers is an extremely important influence on buyer behavior. Word of mouth usually has high credibility because it is perceived as being neutral, honest, and unbiased. It can be especially important at the evaluation stage of the buying decision, after initial awareness has been created and before the customer decides to try the new product.

In designing marketing strategy in general, and especially marketing communication strategy, the marketer needs to carefully consider the nature and extent of social influences on the potential customers for his product or service.

Cultural influences

Cultural influences are the subtlest and deepest influences on the buyer. These influences include social values as well as the influences of language and other sources of meaning in relataionships among people. Other dimensions of social meaning or "message systems" include attitudes toward space, work, social intercourse, time, and play. One generally accepted definition of culture is "that complex whole which includes knowledge, belief, art, morals, law, customs, and any other capabilities and habits acquired by man as a member of society."[1] The notion of culture includes the passing on of something from one generation to the next and the notion of a link between individuals, a mutually shared field of experience, values, and perceptions that provides a basis for mutual understanding.

Cultural influences are so pervasive that they are hard to identify, analyze, and talk about. Subcultures within a population, identified by ethnic or religious groups in the main, can provide an important basis for market segmentation. In the United States, for example, the two most important subcultures from a marketing standpoint are the Black American market and the Jewish market. These distinctions are only relevant for products and services where cultural influences are likely to be significant and different from the larger mass of the public, as for example in matters of food. Language is also an important distinction in some subcultures; this is especially true in foreign markets, of course. The multinational marketer must be especially sensitive to cultural differences in countries where his own background of experience is likely to be misleading and where nuances of language can be of

[1] Bernard Berelson and Gary A. Steiner, *Human Behavior: An Inventory of Scientific Findings* (New York: Harcourt Brace Jovanovich, 1964), p. 646.

critical importance. One of the most serious blunders made by marketers entering new countries is to take advertising that has been run successfully in one country and attempt to have it translated into the language of the new country. Seldom if ever does this result in effective communication.

Culture can be a very important source of predispositions for the buyer; these influences must be carefully assessed by the marketer. In personal selling, care must be taken to understand how the culture creates expectations for such things as appropriate cars for salesmen to drive, size and quality of business cards, relationships between customers and selling companies, attitudes toward promptness in keeping appointments, entertaining, and so on.

In the preceding remarks we have very quickly indicated the major classes of influences determining buyer behavior and developed a simple model of individual buyer behavior. Obviously, there is a large amount of detailed information from behavioral-science and marketing literature on each of the topics and ideas developed. There are few areas in which study by the marketing manager will yield more rewards than the study of buyer behavior. Several excellent books are now available on this subject, and the marketing journals are publishing some excellent and interesting studies that should attract the professional marketing manager's attention.[2]

BUYER BEHAVIOR AS RISK TAKING

Students of buyer behavior have moved toward a concensus that it is best viewed as a form of problem solving or risk taking. One model in particular views buyer behavior as risk taking and information processing.[3] What does it mean to assert that consumer behavior is risk taking? First, it means that there is some uncertainty about the events that will come about as a result of a course of action. Second, it means that some of the possible outcomes are less desirable than others and some are probably negative relative to the status quo. There are two kinds of consequences that buyers worry about: performance consequences, relating to the actual performance of the product and psychosocial consequences, relating to the reaction of both oneself and others to that purchase. Third, considering buyer behavior as risk taking means that we focus our attention on the interaction of buyer char-

---

[2] See for example P. D. Bennett and H. H. Kassarjian, *Consumer Behavior* (Englewood Cliffs, N.J.: Prentice-Hall, 1972); J. A. Howard and J. N. Sheth, *The Theory of Buyer Behavior* (New York: Wiley, 1969); and D. F. Cox, *Risk Taking and Information Handling in Consumer Behavior* (Boston: Harvard Business School, Division of Research, 1967).

[3] Cox, op. cit.

acteristics and the information used to assess risk: information acquisition, processing, and transmission.

Note that we are talking about a subjective assessment of risk—risk as interpreted and acted upon by the buyer. An individual may experience perceived risk any time he has uncertainty or any time there are important consequences. Consequences become important only if they relate to buying goals that are important or to the extent that the individual has to make an investment (of time, money, or self) in the buying decision. These ideas are summarized in Table 2–1.

Ways of reducing perceived risk

There is some minimum acceptable level of perceived risk that must be reached before buyers are willing to take action. This level is not

TABLE 2-1
Components of perceived risk

Uncertainty[a]		Consequences			Perceived Risk[c]	
		Type of Consequences				
Type of Uncertainty	Amount of uncertainty[a]	Importance of buying goals	Amount of investment (time, effort, dollar investment, psychosocial investment)	Seriousness of consequences	Type	Amount of perceived risk
Performance	H M L	Performance (importance of)	(Investment to try to achieve performance goals	H M L	Perform- ance	H M L
Psychosocial	H M L	Psycho- social (im- portance of)	(Investment to try to achieve psychosocial goals)	H M L	Psycho- social	H M L

[a] This can refer to goal *identification* uncertainty, goal-purchase *matching* uncertainty, or both.

[b] Seriousness of consequences is a function of importance of buying goals and amount of investment.

[c] Perceived risk can involve goal *identification* risk, goal-purchase *matching* risk, or both.

Source: Donald F. Cox, *Risk-Taking and Information Handling in Consumer Behavior* (Boston: Division of Research, Graduate School of Business Administration, Harvard University, 1967), p. 8. Reprinted with permission.

zero; in fact, there is some evidence that individuals prefer some positive level of perceived risk (in order to avoid boredom). When risk exceeds that level, however, something must happen to reduce it before buying will occur. Consideration of the structure of the perceived-risk model suggests some strategies for reducing risk.

First, notice that reduction of either the level of uncertainty or the seriousness of the consequences will reduce the amount of perceived risk. This suggests, then, that reduction of uncertainty, decreasing the importance of buying goals, or reducing the amount of investment in decision making will all serve to produce the same end result—a reduction in the level of perceived risk.

UNCERTAINTY REDUCTION
AND INFORMATION HANDLING

Reducing the amount of uncertainty requires the acquisition and processing of information. Information helps us to estimate more accurately the likelihood of various outcomes from a particular course of action. But notice that some sources of information are more likely to reduce the "variance" in those estimates than other sources. A "credible" source is one that is perceived as trustworthy and competent to make the judgments requested.

Consumer-dominated channels are generally regarded as more credible because they are more trustworthy although not necessarily more competent. Informal sources are also uniquely able to help assess psychosocial consequences. This kind of information cannot be supplied by marketer-dominated channels. This is a major stimulus to word-of-mouth activity from the receiver's viewpoint.

Information processing follows certain habits and characteristic methods of operation. Not only are there certain preferred sources of information that people seem to rely on over and over again, but these sources are sought out and used in characteristic ways. Each individual seems to have habitual patterns of information processing that are reflected in the ways he interprets and stores information. For example, some people characteristically take much longer than others to make a decision.

One characteristic that has been found to be significant in producing individual differences in information processing is self-confidence. *General self-confidence* is a more or less pervasive psychological characteristic that can be thought of as a personality trait relating to the individual's need for the approval and support of others. Cox found that people of medium-general self-confidence were most persuasible. Women of high self-confidence were not persuaded by a salesgirl's presentation; the reason seemed to be that the highly self-confident person felt quite capable of making her own judgments. On the other hand, women of low self-confidence were afraid to accept the salesgirl's recommendations because they saw this as "giving in" and were motivated to protect their egos.[4]

Specific self-confidence is specific to a given situation; in buyer behavior the relevant dimension is the extent to which a person feels competent to make judgments about the particular product or service being evaluated. Some individuals perceive some products as more "risky" than other products.

We can work with these few simple concepts to begin to put together some of the findings from perceived risk research. First, it has been found that information acquisition and processing activity is a function of the amount of perceived risk. The greater the degree of uncertainty, the more likely the individual is to seek out and evaluate additional information. Where uncertainty relates primarily to product performance consequences, marketer-dominated channels are likely to prove adequate. Where perceived risk is low to medium, marketer-dominated sources are preferred because of their relatively low cost (time and effort). Where psychosocial consequences are the predominant source of perceived risk, however, informal, personal sources are more likely to be relied upon. Persons of high general self-confidence are less likely to seek significant amounts of additional information, as are those who feel competent in the specific situation.

Information transmission is an interesting case of information handling. There is strong evidence that some individuals *generate* messages as a way of reducing postpurchase doubt. There are several reasons why individuals might initiate word-of-mouth interactions (altruism, goal identification, search for cognitive clarity, etc.), of which reduction of postdecision doubt is only one. Nonetheless, it is important and one of the more interesting aspects of consumer behavior.

DECISION AVOIDANCE

There are several ways in which an individual buyer can avoid having to make a decision. He can maintain the status quo by holding his goals at the level at which they are being satisfied by existing choices. This is one way of looking at brand or supplier loyalty. Here the individual seems to be saying that the amount of risk involved in trying new brands or new suppliers is not worth the possible payoffs. Decision avoidance can also take the form of reducing goals to a previous level after initial search activity has produced no acceptable alternatives. Other strategies that can be logically deduced from the simple model are to reduce the amount of investment—buying the cheapest brand,

[4] D. F. Cox and R. A. Bauer, "Self-confidence and Persuasibility in Women," *Public Opinion Quarterly* 28 (Fall 1964): 453–66.

for example, or reducing the investment in time required to make the decision. Another is to put off the decision, to procrastinate, or to push responsibility onto another person—a strategy followed both in families and in industrial situations.

It has been found that these strategies are more likely to be used when high risk is perceived. That is, people who perceive a product to involve high risk are more likely to be brand loyal, for example.

IMPLICATIONS OF VIEWING
BUYER BEHAVIOR AS RISK TAKING

While there is much more to be done in testing, refining, and elaborating the perceived-risk model, it has proved thus far to be a productive way of viewing buyer behavior. It has been shown to have applicability in both consumer and industrial marketing contexts and predictions based on the model have in most cases been proved by empirical results.

This model has several implications for marketing managers:

1. It emphasizes a very active role for the buyer as a recipient of marketing actions, especially information provided by marketers.
2. It stresses the relationship between marketer-dominated information sources and consumer-dominated channels. It rekindles our interest in word-of-mouth processes and challenges us to consider again how to integrate word-of-mouth stimulation into the marketing communication strategy.
3. It provides a framework within which to assess the significance of product attributes (those relating to amount of perceived risk) for buyer decision making and suggests the kinds and amount of information that consumers will require before they are willing to act.
4. It broadens our understanding of the phenomena of loyalty and suggests at the same time both the opportunity and the difficulty of causing brand or supplier switching.
5. It emphasizes the rational, problem-solving side of buyer behavior. It stresses the fact that buyers react most favorably to, and utilize, information that helps them solve problems. This gets us away from the tendency of a few years ago to think in such esoteric terms as ego-defense, search for status, social compliance, and so on, and brings us back to the real world of day-to-day consumer decision making in which marketer-provided information has a key role to play in helping potential customers solve problems.

ORGANIZATIONAL BUYER BEHAVIOR

To what extent is buyer behavior in complex organizations (industrial firms, government bodies, hospitals, educational institutions, and so on) different from individual buying behavior? There are at least two major ways in which organizational buying is different. First, organizational buying is motivated by organization goals as well as the personal needs and goals of the individuals involved. Second, there is the influence of a formal organization structure. A third distinction is often important: Organizational buying usually involves many decision influencers and is therefore socially more complex. A model of organizational buying behavior, then, must incorporate descriptions and explanations of the impact of these factors on the nature of the buying decision process. A model has been developed that can enhance the marketing manager's understanding of buying behavior in complex organizations as targets for marketing efforts.[5]

The model is a general one. It can be applied to all organizational buying and suffers all the weaknesses of general models. It does not describe a specific buying situation in the richness of detail required to make a model operational for the marketing manager analyzing opportunities to influence buying decisions, but it can be made that specific. However, generality offers a compensating set of benefits. The model presents a comprehensive view of organizational buying that enables one to evaluate the relevance of specific variables. It thereby permits greater insight into the basic processes of industrial buying behavior. It identifies the classes of variables that must be examined by any student of organizational buying—practitioner or academician.

Traditional views

Traditional views of organizational buying have lacked comprehensiveness. The literature of economics, purchasing, and to a limited degree marketing has emphasized variables related to the buying task itself and has emphasized "rational," economic factors. In these economic views, the objective of purchasing is to obtain the minimum price or the lowest total cost-in-use (as in the materials management model).

Other traditional views of organizational buying err in the opposite direction, emphasizing variables such as emotion, personal goals, and internal politics that are involved in the buying decision process but not related to the goals of the buying task. This "nontask" emphasis is seen in models that emphasize the purchasing agent's interest in obtaining personal favors, enhancing his own ego, or reducing perceived risk. Other nontask models have emphasized buyer-salesman interpersonal interaction and the multiple relationships among individuals involved in the buying process over time. The ways in which purchasing agents attempt to expand their influence over the buying decision have

---

[5] F. E. Webster, Jr., and Y. Wind, *Organizational Buying Behavior* (Englewood Cliffs, N.J.: Prentice-Hall, 1972). A brief summary of the model, from which these remarks are abstracted, appeared as "A General Model for Understanding Organizational Buying Behavior" in *Journal of Marketing* 36 (April 1972): 12–19.

also received careful study. These views have contributed to an understanding of the buying process, but none of them is complete. To the extent that these models leave out task or nontask variables, they offer incomplete guidelines for the industrial market strategist and researcher.

A Modern View

An overview of the model   The basic view of the comprehensive model presented here is that organizational buying is a decision-making process carried out by individuals, in interaction with other people, in the context of a formal organization. The organization, in turn, is influenced by a variety of forces in the environment. Thus, the four classes of variables determining organizational buying behavior are individual, social, organizational, and environmental. Within each class, there are two broad categories of variables: those directly related to the buying problem, called task variables and those that extend beyond the buying problem, called nontask variables. This classification of variables is summarized and illustrated in Table 2–2.

It is seldom possible to identify a given set of variables as exclusively task or nontask; rather, any given set of variables will have both task and nontask dimensions, although one dimension may be predominant. For example, motives will inevitably have both dimensions—those relating directly to the buying problems to be solved and those primarily concerned with personal goals. These motives overlap in many important respects and need not conflict; a strong sense of personal involvement can create more effective buying decisions from an organizational standpoint.

Organizational buying behavior is a complex process (rather than a single, instantaneous act) and involves many people, multiple goals, and potentially conflicting decision criteria. It often takes place over an extended period of time, requires information from many sources, and encompasses many interorganizational relationships.

TABLE 2-2
Classification and examples of variables influencing organizational buying decisions

	Task	Nontask
Individual	Desire to obtain lowest price	Personal values and needs
Social	Meetings to set specifications	Informal, off-the-job interactions
Organizational	Policy regarding local supplier preference	Methods of personnel evaluation
Environmental	Anticipated changes in prices	Political climate in an election year

Buying situation and buying center   The organizational buying process is a form of problem solving, and a buying situation is created when someone in the organization perceives a problem—a discrepancy between a desired outcome and the present situation—that can potentially be solved through some buying action. Organizational buying behavior includes all activities of organizational members as they define a buying situation and identify, evaluate, and choose among alternative brands and suppliers. The buying center includes all members of the organization who are involved in that process. The roles involved are those of user, influencer, decider, buyer, and gatekeeper (who controls the flow of information into the buying center). Members of the buying center are motivated by a complex interaction of individual and organizational goals. Their relationships with one another involve all the complexities of interpersonal interactions. The formal organization exerts its influence on the buying center through the subsystems of tasks, structure (communication, authority, status, rewards, and work flow), technology, and people. Finally, the entire organization is embedded in a set of environmental influences, including economic, technological, physical, political, legal, and cultural forces. An overview of the model and a diagramatic presentation of the relationships among these variables are given in Figure 2–5.

Environmental influences   Environmental influences are subtle and pervasive as well as difficult to identify and measure. They influence the buying process by providing information as well as constraints and opportunities. Environmental influences include physical (geographic, climatic, or ecological), technological, economic, political, legal, and cultural factors. These influences are exerted through a variety of institutions, including business firms (suppliers, competitors, and customers), governments, trade unions, political parties, educational and medical institutions, trade associations, and professional groups. The nature of these institutional forms varies significantly from one country to another, and such differences are critical to the planning of multinational marketing strategies. Environmental factors influence the buying process in four ways: (1) by defining the availability of goods and services; (2) by determining general business conditions; (3) by creating the social and cultural norms and values regulating the conduct of negotiations, transactions, and other relationships; and (4) by providing information to the organization, especially about suppliers, products, and services.

The market strategist whose customers are organizations must carefully appraise each set of environmental factors and identify and analyze the institutions that exert those influences in each of the market segments served. This kind of analysis is especially important in entering new markets. For example, economic factors as revealed in

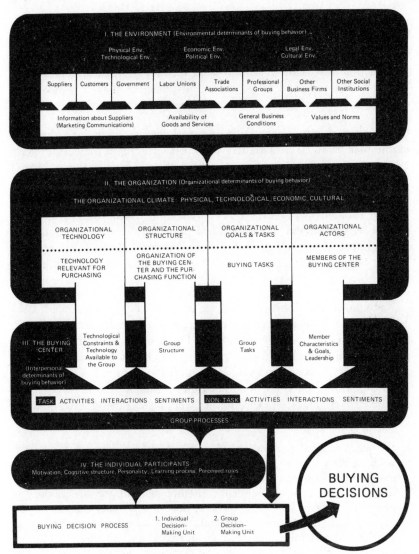

FIGURE 2-5
A model of organizational buying behavior.

Source: From Frederick E. Webster, Jr. and Yoram Wind, "A General Model for Understanding Organizational Buying Behavior," *Journal of Marketing* 36 (April 1972): 12–19.

measures of general business conditions must be continually assessed where market prices fluctuate and buyers make decisions to build or reduce inventories on the basis of price expectations. Similarly, the impact of technological change in markets served must be considered as the basis for strategic decisions in the areas of product policy and promotion. The necessity of analyzing institutional forms is most readily apparent when markets are multinational in scope and require specific consideration of government policies and trade union influences. Environmental factors are important determinants of organizational buying behavior, but they can be so basic and pervasive that it is easy, and dangerous, to overlook them in analyzing the market.

Organizational influences   Organizational factors cause individual decision makers to act differently than they would if they were functioning alone or in a different organization. Organizational buying behavior is motivated and directed by the organization's goals and is constrained by its financial, technological, and human resources. This class of variables is primarily task-related. Four distinct but interrelated sets of organizational variables must be carefully considered in the development of marketing strategies designed to influence that process: buying tasks, organization structure, buying technology, and the buying center.

BUYING TASKS   Buying tasks are a subset of organizational tasks and goals that evolves from the definition of a buying situation. These are pure task variables by definition. The specific tasks that must be performed to solve the buying problem can be defined as five stages in the buying decision process: (1) identification of need, (2) establishment of specifications, (3) identification of alternatives, (4) evaluation of alternatives, and (5) selection of suppliers. Buying tasks can be further defined according to four dimensions:

1. the organizational purpose served—e.g., whether the reason for buying is to facilitate production, for resale, or to be consumed in the performance of other organizational functions.
2. the nature of demand, especially whether demand for the product is generated within the buying organization or by forces outside of the organization (i.e., "derived" demand) as well as other characteristics of the demand pattern such as seasonal and cyclical fluctuations.
3. the extent of programming—i.e., the degree of routinization at the five stages of the decision process.
4. the degree of decentralization and the extent to which buying authority has been delegated to operating levels in the organization.

Each of these four dimensions influences the nature of the organizational buying process and must be considered in appraising market opportunities. At each of the five stages of the decision process, different members of the buying center may be involved, different decision criteria are employed, and different information sources may become more or less relevant. Marketing strategies must be adjusted accordingly.

ORGANIZATIONAL STRUCTURE   The formal organizational structure consists of subsystems of communication, authority, status, reward, and work flow, all of which have important task and nontask dimensions. The communication subsystem performs four essential functions: (1) information, (2) command and instruction, (3) influence and persuasion, and (4) integration. The marketer must understand how the communication system in customer organizations informs the members of the buying center about buying problems, evaluation criteria (both task- and nontask-related), and alternative sources of supply. He must appraise how commands and instructions (mostly task-related) flow through the hierarchy defining the discretion and latitude of individual actors. The pattern of influence and persuasion (heavily nontask in nature) defines the nature of interpersonal interactions within the buying center. The integrative functions of communication become critical in coordinating the functioning of the buying center and may be one of the primary roles of the purchasing manager.

The authority subsystem defines the power of organizational actors to judge, command, or otherwise act to influence the behavior of others along both task and nontask dimensions. No factor is more critical in understanding the organizational buying process because the authority structure determines who sets goals and who evaluates (and therefore determines rewards for) organizational performance. The authority structure interacts with the communication structure to determine the degree of decentralization in the decision process.

The status system is reflected in the organization chart and defines the hierarchical structure of the formal organization. It also expresses itself in an informal structure. Knowing the responsibility, authority, and position in the internal status hierarchy of each member of the buying center is a necessary basis for developing an account strategy for the organizational customer.

The reward system defines the payoffs to the individual decision maker. It is intimately related to the authority system, which determines the responsibilities of organizational actors for evaluating other individuals. Here is the mechanism for relating organizational task accomplishment to individual nontask objectives. People join organizations in anticipation of the rewards given by the organization and agree to work toward organizational objectives in return for those rewards. A careful analysis of the formal and social reward structure of the organization as it affects and is perceived by the members of the buying center can be most helpful in predicting their response to marketing efforts.

Every buying organization develops task-related procedures for managing the flow of paper work, samples, and other items involved in the buying decision process. The flow of paper work also has nontask aspects that reflect the composition of the buying center as well as the authority and communication subsystems of an organizational structure. Needless to say, marketers must understand the mechanical details of buying procedures.

BUYING TECHNOLOGY   Technology influences both what is bought and the nature of the organizational buying process itself. In the latter respect, technology defines the management and information systems that are involved in the buying decision process. More obviously, technology defines the plant and equipment of the organization; these, in turn, place significant constraints on the alternative buying actions available to the organization.

BUYING CENTER   The buying center is a subset of the organizational actors consisting of five roles: users, influencers, deciders, buyers, and gatekeepers. The behavior of members of the buying center reflects the influence of others as well as the effect of the buying task, the organizational structure, and technology. The marketing strategist who wishes to influence the organizational buying process must therefore define and understand the operation of these four sets of organizational variables—tasks, structure, technology, and actors—in each organization he is trying to influence. The marketer's problem is to define the locus of buying responsibility within the customer organization, to define the composition of the buying center, and to understand the structure of roles and authority within the buying center.

Social (interpersonal) influences   Within the organization as a whole, only a subset of organizational actors is actually involved in a buying situation. The buying center includes five roles:

Users—the members of the organization who use the purchased products and services.
Buyers—those with formal responsibility and authority for contracting with suppliers.
Influencers—those who influence the decision process directly or indirectly by providing information and criteria for evaluating alternative buying actions.
Deciders—those with authority to choose among alternative buying actions.
Gatekeepers—those who control the flow of information (and materials) into the buying center.

Several individuals may occupy the same role; for instance, there may be several influencers. Also, one individual may occupy more than one role—the purchasing agent is often both buyer and gatekeeper.

As illustrated in Figure 2-5, the nature of group functioning is influenced by five classes of variables: the individual members' goals and personal characteristics, the nature of leadership within the group, and external (organizational and environmental) influences. Group processes involve not only activities but also interactions and sentiments among members, which have both task and nontask dimensions. Finally, the output of the group is not only a task-oriented problem solution (a buying action) but also nontask satisfaction and growth for the group and its members.

In analyzing the functioning of the buying center, it helps to focus attention on the buyer role, primarily because a member of the purchasing department is most often the marketer's primary point of contact with the organization. Buyers often have authority for managing the contacts of suppliers with other organizational actors and thus also perform the "gatekeeper" function. While the buyer's authority for selection of suppliers may be seriously constrained by decisions at earlier stages of the decision process (especially the development of specifications), he has responsibility for the terminal stages of the process. In other words, the buyer (or purchasing agent) is in most cases the final decision maker and the target of influence attempts by other members of the buying center.

Buyers who are ambitious and wish to extend the scope of their influence will adopt certain tactics and engage in bargaining activities in an attempt to become more influential at earlier stages of the buying process. These tactics or bargaining strategies define the nature of the buyer's relationships with others of equal organizational status and structure the social situation that the potential supplier must face in dealing with the buying organization. An understanding of the nature of interpersonal relationships in the buying organization is an important basis for the development of marketing strategy.

The influence of the individual   In the final analysis, all organizational buying behavior is individual behavior. Only the individual as an individual or a member of a group can define and analyze buying situations, decide, and act. In this behavior the individual is motivated by a complex combination of personal and organizational objectives, constrained by policies and information filtered through the formal organization, and influenced by other members of the buying center. The individual is at the center of the buying process, operating within the buying center, which is in turn bounded by the formal organization, which is likewise embedded in the influences of the broader environment. It is the specific individual who is the target for marketing efforts, not the abstract organization.

The organizational buyer's personality, perceived role set, motivation, cognition, and learning are the basic psychological processes that affect his response to the buying situation and marketing stimuli provided by potential vendors. As in the case of consumer markets, it is important to understand the organizational buyer's psychological characteristics and especially his predispositions, preference structure, and decision-making styles as the basis for marketing strategy decisions.

The organizational buyer can therefore be viewed as a constrained decision maker. Although the basic mental processes of motivation, cognition, and learning as well as the buyer's personality, perceived role set, preference structure, and decision style are uniquely individual, they are influenced by the context of interpersonal and organizational influences in which the individual is embedded. The organizational buyer is motivated by a complex combination of individual and organizational objectives and is dependent upon others for the satisfaction of these needs in several ways. These other people define the role expectations for the individual, determine the payoffs he is to receive for his performance, influence the definition of the goals to be pursued in the buying decision, and provide information with which the individual attempts to evaluate risks and come to a decision.

Task and nontask motives

The organizational buyer's motivation has both task and nontask dimensions. Task-related motives relate to the specific buying problem to be solved and involve the general criteria of buying "the right quality in the right quantity at the right price for delivery at the right time from the right source." Of course, what is "right" is a difficult question, especially to the extent that important buying influencers have conflicting needs and criteria for evaluating the buyer's performance.

Nontask-related motives may often be more important, although there is frequently a rather direct relationship between task and nontask motives. For example, the buyer's desire for promotion (a nontask motive) can significantly influence his task performance. In other words, there is no necessary conflict between task and nontask motives, and in fact the pursuit of nontask objectives can enhance the attainment of task objectives.

Only rarely can the organizational buyer let purely personal considerations influence his buying decisions: In a situation where "all other things are equal," the individual may be able to apply strictly personal (nontask) criteria when making his final decision.

Broadly speaking, nontask motives can be placed into two categories: achievement motives and risk reduction motives. Achievement motives are those related to personal advancement and recognition. Risk reduction motives are related but somewhat less obvious and provide a critical link between the individual and the organizational decision-making process.

The perceived-risk model developed earlier can be very helpful in analyzing organizational buyers, but care must be taken to understand the personal risk perceived by the buyer. For example, the buying decision may involve a major financial commitment, but this is not "risky" for the individual. Rather, the risk for him relates to how he will be evaluated and rewarded as a result of that decision. A preference for the status quo is perhaps the most common mode of risk reduction, since it removes uncertainty and minimizes the possibility of negative outcomes. This is one explanation for the large amount of source loyalty found in organizational buying.

SUMMARY

An understanding of buyer behavior should be the basis for all marketing decisions, since buyer response must be predicted in making those decisions and is the ultimate criterion of marketing effectiveness. Models of buyer behavior can help the manager plan market research and analyze market data as well as, less frequently, aid in making specific predictions of market response. A simple model of individual buyer behavior was presented in this chapter, followed by a model of buyer behavior as risk taking. Finally, the model of organizational buying behavior was outlined as a framework for analyzing the complexities of formal organizations as buyers.

MARKET SEGMENTATION STRATEGY

Market segmentation is a method for achieving maximum market response from limited marketing resources by recognizing differences in the response characteristics of various parts of the market. It is a strategy of "divide and conquer" that adjusts marketing strategy to inherent differences in buyer behavior. Segmented marketing means careful attention to the selection of customers and an appropriately different marketing mix for each chosen segment.

Every market is a heterogeneous collection of smaller, more homogeneous segments. Buyer behavior in each segment will be different in one or more important respects. These differences call for different strategies. Thus, segmentation is an operational link between analysis of buyer behavior and development of marketing strategy.

THREE STRATEGIC OPTIONS

When the concept of market segmentation was briefly introduced in Chapter 1, three strategic options were identified: concentrated, differentiated, and undifferentiated marketing. Here they can be examined in greater detail.

Concentrated marketing   *Rolls Royce*

Concentrated marketing is a strategy of focusing all available resources on one segment within the total market. It is an attempt to match what the firm can do best with a market niche devoid of strong competitors, a strategy of differential advantage. When done successfully, concentrated marketing results in a quasimonopoly position. Highly satisfied customers develop strong loyalties, and the market niche is reasonably well insulated from competition.

Concentrated marketing takes a variety of forms. Specialty retailers often appeal to a rather narrow market segment, as in high-fashion boutiques and design-oriented housewares shops. Rolls-Royce automobiles have followed a concentrated marketing strategy, as have certain watch brands like Coram, Rolex, and Girard-Perregaux. Steuben Glass is a well-known example of concentrated marketing. In industrial marketing, especially for high-technology products, concentrated marketing is even more common. Many industrial companies have successfully developed a new market by concentrating all marketing resources on one or a few potential customers—using the possible competitive advantage for these potential users of the new product as a selling tool.

The problem with concentrated marketing is that it is an "all-the-eggs-in-one-basket" strategy. As customer preferences evolve, there is the risk of decreasing effectiveness without offsetting growth opportunities in other segments. Concentrated marketing puts a premium on ability to innovate and to develop new products to ensure continued favor in the chosen market niche.

Marketing Mix?

There is a tendency to equate concentrated marketing with high-quality, high-price strategies, but this is not necessarily so. For example, small industrial manufacturers often find highly profitable market niches by serving nearby, large-volume users on a quick delivery, low price basis. Timex watches have followed a concentrated strategy aimed at the "low end" of the market, although this part of the market undoubtedly has several segments.

Concentrated marketing generally means one marketing mix, a rather narrow product line, and some unique competence, which is the basis for the firm's competitive advantage in the chosen segment. It is often the basis on which smaller firms compete successfully against much larger ones.

Differentiated marketing   *Diff mix for every segment*

This is the strategy followed by most medium-sized and large firms doing business in many markets with a broad product line. Differentiated marketing adopts a unique marketing mix for each segment, and the company attempts to do business successfully in several segments.

Differentiated marketing usually involves some differentiation among products and brands as well as in pricing, promotion, and distribution. Many large, consumer packaged-goods companies often sell competing brands of similar products, each aimed at different segments. For example, Proctor and Gamble markets both Crest and Gleem toothpaste; Zest, Ivory, Camay, and Lifebuoy bath soaps; Tide, Duz, Cheer, and Oxydol laundry detergents; and so on. Industrial companies often develop different product lines of similar products to more effectively serve specific applications (market segments). To illustrate, Atlas Copco manufacturers both vane and piston types of air motors; the former is somewhat less expensive and the latter is better suited to applications requiring the ability to handle heavy loads at slow speeds.

Differentiated marketing may involve different marketing mixes for the same product. Some food processors offer both their own brand, supported by national advertising and commanding a premium price, and private (that is, store-owned) labels, without advertising and at a much lower price, of identical products. European automobile manufacturers significantly alter their marketing strategies to reflect market characteristics and competitive conditions in each country. Pricing and advertising are distinctly different for the same automobile models in different countries.

Differentiated marketing often calls for an organization using product managers or market managers as decentralized profit centers. It can be criticized on the basis that company resources are wasted when company brands compete with one another. But the defense against this criticism gets at the essential feature of differentiated marketing: The brands are really competing in distinctly different market segments. To justify the practice, however, it is necessary to show that the product concepts and market segments are in fact distinct, or else one must argue that the segments are large enough, and the economies of the business are such, that multiple-brand competition is efficient.

Differentiated marketing has become so characteristic of affluent markets, and consumer needs and wants have become increasingly so precisely defined, that a "pathological" form of differentiated marketing may be emerging: fragmented marketing. This condition evolves as markets become more and more segmented and subdivided to such an extent that the segments are no longer large enough to be profitable. Increasingly refined strategies for competing for the buyer's favor can reach a point of diminishing returns.

Undifferentiated marketing 1 mix for all segments

Undifferentiated marketing is an attempt to compete successfully in several market segments using the same marketing mix. Sometimes it is the result of a conscious choice by a management that says, "We know segments exist, but we judge it to be more efficient to have one consistent strategy." More often, it reflects incomplete market analysis and inadequate understanding of the strategic choices available to the firm.

The marketer using an undifferentiated strategy is likely to find that he has a relatively weak position in each segment because he faces more specialized competition in each one. Coca-Cola Company for many years followed an undifferentiated strategy in the United States—one product for one big market. Then competitors began to whittle away at the giant's market by using more concentrated and differentiated strategies. In particular, Pepsi-Cola went after the youth market, a segment of heavy soft-drink users, with a concentrated strategy that took valuable market share from Coke. Today Coca-Cola has a broad product line extending well beyond soft drinks and follows a differentiated strategy.

The choice of a concentrated, differentiated, or undifferentiated marketing strategy depends on a variety of factors, including competitors' strategies, company strengths and weaknesses, the size of the market and of individual segments, and the availability of distribution channels and promotional media as required to implement the chosen strategy. Chosen segments should be distinctly different from one another, large enough to be profitable, and reachable through available media and distribution options.

SEGMENTATION STRATEGY VERSUS TACTICS

Market segmentation strategy is concerned with the development of different marketing mixes for different groups of customers on a medium- to long-term basis. It is an answer to the question, "To whom should we sell our products, and what should we sell them?" Segmentation is concerned with groupings of customers and is a *strategic* choice—it is concerned with "doing the right things" as opposed to "doing things right," the concern of operational problems.

Segmentation decisions are less concerned with tactical or operational problems. For example, every buying organization has a "buying center," as defined in Chapter 2, composed of several individuals playing a variety of roles—influencers, users, buyers, deciders, and gatekeepers. Should each role be considered a distinct market segment? Not according to my terminology, since this now becomes a tactical question— how to approach each member of the buying center—and because the answer is likely to be peculiar to each individual situation. The concept of segmentation is a strategic concept, not a tactical one. It takes on meaning in the aggregation of customers and generally loses meaning when it is taken to extremes such as talking about each member of the buying center, each advertising medium's audience, each family member, or the customers of different types of distributors as distinct segments. As a quick test one can ask "Do these people buy the product for roughly the same reasons and in roughly the same way?" If the answer is yes, they are probably not distinct segments from a strategic viewpoint, although tactically they may present distinct challenges.

OPTIMAL SEGMENTATION

How many segments should there be, and how large should each segment be? Determining a precise answer to that question is a complex undertaking requiring familiarity with economic theory and mathematics.[1] The optimal number of segments also depends, of course, on the structure of the market and the characteristics of the various strategic alternatives (advertising media, distribution channels, etc.) available to the decision maker. More precisely, it depends on the quality and detail of information available to the decision maker concerning strategic alternatives. A large amount of detailed information is needed to plan an optimal segmentation strategy. Such techniques as have been developed for precise market segmentation are based almost entirely on sophisticated statistical analysis of aggregate data banks (especially consumer panels) concerning frequently purchased consumer packaged goods.

It is always possible that meaningful segments will not exist in a particular market. In highly concentrated industrial markets with only a few potential customers, each individual customer may be a distinct target for marketing effort, making the development of segments a meaningless exercise. (It is better to think of segmentation as an aggregative process of grouping customers with similar response characteristics rather than as a disaggregative process.)

In very general terms, segments should be developed such that the members of each segment have maximum similarity on relevant characteristics and maximum difference from members of other segments . . . maximizing within segment similarity and among segment difference.

A general approach to the segmentation process can be proposed as follows:

1. *Determine what product characteristics and appeals are meaningful and important to potential customers and weight their relative importance.*

[1] Those who are so inclined are referred to the best book on this subject: R. E. Frank, W. F. Massy, and Y. Wind, *Market Segmentation* (Englewood Cliffs, N.J.: Prentice-Hall, 1972).

2. *Determine the distribution of preferences in the population for each relevant dimension.*
3. *Find the optimal position for the product or appeal on each dimension, taking into account the distribution of preferences and the positions of existing brands.*[2]

This approach implies a concentrated marketing strategy, looking for one niche in the "product preference space" of potential customers. But the analysis of preferences may reveal several places where customer preferences cluster and competitive offerings are weak, creating opportunity for differentiated marketing.

In searching for market niches, the "majority fallacy"—the assumption that the product should appeal to a majority of potential customers—is to be avoided. The reason is simple: Competitive activity is likely to be strongest in that segment. A better opportunity is often represented by smaller segments where customer preferences have not been precisely identified and responded to by competitors. Small market shares can often be highly profitable due to more efficient promotion and high loyalty.

The allocation rule

In thinking about optimal segmentation strategy, the simple allocation rule from economics can be helpful—optimum allocation of marketing effort to market segments occurs when the marginal returns (the slopes of the curves relating effort and results in each segment) are equal for all segments. If this condition is not met, increased returns can be realized by shifting resources among segments from lower to higher incremental (or marginal) returns. Return may be defined in a variety of ways—gross margin contribution, net sales, or profit after taxes, for example. The marginal return is the incremental change in the desired variable (sales, etc.) attributable to an increase of one unit of marketing effort. Again, marketing effort can be measured in a variety of ways—number of sales calls, advertising dollars, and so on.

In mathematical terms, the optimum allocation of marketing effort to market segments occurs when

$$\frac{dR_1}{dE_1} = \frac{dR_2}{dE_2} = \ldots = \frac{dR_n}{dE_n}$$

where

R_i = the response in the ith segment
E_i = the effort allocated to the ith segment

and

n = the number of segments

[2] Ibid., p. 7.

TABLE 3-1
An example of different response[a] to marketing effort (monthly)

	Segment 1		Segment 2		Segment 3	
Units of Effort (Sales Calls)	Total Response	Marginal Response	Total Response	Marginal Response	Total Response	Marginal Response
100	$ 2,000	2,000	$ 2,500	2,500	$ 2,000	2,000
200	3,900	1,900	4,900	2,400	3,000	1,000
300	5,800	1,900	7,100	2,200	4,000	1,000
400	7,650	1,850	9,000	1,900	5,000	1,000
500	9,450	1,800	10,600	1,600	6,000	1,000
600	11,150	1,700	11,800	1,200	7,000	1,000
700	12,750	1,600	12,500	700	8,000	1,000
800	14,200	1,450	12,700	200	9,000	1,000
900	15,500	1,300	12,700	0	10,000	1,000
1,000	16,600	1,100	12,700	0	11,000	1,000

[a] Response = gross margin contribution after sales expense.

This decision rule assumes that the returns in each segment are positive and that they are increasing at a decreasing rate (mathematically, that the second derivative of the response function is negative). This simple rule applies to any allocation problem in marketing where there are competing uses for scarce marketing resources.

It is possible that all marketing resources could be efficiently used up in one segment before returns in that segment decreased to the point where they were equal to the highest returns available from any other segment. In that case, a concentrated (one-segment) marketing strategy is indicated.

The simple numerical example in Table 3-1 may help illustrate the basic logic of the simple allocation rule. Assume that one salesman can make 100 calls per month. If the company has only one salesman, then all sales efforts should go into Segment 2. In fact, the total time of up to three salesmen could be most profitably spent in this segment. But if four salesmen are available, then one should spend his time in Segment 1. If a fifth, a sixth, and a seventh salesman become available, then one more could be assigned to Segment 2 and two more to Segment 1 *in any order* up to a total of three in Segment 1 and four in Segment 2. It makes no difference how they are assigned (1–1–2 or 2–1–1) because marginal rates of response are equal at this stage ($1900). The differing marginal response in the three segments means that Segment 1 is always more profitable than Segment 3, but a maximum of six salesmen should be assigned to Segment 2 before shifting effort into Segment 3. If we had 20 salesmen, for example, the optimum allocation would be:

Segment	Number of Salesmen	Total Response
1	10	$16,600
2	6	10,600
3	4	4,000
	20	$31,200

You can play with alternative allocation schemes and easily prove that no other scheme would produce better results.

Choosing segmentation variables

The best segmentation variables to use depend primarily on the data available to the decision maker. Without data, the segmentation cannot be made operational. Given data on several variables describing potential customers, the variable or variables chosen should meet three criteria:

1. The segmentation variable should be related to the response variable of interest (i.e., sales, profit contribution, rate of product usage, etc.).
2. The segmentation variable should be related to one or more decision variables (product appeals, prices, advertising media, etc.).
3. The segmentation variable should divide the total market into segments that tend to respond differently to marketing effort.

BASES FOR SEGMENTATION

Almost any variable describing customers is a candidate as a basis for segmentation, including geographic location, age, sex, income, occupation, number of children, education, race, language, frequency of purchase, shopping habits, personality, brand loyalty, media usage, price sensitivity, attitudes, preferences, perceptions, number of employees, area of business activity, payment terms, method of product use, sales volume, and so on and on. Every marketing author seems to prefer to develop his own slightly different categories describing these variables. Frank, Massy, and Wind make the following distinction:

General customer characteristics—*those which can be assumed to influence buying behavior for several products, including demographic, socio-economic, life style, and personality characteristics.*

Situation-specific customer characteristics—*those relating to individual products and brands, including usage, loyalty, influences, information-handling habits, innovativeness, intentions, attitudes, perceptions, and preferences.*[3]

[3] Ibid., p. 87.

They conclude that the decision as to which variables to use should be based on a specific model of the market behavior for the individual product and that it is quite likely that analysis will show the need for a model incorporating a number of general and situation-specific characteristics. General customer characteristics are likely to have low correlation with actual buying behavior, but situation-specific characteristics are harder to measure and tend to change over time.

In the following paragraphs evaluating alternative bases for segmentation, a simple three-way classification will be used: geographic location, demographic and socioeconomic variables, and predispositions. The relationship between the latter two is especially important and might be modeled as follows:

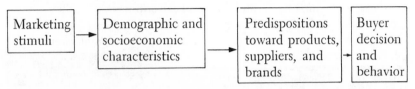

This simple model is adequate to convey a few very important notions about the segmentation process. First, marketing stimuli influence predispositions *in interaction with* the demographic and socioeconomic characteristics of the individual. Second, demographic and socioeconomic characteristics of buyers have an indirect influence on buyer decision and behavior through the determination of predispositions. Third, the same marketing stimuli can produce markedly different buyer decisions and behavior depending on complex interactions among marketing stimuli, demographic and socioeconomic characteristics, and predispositions.

Geographic location

Geographic location of customers is perhaps the most common basis for segmentation simply because so many marketing institutions and marketing variables are organized on this basis. Furthermore, many industrial markets are likely to be highly concentrated geographically, and consumer markets may show very important regional differences. Nowhere is this more obvious than in multinational marketing, where each country presents a unique situation in terms of preferences, habits, language, buying power, marketing channels, and so on. Within a country, differences among regions may be even more important than differences among countries—especially where there are language differences within the country.

One of the most important distinctions to make within any market is between urban and rural customers. The urban population is often better educated, with higher incomes and more mobility. Innovators are more likely to be urban dwellers, and the city offers a much broader range of information sources. Urban populations may be somewhat younger and generally more affluent than rural market segments. In addition, of course, cities offer the marketer highly concentrated populations as targets for marketing effort and thus the opportunity for greater marketing efficiency.

Demographic and socioeconomic variables

The marketing literature is full of examples of segmentation studies using demographic and socioeconomic variables. Demography (the study of population) is conducted by most national governments and by most state, provincial, and cantonal governments and their equivalents. The availability of demographic data is a major reason for their wide use in consumer market segmentation. *Demographic* and *socioeconomic* are not mutually exclusive terms; demographic usually refers to such objective characteristics as age, sex, occupation, size of family, income, and place of residence, whereas *socioeconomic* variables include more subjective and complicated variables such as stage in family life cycle, social class, religion, and culture.

For industrial markets, the functional equivalents of demographic data are industry affiliation, size of company in terms of sales volume or number of employees, product line, and number of plants. Such data are often provided by industry groups, trade associations, and similar institutes, as well as by governmental units.

For frequently purchased consumer products (among the most studied are coffee, beer, toothpaste, fruit juices, toilet paper, and detergents), a very large number of studies have found strong relationships with demographic and socioeconomic variables.[4] The most commonly used variables are

Dependent Variables	Independent Variables
Amount purchased	Age, occupation of head
Brand loyalty	of household, number
Store loyalty	of children (by age
Deal proneness	groups), education, race,
	and income

However, despite strong relationships (as measured by the beta coefficients in a regression equation), the total amount of variance in the dependent variable explained (measured by R^2) by the regression

[4] For the reader interested in such studies, the results have been summarized in several books, among them Frank, Massy, and Wind, op. cit.; W. Massy, R. E. Frank, and T. M. Lodahl, *Purchasing Behavior and Personal Attributes* (Philadelphia: University of Pennsylvania Press, 1968); and J. F. Engel, D. T. Kollat, and R. D. Blackwell, *Consumer Behavior* (New York: Holt, Rinehart & Winston, 1968).

equation has usually been quite small, seldom higher than 20 percent. The reason for this is explained by the simple model presented earlier: These studies have not included data on predispositions, the link between marketing stimuli, demographic and socioeconomic characteristics, and buyer behavior.

FAMILY LIFE CYCLE is a complex variable based primarily on age and number of children. Each family progresses through seven stages:

1. bachelor—young and single
2. newly married couple—young, no children
3. the full nest I—young couple, youngest child under six
4. the full nest II—young couple, youngest child over six
5. the full nest III—older couple, dependent children
6. the empty nest—older couple, no children living with them
7. solitary survivor—old and single

(The term *young* means that the head of the family is under 45). Obviously, need for and purchase of a variety of important goods and services is highly correlated with these stages; this is especially true of furniture, appliances, insurance, installment credit, toys, medical care, recreation, and education. The market for a company's products might very well be limited to one or two of these stages.[5]

SOCIAL CLASS is another complex combination of demographic variables—income, occupation, education, and place and type of residence. A distinction is made between inherited and earned wealth, and the residence variable is analyzed with specific reference to a particular community. Members of a social class are believed to have similar life styles, values, interests, and behavior. Several social-class schemes have been proposed, but the most commonly used is Warner's six classes, summarized in Table 3–2. Note the relatively low percentage of the population in the upper classes (3 percent) compared to the high percentage (almost 60 percent) in the lower classes. Even the upper-middle class contains only 10 percent, which means that almost 90 percent of the population is lower-middle class or below. These comparisons suggest that the concept itself, despite the fact that it is often used in marketing, is rather outdated. At the minimum, the percentages considered to be in each segment need to be revised, with perhaps the majority of the population in the affluent societies assigned to the lower-upper, upper-middle, and lower-middle classes.

As in the case of simple demographics, so with social class: The

---

[5] Further development of the family life cycle concept can be found in W. D. Wells and G. Gubar, "Life Cycle Concept in Marketing Research," *Journal of Marketing Research* 3 (November 1966): 355–363.

TABLE 3-2
Warner's social classes

Class	Definition	Percentage
Upper-upper	Aristocracy, "old families," inherited wealth	1.4
Lower-upper	Similar to upper-upper in income, occupation, costly homes but lacking distinguished ancestry	1.6
Upper-middle	Professionals and substantial businessmen, civic leaders but not "society"	10.2
Lower-middle	Small businessmen, white-collar workers, smaller homes, "good common people"	28.1
Upper-lower	Semi-skilled workers, lower incomes, less desirable homes "poor but hard-working people"	32.6
Lower-lower	Semi-skilled and unskilled, poor homes, often on relief, low incomes, "level below the common man"	25.2
Unknown		0.9
		100.0

Source: W. L. Warner and P. S. Lunt, *The Social Life of a Modern Community* (New Haven, Conn.: Yale University Press, 1941), p. 88.

impact on buyer decision and behavior occurs through influence on predispositions rather than directly. One source suggests, for example:

Members of the upper-middle *class place an emphasis on professional competence, indulge in expensive status symbols, and more often than not show a taste, real or otherwise, for theater and the arts. . . .*

Members of the lower-middle *class cherish respectability, savings, a college education and good housekeeping. . . .*

Members of the upper-lower *class try hard to keep up with the times, if not with the Joneses. They stay in older neighborhoods but buy new kitchen appliances. They spend proportionately less than the middle class on major clothing articles, buying a new suit mainly for an important ceremonial occasion. They also spend proportionately less on services, preferring to do their own plumbing and other work around the house. . . .*[6]

Despite its intuitive appeal as an aid in thinking about the nature of the market for various goods and services, the social-class concept is hard to make operational. Although there have been many studies attempting to segment markets on the basis of social class, measurement is difficult; simpler variables, especially occupation, may do almost as

[6] P. Kotler, *Marketing Management: Analysis, Planning, and Control,* 2d ed. (Englewood Cliffs, N.J.: Prentice-Hall, 1972), pp. 110–111.

well as predictors. The focus of such studies has often been on the relationship among social class, media usage, promotional appeals (to achievement, conformity, and other social motives), and purchasing behavior. One interesting study found that social class by itself is not a strong predictor of durable-products purchases, especially automobiles. However, if the market is further segmented within each social class according to income, producing a definition of those who are "over-privileged" and "underprivileged" in terms of income relative to others in that social class, then some meaningful patterns appear.[7] The over-privileged within each class are more likely to own high-priced luxury cars and expensive color TV sets, for example, whereas the under-privileged are more likely to own small economy cars and less likely to own color TV sets, especially during the early stages of the life cycles for these products.

On balance, we may conclude that demographic and socioeconomic variables are probably best used as a "first cut" at segmentation, before more detailed analysis of predispositions. Even the more complex variables such as family life cycle and social class may be relatively weak predictors of buying behavior, especially in the highly compli-cated and fragmented markets of the 1970's where the determinants of buying behavior are increasingly complex.

Predispositions

As used elsewhere in this book (especially in Chapters 2 and 11), the term *predispositions* is meant to include all motivational and cognitive states predisposing the buyer to behave in a particular way toward a brand, product, dealer, advertising medium, or company. It includes such familiar concepts as needs, values, beliefs, goals, atti-tudes, and memory. Predispositions can also be thought of as categories of meaning stored in the buyer's mind, with which marketing stimuli are interpreted and responded to. In the marketing literature the re-lated concept of attitudes is most commonly found. In the terms used earlier, predispositions can be both general and situation-specific cus-tomer characteristics because they may be general predispositions like personality and life style or specific to particular brands, suppliers, and product categories.

The record for segmentation studies based on predispositions is much better than for demographic and socioeconomic variables. The reasons for this are familiar to the reader, having to do with the interaction between these two classes of variables in mediating the influence of marketing stimuli on buyer response. As we saw earlier,

---

[7] Richard P. Coleman, "The Significance of Social Stratification in Selling," in M. L. Bell, ed., *Marketing: A Maturing Discipline* (Chicago: American Marketing Association, 1961), pp. 171–184.

social class, for example, probably influences buyer behavior primarily by creating shared values, interests, and other predispositions toward products.

Personality variables have often provided the basis for attempted segmentations; they have a definite appeal, due to their very nature. But because such variables are general rather than situation-specific, such studies have not always produced positive results. There are two related problems with personality variables. First, they are hard to measure; people can't be categorized in personality terms as easily as in demographic and socioeconomic terms. Second, the variables are often exceedingly complex and esoteric. Even psychologists have a hard time agreeing to a definition of personality, let alone specific personality characteristics such as ascendancy or conformity.

Common definitions of personality emphasize the organization of a person's views of the world rather than their individuality, their totality and not their specificity. Thus, a recent book on buyer behavior calls personality "the individual's consistent reactions to the world about him."[8] Two authorities in the field of psychology have written that the definition of personality used depends on the particular theory favored by the person doing the study:

Personality consists concretely of a set of values or descriptive terms which are used to describe the individual being studied according to the variables or dimensions which occupy a central position within the particular theory utilized.[9]

In the past twenty years or so, a number of standardized personality tests have been developed and have received widespread use. Among the most popular are the Edwards Personality Preference Schedule, the Minnesota Multiphasic Personality Inventory, the Guilford-Zimmerman Temperament Survey, and the Thurston Temperament Schedule. (The question of the usefulness and validity of such tests comes up again in Chapter 13 in a discussion of their use for selecting salesmen.) The tests attempt to measure such characteristics as dominance, aggressiveness, objectivity, achievement motivation, neuroticism, and the like, depending on the personality theory underlying the test. Scores on the personality test become independent variables in models designed to predict volume of product usage, brand preference, and so on.

In one of the best-known such studies, scores on the Edwards Personality Preference Schedule were used to discriminate between owners of Ford and Chevrolet automobiles. Ford owners were found to have somewhat higher scores on need for dominance, but other

    [8] P. D. Bennett and H. H. Kassarjian, *Consumer Behavior* (Englewood Cliffs, N.J.: Prentice-Hall, 1972), p. 59.
    [9] C. S. Hall and G. Lindzey, *Theories of Personality* (New York: Wiley, 1957), p. 9.

differences were not significant.[10] Others analyzed the same data and came to different conclusions, and a battle went on in the literature for some years over both methodology and conclusions, indicating as well as anything could that the use of personality measures is a troublesome and controversial approach to market segmentation. In general, results from such studies have been disappointing.

Once again, the problem may be one of generality and oversimplification. When personality measures can be developed in reference to specific products and buying situations—relating self-concept to product or brand image—more useful measures may be found. In one such study, for example, J. N. Fry was able to find significant relationships between cigarette brand choice and a variety of personality measures including achievement, affiliation, aggression, autonomy, dominance, harm avoidance, change, sentience, social recognition, femininity, and self-confidence.[11] Instead of looking for relationships between brand choice and such personality measures as were available, Fry had a modest theory to suggest what variables should be examined, and they were taken from several different personality tests rather than one.

Personality variables would appear to offer at least one advantage over easier-to-measure demographic and socioeconomic variables—they come closer to dealing with the reasons why people buy. Depending on his personality, a beer drinker may buy beer to reward himself, to escape, or for social satisfactions, and each of these three segments may be the province of distinctly different brands and appeals. To use another example, a relatively recent study found that two variables, venturesomeness and social mobility, were capable of differentiating between innovators and noninnovators in the purchase of new home appliances.[12] As with demographic and socioeconomic variables, the predictive power of personality variables may be enhanced by combining them into more complex variables such as life style.

LIFE STYLE refers to a variety of other concepts such as leisure, social class, status, mobility, and conformity, as well as being related to family life cycle. It is most usefully thought of as a patterned way of life into which individuals fit various products, events, or resources, often with emphasis on their roles as members of the family.[13] It is a

---

[10] F. B. Evans, "Psychological and Objective Factors in the Prediction of Brand Choice: Ford Versus Chevrolet," *Journal of Business* 32 (October 1959): 340–369.

[11] J. N. Fry, "Personality Variables and Cigarette Brand Choice," working paper, Graduate School of Business Administration, University of Western Ontario, 1970: referred to in Frank, Massy, and Wind, op. cit., pp. 57–58.

[12] T. S. Robertson and J. N. Kennedy, "Prediction of Consumer Innovators: Application of Multiple Discriminant Analysis," *Journal of Marketing Research* 6 (February 1968): 65–69.

[13] D. G. Moore, "Life Style in Mobile Suburbia," in S. A. Greyser, ed., *Toward Scientific Marketing* (Chicago: American Marketing Association, 1963), pp. 151–163.

concept that focuses on the symbolic value of products, and it would therefore be most useful for products with high symbolic content such as fashions, boats, diet foods, sporting goods and services, furniture, automobiles (models and brands), and so on. For example, the Jell-O Division of General Foods has been able to divide its market for dessert products into four segments using several life style factors variously labeled control of children, the planned homemaker, the social entertainer, the economy-oriented, the homemaking avoider, the diet-conscious, the self-indulgent, and the creative homemaker.[14]

The use of predispositions in segmentation studies is not as straightforward as the use of demographics and socioeconomic variables. Acceptable definitions of personality measures are harder to come by, and a large component of creativity is called for in their definition and development into more complicated variables such as life style. But the payoff for this incremental effort may come in the form of higher degrees of predictability of buyer behavior and more practical and meaningful bases for segmentation.

It is virtually certain, then, that the company wishing to develop a meaningful segmentation strategy for its products must be willing not only to analyze publicly available information but also to conduct its own studies of predispositions toward brands, products, and suppliers. Such specific information is necessary in order to understand the determinants of buyer decisions and behavior.

METHODS OF SEGMENTATION ANALYSIS

What are meaningful market segments, and what is their potential value to the marketer? In very general terms, there are two broad classes of studies that can help answer these questions—market surveys and statistical studies.

Market surveys

The next chapter will be concerned with marketing research, and the nature of market surveys will be discussed in more detail. In connection with the problems of developing meaningful market segmentation strategies, the following observations can be made about market surveys.

For established products it is always possible to look at available customer records and to determine if there are significant groups of customers that respond differently to marketing efforts. One method used by many industrial companies is to interview buyers in different industries and different types of customers and ask questions relating

[14] Reported in Frank, Massy, and Wind, op. cit., p. 60.

to how the product is bought, why it is purchased, who is involved in the buying decision process, and what are the major criteria used in evaluating suppliers. Such analysis can reveal distinctly different market segments.

Similar studies can be conducted for new products—interviewing potential customers in a variety of potential market segments in order to determine degree of possible interest in the product, uses in which it would be most effective, and criteria to be used in deciding whether to buy. Obviously, the selection of the sample for such studies is a critical issue—all potential segments should be explored, but money can be wasted by exploring a variety of unlikely segments. Analysis of customer records (and industry information) for similar products can provide useful guidance. It is quite common to do research on the potential market for any new product, and it makes good sense to include segmentation analysis in such studies.

Even in mature markets, segmentation studies can point to major opportunities for increased marketing efficiency and effectiveness. In addition to differences in product benefits and appeals, a variety of other segmentation possibilities can be usefully explored, including price sensitivity, dealer preference, service and delivery requirements, and composition of the buying center. For example, one segmentation study for industrial chemicals identified eight market segments using traditional variables of products bought and industry affiliation, but within each segment there were between two and five subsegments defined by the composition of the buying center—distinctly different targets for marketing effort.[15]

Statistical studies

Advanced statistical approaches have been the hallmark of segmentation analysis. This is because the vast majority of segmentation studies have been concerned with frequently purchased consumer packaged goods, products for which aggregate data such as consumer panels and retail-store audit data are more readily available.

Some of the more traditional statistical techniques such as cross-classification analysis and regression analysis have been used successfully in segmentation studies. Cross-classification techniques simply measure the relationship between pairs of variables such as consumption and income. Regression analysis can analyze the relationship between one dependent variable and a large number of independent variables.[16] A major shortcoming of regression analysis for segmentation research is that the technique requires the assumption that the independent vari-

---

[15] F. E. Webster, Jr., "Modeling the Industrial Buying Process," *Journal of Marketing Research* 2 (November 1965): 370–377.

[16] For an extended discussion of regression analysis, see Chapter 6.

ables are not correlated with one another. When the independent variables are demographic and socioeconomic, such as age, income, education, and occupation, this assumption is not correct and mistakenly large measures of correlation with the dependent variable will result.

Under such circumstances, several newer and somewhat more sophisticated techniques are available that use these interdependencies to advantage in the search for relationships. Among these techniques are factor analysis, cluster analysis, and multidimensional scaling techniques. These techniques, which have recently received a great deal of positive attention, lead to the identification of groups of buyers with common preferences, attitudes, perceptions, and other predispositions. One of the advantages of multidimensional scaling techniques is that research respondents are required to make only rank order judgments (such as paired comparisons) among alternative products, brands, or product characteristics, rather than more difficult and more likely biased ratio scale judgments. The results of such studies can be presented as "perceptual maps" showing the positions of existing brands along two or more dimensions of consumer perceptions.[17] An example of such a preference map is presented in Figure 3–1.

Such maps can be used to define new-product and promotional opportunities, to predict likely brand-switching patterns, and to understand market structure. In Figure 3–1 there appear to be some gaps in the market that could be occupied profitably by new brands—a heavy

[17] For a detailed technical discussion, see P. E. Green and F. J. Carmone, *Multidimensional Scaling and Related Techniques in Marketing Analysis* (Boston: Allyn & Bacon, 1970).

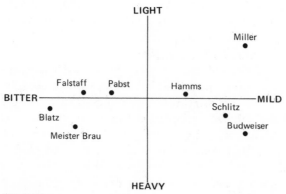

FIGURE 3-1
A perceptual map of beer brands.

Source: From R. M. Johnson, "Market Segmentation: A Strategic Management Tool," *Journal of Marketing Research* 9 (February 1971): 16.

beer that is neither bitter nor mild, for example, or a light but bitter beer. Of course, it might turn out that such combinations of brand characteristics would prove to have little consumer appeal.

Such analytical techniques are clearly the appropriate place to use experts. When properly used, these segmentation methods can be very powerful and helpful.

SUMMARY

Market segmentation is one of the pillars of the modern marketing concept. It is the link between corporate strategy, market structure, and buyer behavior, and points the way to achieving unique competitive advantage. Because buyer decision and behavior are influenced by a complex interaction of marketing stimuli, demographic and socio-economic characteristics, and predispositions, simple segmentation models are likely to have relatively little predictive ability. Newer statistical techniques such as multidimensional scaling have major promise for developing segmentation models with specific relevance to particular product/market interactions.

MARKETING RESEARCH

The marketing concept calls for customer orientation, which in turn requires current, complete, and accurate information about potential buyers and all other aspects of the market environment. Likewise, the development of a professional approach to marketing management decision making requires objective analysis of such information, aiding managerial judgment and extending it. It is through marketing research, then, that the firm implements the marketing concept and takes a scientific approach to marketing management.

Marketing research is a field for experts, requiring special training. The purpose of this chapter is certainly not to tell you how to do marketing research—an impossible task in this brief treatment. Rather, it attempts to describe the major determinants of marketing research quality and to improve your ability to understand and use such research wisely. It will focus on areas where one can usefully ask questions in appraising research one hopes to use in decision making.

In writing this chapter, I have decided to avoid technical detail in favor of providing an overview of issues of research planning and management. Many important research topics, such as the measurement of sampling error, have been left out entirely. The reader desiring a deeper treatment of the marketing research area is encouraged to consult the suggestions for additional reading for this chapter in the back of the book.

Marketing research and marketing information systems are not separate. I use the term *marketing research* to mean special projects and studies of various kinds, including the purchase of outside services on an ongoing basis, designed to improve understanding of the marketing system, especially the behavior of buyers, resellers, and competitors. Marketing research is usually designed to aid planning and often involves evaluation of previous marketing efforts.

The marketing information system is broader, as we shall see in the next chapter. Marketing research is one source of data inputs into the marketing information system, which also includes ongoing information provided by the company's internal accounting system, as well as models, information-processing facilities, and information users. Of course, internal accounting data can also be used in marketing research studies—as when sales records are analyzed to answer questions about patterns of buyer behavior overtime. The distinctive feature of marketing research is its project orientation, designed to answer specific questions, as opposed to routine information gathering through record keeping.

SCOPE OF RESEARCH ACTIVITIES

The extent to which various kinds of marketing research activities are used by American companies was the object of a 1968 study by the American Marketing Association.[1] It was found that 82 percent of all companies with annual sales over $500 million had formal marketing research departments. The number of companies with such departments had approximately doubled in a decade. For companies doing marketing research, the average research budget had increased by 93 percent between 1963 and 1968, running as high as 1.2 percent of sales for advertising and media firms and between 0.15 and 0.50 percent of sales for consumer products companies. For industrial companies, the figure ranged between 0.04 and 0.30 percent of sales. Consumer products companies were only slightly more likely than industrial products companies (64 percent versus 58 percent) to have research departments.

The types of research done by the firms responding to this survey

[1] Dik Warren Twedt, ed., *1968 Survey of Marketing Research: Organization, Functions, Budget, Compensation* (Chicago: American Marketing Association, 1968).

are shown in Table 4–1. In this tabulation one sees a description of all kinds of marketing research, of which market research (research into markets as distinct from research about marketing effectiveness) is only a subset. We will be discussing marketing research throughout this textbook, wherever specific marketing research tools can aid decision making. The next chapter will look at management science and marketing information systems. In Chapter 6, market measurement and forecasting are discussed as part of the marketing planning process. Product research is discussed in Chapter 8 and advertising research in Chapter 12. In this chapter we emphasize data collection procedures of general importance in all kinds of marketing research.

BASIC RESEARCH APPROACHES

There are five distinctly different approaches to marketing research:

1. *Analysis of sales records*—the use of normal sales-accounting and order-processing data to analyze particular questions such as the distribution of customer order size, the location of major customers, historical market potentials, ratios of orders to bid quotations, and so on.
2. *Use of published market information*—relying on government, industry, and trade sources to provide information about market characteristics and behavior. Such research can be highly productive and quite inexpensive. Every research project should begin with library research.
3. *Observational studies*—going into the field to observe customers, dealers, salesmen, and competitors. Observation may be direct, as when the observer makes calls with salesmen, or concealed, as with the use of hidden TV cameras in supermarkets. Data may be collected by tabulating events of interest (e.g., people stopping at a display), by simple note taking, or by tape recording.
4. *Sample surveys*—data collection, usually with interviewing, from a sample of individuals drawn from the population of interest to measure one or more variables such as attitudes toward brands, shopping habits, or product usage.
5. *Experiments*—systematic manipulation of one or more variables while controlling all other variables expected to influence the (dependent) variable of interest, as when advertising budget levels are varied in controlled markets to determine the influence on sales. Experiments often involve other research techniques such as observation and sample surveys.

Accuracy costs money. Although experimental designs may produce the most reliable information, they are complicated and expensive when done properly, requiring great attention to details of design and execution. The costs of research design should be compared with the benefits to be expected by the decision maker who will use the information generated. The greater the decision maker's uncertainty and the greater

TABLE 4-1
Marketing research activities

Type of Research	Percentage Performing		
	All Companies	Consumer Companies	Industrial Companies
Advertising research			
Motivation research	32	60	22
Copy research	38	71	38
Media research	47	70	51
Studies of ad effectiveness	49	81	58
Other	13	17	14
Business economics and corporate research			
Short-range forecasting (up to one year)	61	95	95
Long-range forecasting (over one year)	59	90	94
Studies of business trends	60	87	93
Profit and/or value analysis	53	90	87
Plant and warehouse, location studies	46	83	81
Diversification studies	49	85	86
Purchase of companies, sales of divisions	45	79	86
Export and international studies	41	75	78
Linear programming	33	68	51
Operations research	36	62	55
PERT studies	29	55	52
Employee morale studies	36	64	62
Other	7	8	9
Product research			
New-product acceptance and potential	63	98	95
Competitive product studies	64	95	95
Product testing	53	95	81
Packaging research design or physical characteristics	45	86	62
Other	6	9	8
Sales and market research			
Development of market potentials	67	98	97
Market share analysis	66	98	97
Determination of market characteristics	69	98	97
Sales analyses	65	99	96
Establishment of sales quotas, territories	56	95	94
Distribution channels and cost studies	50	91	83
Test markets, store audits	37	87	35
Consumer panel operations	41	80	20
Sales compensation studies	43	85	78
Studies of premiums, coupons, sampling, deals	32	77	11
Other	5	7	6
Number of companies answering	1,703	186	311

Source: Adapted from Dik Warren Twedt, ed., *1968 Survey of Marketing Research* (Chicago: American Marketing Association, 1969), pp. 41 and 44. Reproduced, with permission, from Kenneth R. Davis, *Marketing Management,* Third Edition. Copyright © 1972 The Ronald Press Company, New York, p. 344.

the economic implications of the decision, the larger the research expenditure can and should be.[2]

The first two research methods listed, analysis of sales records and use of published market information, have the advantage of making use of existing information and therefore lead to research efficiency. An important criterion for evaluating a research design is the extent to which it makes good use of existing information. But information from sales records and published sources is likely to be incomplete for the specific research questions involved.

Observational, survey, and experimental studies share several common methodological problems. These include sample selection, managing field personnel, designing data collection instruments, interacting with respondents, and analyzing results. All research must be carefully planned and managed.

ISSUES OF RESEARCH DESIGN

One way to think about the issues of research design is to identify the possible sources of error. These include

- The sample—the extent to which it is not representative of the population of interest.
- The research setting—especially for observational studies, and the extent to which it is not representative of actual operating conditions.
- The research instrument—such as a questionnaire, and the extent to which it creates bias or omits key pieces of information.
- The interviewer—the extent to which he introduces bias, fails to execute plans, omits data, or makes up false responses.
- The respondent—who may be unwilling or unable to provide requested information, especially about attitudes or past events.
- The data analysis—including errors in data recording, coding, tabulating, interpretation, and reporting.

Sampling

A *sample* is a selection of units from the population of interest. Researchers often use the word *universe* to mean the population from which the sample is to be drawn. Defining the universe is often a difficult and important research task. The sample universe is usually the market segment that is the target for the marketing decisions that will be influenced by the research. The sample units can be firms,

---

[2] For a rigorous presentation of this argument, see F. M. Bass, "Marketing Research Expenditure: A Decision Model," *Journal of Business* (January 1963): 77–90.

housewives, retailers, families, city blocks, or whatever individual respondents are best suited to provide the desired information.

Selecting the sample is a technical process for picking sample units from the universe. The type of sampling method used is determined by questions of cost and convenience as well as by the degree of accuracy desired in research results and the intended statistical tests. A *probability* sample is one in which every population unit has an equal and known probability of being included in the sample. It is also called a *random* sample, meaning that sample selection is random in the sense of being unbiased (not "haphazard"). A probability sample permits the use of statistical inference to judge the extent to which data collected are representative of the total population.

A true probability sample is possible only if the researcher has at his disposal a list or *sampling frame* containing all units of the population. Otherwise he cannot ensure that all units have an "equal and known" probability of being included in the sample. A telephone directory is a poor sampling frame in consumer research, for example, because not all families have telephones and not all telephone numbers are listed.

A *simple random sample* is most often drawn by selecting every *n*th item in the sampling frame where *n* is determined by desired sample size and the list is entered at a point determined by drawing a number at random, usually a number between 1 and 10. Such a procedure is sometimes called *systematic sampling*. Simple random samples have a disadvantage in that they are neither as economically nor as statistically efficient as other random sampling methods.

A *stratified random sample* introduces a higher degree of statistical efficiency by allowing the researcher to use his knowledge about the distribution of population characteristics to ensure a more representative sample than would occur with simple random sampling. For example, suppose an auto-leasing company wanted to survey companies that lease fleets of cars. It knows that larger companies are more likely to do so. The representativeness of the sample would be improved by having larger companies represented in the sample in proportion to their importance. Thus sampling error could be reduced by stratifying the population of companies according to size and selecting a sample from each of the strata in relation to their importance, the percentage of the total sample drawn from each stratum being equal to the percentage of total leased automobiles accounted for by companies in this size category.

Cluster sampling is a method of improving the economic efficiency of the research by selecting sample units in clusters or groups (using random sampling procedures). *Area sampling* is a common form of cluster sampling in which geographic areas such as city blocks or counties are the sample units, a procedure that permits research workers to minimize time and travel distance, thus improving economic efficiency. All population units within a cluster can be included in the sample, or units can be chosen at random from within the cluster; the latter is called a *two-stage* sampling procedure. Cluster sampling has the disadvantage of reducing statistical efficiency because population units within a cluster tend to be similar, thus decreasing the representativeness of the sample. This problem can be minimized by an attempt to achieve maximum variation within clusters—for instance, by choosing areas that are believed to be closely representative of the total population.

Nonrandom samples or nonprobability samples are also called *convenience samples*. These may be used to reduce the costs associated with random sampling or because an adequate sampling frame is not available. Strictly speaking, convenience samples do not permit the use of statistical inference to judge the representativeness of the data collected. In point of fact, one often sees statistical tests performed on nonprobability samples, but an essential feature of probability sampling is missing. With a true probability sample the researcher can estimate *sampling error*—that is, the amount of error in the data due to the fact that a sample has been investigated rather than the total population. No such estimate of sampling error is possible with a nonprobability sample.

Perhaps the most common type of convenience sample is a *quota sample*, in which the research worker is given a quota of respondents with particular characteristics. The purpose of assigning quotas is to achieve a degree of sample representativeness above what might be expected if the research worker were left to his own devices. For example, instead of instructing an interviewer to interview 40 housewives, he might be instructed to interview 5 nonwhite housewives and 35 white, and to have equal numbers of housewives 35 years old or less and over 35. Or, within an industrial firm, the interviewer's instructions may call for interviewing a member of the purchasing department, an engineer, and a production supervisor. The fact that the researcher can exercise discretion in selecting the specific people to be interviewed means that the requirement for random sampling (that all population units must have an equal and known probability of being included in the sample) is no longer met. The interviewer's preferences, prejudices, and desire to minimize effort are all sources of bias in a quota sample.

Nonetheless, convenience samples can be adequate for many research purposes. It is not always essential that a sample be truly representative of a population, especially where the research is of an exploratory and qualitative nature, as in product concept testing, rather than designed to estimate specific population parameters. Furthermore, concern for sampling error, which is the central focus of statistical inference and the analysis of variance, can obscure other, possibly more serious, sources of error such as interviewer error and respondent error.

Research setting

The importance of the research setting, the physical environment in which data are collected, is often ignored in research design. In experimental settings such as in-store tests of promotional displays, there is the obvious problem of duplicating actual market conditions. For example, an attempt to measure response to different prices for a product may produce meaningless results if the product is featured in a more-attractive-than-usual location and if inventories are expanded and carefully monitored during the test.

In other kinds of research the problem may be somewhat less obvious. In advertising tests it makes a great deal of difference whether respondents are exposed to the advertising under forced or natural exposure conditions. When interviewing is done, the physical environment can be a major determinant of data quality. Busy offices, noisy shop floors, living rooms with television sets and radios playing, busy streets and supermarkets, all are settings that reduce attentiveness and communication efficiency.

Research instrument

A questionnaire is the most common research instrument. Others are interview guides, attitude scales, and tabulation sheets. The design of the research instrument requires painstaking effort to avoid bias and to develop a device that will facilitate efficient communication. Some general guidelines can be offered:

1. Keep focused on research objectives; avoid the temptation to complicate the research instrument by asking for unnecessary information.
2. Develop a logical sequence in questionnaires and interviews. Ask easy questions first; save the most difficult and sensitive (e.g., questions about age and income) for last. Use early questions to establish rapport and set the respondent at ease.
3. Ask only questions that the respondent is capable of answering; avoid those making excessive demands on memory and personal insight.
4. Avoid questions that suggest their own answers. Remember that respondents are often too polite and will give the answers they think the researcher would like to hear. Question sequence can also suggest expected answers.
5. Make sure all words and phrases will be understood by respondents and interviewers.
6. Make all interviewer instructions clear and explicit.
7. Make the research instrument itself easy to use—answers quickly recorded, enough space, no overlapping or incomplete response categories, brief, and legible.
8. Pretest all versions of the research instrument in the field with representative research workers and respondents.

Interviewer

Interviewing is not something that everybody does well. Good marketing research requires a carefully trained and supervised field interviewer, for the interviewer's ability and carefulness are the major determinants of the quality of the information collected. A major benefit of using professional market research firms is that they can provide trained field staffs. At the same time, one must recognize that most of these staffs consist of part-time workers, often housewives or students, who may not be quite as professional as their employers claim. Firms specializing in industrial marketing research are somewhat more likely to have full-time and more professional part-time staffs, such as business school professors.

The central problems in managing interviewers are to make them aware of the ways in which they influence the quality of the information obtained in the interview and to make sure that requested work is actually completed, accurately and on time. A poorly trained interviewer who doesn't understand his job is more likely to be frustrated and, as a result, to falsify reports or fail to submit completed work.

Interviewers can be a major source of bias and other forms of error. It is easy for the interviewer to react to answers in ways that influence subsequent responses. There is a narrow line between "probing," something every good interviewer must learn to do well, and suggesting answers to the respondent. Like a good salesman, an interviewer must have empathy—the ability to sense the way he is influencing the other person. Such sensitivity can and must be developed through training before the interviewer is turned loose on respondents.

There are a variety of ways of supervising and monitoring interviewer performance. Field supervisors are essential in a high-quality field research operation. It is a common research practice to follow up with a subsample of respondents to make sure that reported interviews were actually completed. Sometimes information about the interviewer's conduct is also solicited. The work of every field interviewer should be appraised from time to time, both by the field supervisor and by checking completed interviews and questionnaires.

Selection of a marketing research firm should be based in part on the quality of the field interviewers and the care with which they are selected, trained, supervised, and evaluated.

Respondent

Respondent error in survey research is a result of the respondent's inability or unwillingness to provide the requested information. It can be minimized by careful design of the research instrument and by the way the interview is conducted. But there is always likely to be some residual of respondent error due to ignorance, confusion, mis-understanding, lack of motivation, and fatigue, and its presence should be recognized in appraising survey results.

But this is not to imply that all respondent error reflects reluctance to cooperate in the research. In fact, cooperativeness is itself a major source of respondent error. It is true that most respondents will go out of their way to be helpful and that they feel a sense of importance in being included in the research. The problem is that this desire to help can cause the respondent to fabricate answers and to give responses that he believes the researcher wants to hear. Generally these are responses favorable to the company and its products, assuming that the respondent can identify the research sponsor.

A related problem is the respondent's desire to project the best possible image of himself. This can lead to an upward bias in answers to questions about income, education, and occupation. It also takes a more subtle form in responses about consumption patterns, media usage habits, brand preferences, and other behavioral dimensions that reveal something about the individual. There is a tendency for an idealized self-concept to interfere with objective reporting. Respondent error can be reduced if the design of the research instrument takes into account these tendencies.

Data analysis

The final source of error to consider is data analysis. Most obvious are problems of recording, coding, and tabulation of responses. These problems are common in both hand tabulation and electronic data processing, and can be controlled by spot-checking. Special care must be exercised in developing coding systems for responses to open-ended questions, those in which responses are not specified for the respondent to choose among. Problems of data analysis should be considered in the design of the research instrument.

In addition to such mechanical and clerical sources of error, the research user must also be sensitive to potential errors of interpretation. Are the conclusions justified and supported by the data? Are other explanations possible? Answering such questions requires some familiarity with research design and methodology—how the sample was drawn, how the interviews were conducted, and so on.

One of the dimensions on which to measure the quality of market research contractors is their ability to use the powerful statistical tools now gaining popularity and importance in the marketing research field, including cluster analysis, factor analysis, discriminant analysis, and multidimensional scaling techniques. Such methods can significantly extend the insights generated from a research study beyond those possible with such simple mathematical approaches as cross-tabulation, correlation, measures of central tendency and dispersion, and analysis of variance. Of course, research design must be tailored to the intended data analysis and vice versa.

In this discussion of research design, we have reviewed the major dimensions of a research study, especially as they determine the quality of the research and the potential sources of error. So far, the chapter has considered primarily sample surveys as a market research technique. Now, several other sources of market research data will be considered.

PANELS

Panels are made up of respondents who regularly and routinely report on their buying behavior. Common practice is to keep a diary of purchases, advertising exposure, shopping activity, or whatever the researcher wishes and to return this periodically, say monthly to the company that maintains the panel. One of the best-known panels is the Market Research Corporation of America (MRCA) consumer panel, which reports on household purchases of consumer products. Marketers can buy these data on a subscription basis. General Electric has maintained its own panel, asking each panel family to report changes in its inventory of electrical appliances (beginning with an initial inventory) at six-month intervals for a total of three reporting periods; one-third of the panel is new at each interval. There is also a panel of physicians who keep track of their prescription writing for a one-year period. There are panels in other areas, including agricultural products, but they seem to be nonexistent in the industrial marketing field.

Panels have three important benefits: (1) buyer behavior data can be related to buyer characteristics, (2) changes in buyer behavior can be monitored over time, and (3) changes in buyer behavior can be related to changes in the marketing mix. There are two major problems with using panels in marketing research. First, it is hard to maintain a representative panel. Higher income groups and minority groups tend to be underrepresented. There is always a problem of lack of response from those who agreed to cooperate, and as with other forms of marketing research, nonrespondents tend to be different from respondents. Furthermore, respondents may be careless in completing their diaries, filling them out when they are due to be returned rather than when purchases occurred and thus introducing the error that is inevitable when memory is relied upon too heavily. Special care must be exercised in replacing panel members who drop out so as to maintain a representative panel. Finally, the panel members who are most reliable and dedicated may be atypical, not like the average buyer at all, too "professional" in their approach to buying.

The second problem in using panels concerns the extent to which potential and actual customers are to be found in the sample. For the

average marketer with a reasonably small market share, a truly representative national sample may have little value for him in understanding
his own market. This is especially true for marketers with narrow
market segments or highly specialized products.

TRADE AUDITS

Instead of surveying buyers, it may be easier, more economical, and
more accurate to measure changes in stocks and flows in the channel
of distribution. Retail-store audits, especially for grocery and drug
products, are commonly used, the two most popular suppliers being
Audits and Surveys, Inc., and the A. C. Nielsen Company. In addition
to regular services to which the marketer can subscribe, it is quite
possible for a marketer to develop his own retail-store audit, but the
expense may be prohibitive. Store audits have the advantage of relying
on objective count-recount measures of product movement rather than
potentially biased consumer reporting, and they provide comparable
data for all competing products. Obtaining a representative sample
can be a problem if several large retailers refuse to cooperate. Retail
movement may be a better measure of the effectiveness of certain promotions than reported changes in consumer purchasing.

Changes in product stocks and flows can be measured at several
stages in the channel of distribution, not just at the retail level. For
example, SAMI (Selling Areas—Marketing, Inc.), a division of Time,
Inc., offers a service that reports warehouse withdrawals by all major
food chains in several major metropolitan areas, accounting for as
much as 90 percent of total food sales in some markets. Key metal
distributors in selected markets could provide similarly interesting data
to metals producers.

MARKET TESTS

In a market test, a product is marketed in one or a few selected market
areas under conditions similar to those that will prevail when it is
marketed nationally. Market tests are often associated with new products but may also be used for all other elements of the marketing mix,
including new prices, packaging, retailers, displays, advertising, and
sales promotions. A market test is a simulation of a full-scale marketing
program. Even when a new product is involved, the purpose of a
market test (or test market) is not to test the product (which is done
in laboratory and field tests of various kinds) but to test the marketing
plan for the product.

Selecting the markets to be used for a test is often difficult. Very few markets are truly representative of the national market in terms of buyer characteristics, distributor availability and characteristics, media availability, and competitive conditions. Those that are quite representative (Seattle-Tacoma, Rochester, Syracuse, Columbus, Albany-Schenectady-Troy, and a few others) are heavily used as test markets—a fact that has probably reduced their representativeness. In addition, competitive attention has been attracted to these markets, making it hard to proceed in the market test without competitive response. This can destroy the validity of the market test itself.

It is important to emphasize again that the market test is a test of the marketing plan as a whole. Results should be analyzed in this light, with a sharp awareness of the important interrelationships among elements of the marketing mix. If test results suggest that a variable should be changed, then the new decision should also be tested to determine its impact on other parts of the mix. For example, assume that the market test shows a rate of trial lower than expected and analysis suggests that the reason is inadequate price inducements. Lowering the introductory price is now likely to have a substantial impact on advertising response and may call for new decisions about the level of advertising effort. The new price-advertising budget levels will have important implications for return on investment and should be tested. Projections based on the old test market would no longer be valid.

In the test market itself, data may be collected using any of the techniques we have already examined—surveys, store audits, observation, and so forth. Given the complex combination of variables being tested, a variety of data collection techniques may be called for.

EXPERIMENTS

Experiments are the most sophisticated form of marketing research. Only an experiment can establish a true cause-and-effect relationship between a marketing decision variable and a change in buyer behavior and market response. An experiment involves the systematic variation of certain factors (say, three different levels of sales-calling activity and use of advertising versus no advertising) and the careful control of other variables thought to influence response (such as credit terms, distributor stock levels, and delivery time). Some of these variables can be controlled by the actions of the firm. Others, such as competitors' selling activities and customer buying potentials, cannot be controlled by the firm but can be controlled statistically through research design and data analysis.

The complexity of a research design is determined by the number of variables to be examined and controlled. A common approach to the problem of experimental control is to use matched groups of respondents, some treated with the experimental variables and others simply monitored, in order to determine the effect of "environmental variables" on subjects' responses as differentiated from "experimental variables." Experimental designs from simple to complex can be described as follows:

* Simple time-series design   *Observing subjects for a period, then introducing the experimental variables and monitoring response for a period.*
* Recurrent time-series design   *Periods of observation are interspersed between periods when the experimental treatment is performed, with changes in response observed over time. An averaging of results can control for the impact of unique environmental events.*
* Before-after with control-group design   *A common design in which experimental groups and control groups are monitored for a time followed by introduction of the experimental variables with the experimental groups. The response of both sets of groups (perhaps with recurrent time-series design) is monitored and differences tested for statistical significance.*
* Factorial design   *A complex design for testing several variables simultaneously, to achieve more efficient use of research resources. The number of groups required depends on the number of variables; for example, a test of two levels of advertising and two prices would require at least 4 groups. In a factorial design, interactions among experimental variables can be assessed as well as their individual effects.*
* Latin-square design   *A Latin square is a simplified factorial design which can be used if interaction among the experimental variables is believed to be unimportant. They are also used to obtain a "balanced" design where treatments must be assigned efficiently to different groups in different time periods.*[3]

The great advantage of experiments in marketing is their precision and their ability to trace the effects of multiple variables and their interactions. Their major disadvantages come from their complexity, which makes them expensive and difficult to administer. Furthermore, the market environment is often so complex that true control over the conditions under which the experiment is conducted is a virtually unattainable ideal. Nonetheless, a variety of well-known companies, including Ford Motor, E. I. du Pont de Nemours, Scott Paper, General Electric, and Anheuser-Busch, have published results of experimental research on such problems as advertising media selection, sales force call schedules, advertising budgets, and product display. Experiments can be used in multiple test markets to evaluate alternative

[3] P. Kotler, *Marketing Management: Analysis, Planning, and Control,* rev. ed. (Englewood Cliffs, N.J.: Prentice-Hall, 1972), pp. 319–320.

marketing strategies. Experimentation is bound to become increasingly important as marketing practice becomes more professional, scientific, and sophisticated.

PLANNING AND MANAGING RESEARCH

Although the design and execution of marketing research is a field for experts, it does not follow that marketing research should be left to the experts. On the contrary, good research requires close cooperation and communication between management and the marketing research department or agency. It should never be forgotten that the research is undertaken to assist managerial judgment (but not to replace it) in making certain marketing decisions; the nature of those decisions should guide research design and execution.

The planning of marketing research should begin with a clear statement of research objectives. As explained in Chapter 2, models of buyer behavior can be especially helpful in defining what information management needs and, in interpreting the data collected. Explication of such models of buyer behavior can be one of the first stages in the design of marketing research. A good statement of research objectives serves the related purposes of facilitating communication between researchers and management information users and improving research efficiency. Data collected should be meaningful for specific marketing decisions; the temptation to get "just a bit more" information must be avoided, as it leads to lengthy and costly research designs and research instruments, and blurs the focus on key decision issues. On the other hand, a good statement of research objectives will help ensure that all relevant information is obtained and some key variables are not ignored.

A timetable of research activities, perhaps in the form of a Program Evaluation and Review Technique plan (PERT), will help keep research on schedule and to make sure information is available when management needs it. Again, such a schedule can help avoid misunderstandings between researchers and management.

SUMMARY

Marketing research is part of the marketing information system and, as such, a key to the implementation of the marketing concept. Intelligent use of marketing research requires that the manager have some understanding of the major dimensions of research design—the sample, the research setting, the research instrument, the interviewer, the respondent, and data analysis. Any research project should be evaluated in part on the extent to which it makes good use of already available information from company records and published sources. In addition, observational studies, surveys, and experiments may be used, perhaps in the form of a market test. Finally, syndicated services such as panels and trade audits are available. Each of these was described briefly in this chapter. In the following chapter our view is broadened to include the entire marketing information system and management use of research results in decision making.

MANAGEMENT SCIENCE AND INFORMATION SYSTEMS IN MARKETING

For several years the computer and sophisticated quantitative techniques for analyzing market data have been expected to bring major, even revolutionary, changes to the practice of marketing management. The initial interest of the early 1950s reached fad proportions in the early 1960s, but by the end of the decade a kind of disillusionment had set in as visions of tremendous payoffs from computerization in the marketing field remained largely unfulfilled. In fact, some rather expensive failures and a general sense of frustration with the lack of progress in finding important management benefits had created a pessimistic view among practicing marketing managers about the value of such sophisticated approaches. At the beginning of the 1970s, however, a more realistic set of expectations began to emerge, and the promises being made by management scientists took on a new degree of realism. Once again there is hope for some major improvements in marketing management effectiveness and efficiency through the intelligent application of computers and mathematical techniques to data analysis and decision making. With a more realistic set of expectations and a somewhat more complete understanding of the proper role of the computer in marketing, the gap between potential value and actual accomplishment is more likely to be closed.

MANAGEMENT SCIENCE

It is always helpful to begin with a definition of terms: *Management science* involves the application of concepts and techniques from economics, mathematics, statistics, and related areas such as industrial engineering to the problems of management. To many people, management science and operations research are essentially the same thing; both describe a problem-solving approach characterized by rigorous descriptions and analytical techniques. A common objective of many operations research studies is to develop "decision rules," guidelines for evaluating the profitability of alternative courses of managerial action. Management science approaches also generally try to develop an understanding of the relationships among key variables in the decision environment, both those that are under the control of the decision maker and those that are not, as these interactions are likely to affect the outcomes of management actions.

Models

A central feature of management science is the use of *models*—simplified representations of more complex systems. We are all familiar with models in everyday life—model airplanes assembled by young boys, architects' models of building projects, and so on. In management science, models are commonly expressed in mathematical language. Wagner sees model-building in management science as the counterpart to laboratory experimentation in the physical sciences:

Constructing a model helps you put the complexities and possible uncertainties attending a decision-making problem into a logical framework amenable to comprehensive analysis. Such a model clarifies the decision alternatives and their anticipated effects, indicates the data that are relevant for analyzing the alternatives, and leads to informative conclusions.[1]

---

[1] Harvey M. Wagner, *Principles of Operations Research* (Englewood Cliffs, N.J.: Prentice-Hall, 1969) p. 10.

All models involve simplification. This simplification is one of the virtues of modeling, for it permits the analyst to focus on the most important variables and relationships, and to overlook the unimportant aspects of the real-world system. Of course the model should be complex enough to be a good approximation of the real-world problem. With any model, the problem solutions suggested by manipulation of the model must be modified to take into account the differences between the model and the real world. This sequence might be visualized as follows:

Real-world → Model of → Manipulation → Model → Real-world
  Problem   Problem   of Model   Solution   Solution

It is a common failing of management scientists to forget that their models are not the real world in all respects. Likewise, it is a common failing for the manager-client of the operations researcher to ask for more complexity in the models being used, to make them more like the real-world problem. Often further complexity is not the best way for the investigation to proceed, but the analyst loves complexity and goes along with the request, further reducing the likelihood of a productive conclusion to the research.

Management science and the computer go hand-in-hand because management science usually requires the analysis of large amounts of data describing companies, markets, and marketing operations. One of the most common tools of management science is computer *simulation*—a technique whereby models are analyzed by making systematic changes in one or a few variables and evaluating the impact on system performance. For example, the management scientist might wish to know, What will happen if we reduce prices by 1 percent? by 2 percent? 5 percent? 10 percent? By changing this one variable and letting the computer perform the mathematical operations implied by the descriptive model of the market system, some implications can be developed. Simulation is often used to explore system performance over time; for example, a distribution system simulation could be run for a specified number of periods (say, 13 weeks) to trace the effects of some changes made at the beginning of the period, such as a reduction in order processing time or an increase in starting inventories. Simulation is simply the use of a computer-based model to ask "what if?" questions about system performance.

The "scientific approach"

Management science and marketing information systems are part of the general evolution of a more scientific approach to marketing decision making. This scientific approach involves not so much a replacing of management intuition and judgment with more rigorous analytical techniques as a redefinition of the relationship between the manager and the information available to him, the relationship between judgment and analysis, in such a way that the quality of required judgments is improved. The scientific approach is as much a question of attitude and viewpoint concerning the manager's decision-making responsibilities as it is one of techniques. With a scientific approach, the emphasis is on attacking problems systematically, obtaining facts by measurement procedures with known properties, defining the problem and management objectives as precisely as possible, and evaluating alternative courses of management action objectively and thoroughly. Furthermore, the scientific approach involves acting in such a manner that the results of a course of action can be systematically evaluated after the fact in a way that improves understanding of system performance and enhances the quality of future decisions.

Steps in the scientific approach

One way of understanding the nature of management science in marketing is to think of the steps required to implement a "scientific approach" to the solution of a marketing problem. A possible conceptualization of the process is the following:

1. Make the problem definition as explicit as possible, including definition of key variables, probable relationships among them, and management objectives with respect to system performance.
2. Develop a logical flow analysis of the system, tracing the sequence of management analysis and decision required and showing the impact of information about key variables. Figure 5–1 illustrates what such a logical flow analysis could look like.
3. Quantify the variables in the model, gathering necessary information according to carefully planned and generally accepted research procedures.
4. Manipulate the model to test alternative courses of action and to indicate action recommendations.
5. Attempt to implement the recommendations in a controlled environment where adjustments can be made to account for differences between the model and the real world.
6. Use the results of controlled implementation to validate and refine the model.
7. Implement the model recommendations on a full scale but with provision for systematically monitoring changes occurring in the real world that will tend to invalidate the model over time.

These steps in the scientific approach can be labelled (1) explication, (2) logical flow analysis, (3) measurement and quantification, (4) manipulation, (5) experimental implementation, (6) validation and refinement, and (7) full-scale implementation and monitoring.

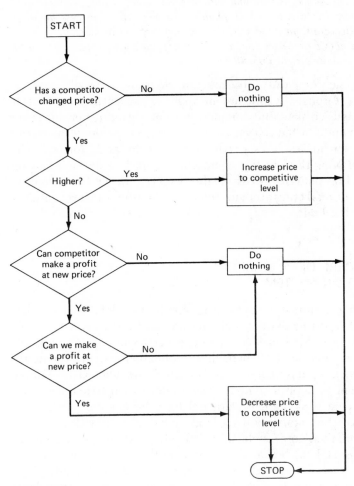

FIGURE 5-1
A simple logical flow analysis for a pricing decision.

Marketing complexity

Many will argue that marketing problems are so complex and the outcomes of marketing decisions so hard to predict that the simplification and precision of management science make it inapplicable to marketing problems. It *is* probably true that marketing decisions *are* more complex and their outcomes more difficult to predict than the traditional areas of management science concern such as inventory management, cash flows, and production scheduling. As one author has put it,

The variables in a marketing problem do not generally exhibit the neat quantitative properties of many of the problems in production,

accounting, or finance. Attitudinal variables play a larger role in marketing;
marketing plans intimately affect planning in the other business areas.
Marketing decisions must be made in the context of insufficient
information about processes that are dynamic, nonlinear, lagged, stochastic,
interactive, and downright difficult.[2]

The basic complexity of marketing decisions is usually cited as
one of the reasons why progress in applying management science to
this area has been slow. But complexity is not a good reason for giving
up the attempt. On the contrary, it is the very complexity of marketing
decisions that makes it especially important to press forward with
attempts to bring the scientific approach to marketing decision making.
The marketing manager needs all the help he can get. The inherent
complexity of marketing decisions soon stretches the manager's intuitive
abilities to the limit.

THE CONCEPT OF A MARKETING INFORMATION SYSTEM

A marketing information system is simply the data sources, data
storage and reporting devices, and data uses that assist marketing managers in their decision making. In this general sense, every marketing
manager has some kind of marketing information system. Today, the
phrase *marketing information system*, which we abbreviate MIS, is
usually meant to imply a computer-based information system consisting
of a large data bank, various statistical tools for analyzing data, computer devices for information retrieval and display as well as storage
and computation, and sophisticated models. Although information
systems existed long before the computer, their design and use was
not always carefully planned and managed. One of the benefits of the
introduction of computers into business organizations has been to bring
management attention into the area of formally planning and analyzing
the flows and uses of information. The people who use the information
and the uses to which it is put are the most important parts of the MIS,
not the computer or the numbers.

Management benefits

Computer-based information systems have the potential to offer several
benefits to the marketing manager. Chief among these are (1) more
timely information, (2) more complete information, (3) more thorough
analysis of available data, (4) a better understanding of relationships

[2] Philip Kotler, *Marketing Management* (Englewood Cliffs, N.J.: Prentice-
Hall, 1967), Preface.

among the elements of the marketing system, and (5) more thorough evaluation of alternatives and consideration of more alternatives.

Three types of systems

There are three stages of marketing information system sophistication and complexity. The simplest MIS is an information-reporting system, giving the manager current data about marketing performance—orders booked during period, sales as a percentage of quota, advertising expenditures, profit margins realized, number of sales calls, and so on. The next level of sophistication is the information storage and retrieval system, in which data are available to the analyst to permit the study of past performance and the development of an understanding of the relationships between the variables controlled by the marketing manager and marketing performance results. The availability of on-line remote computer terminals has made it relatively easy for the manager to have almost immediate access to marketing data banks if he wishes. The third level of sophistication is the use of decision models in the information system. As explained earlier, normative decision models can be used to evaluate alternative courses of action and to select those that best meet the objectives and other decision criteria determined by management and incorporated into the model.

Computer-based systems

In more detailed terms, the stages of analytical sophistication in a computer-based MIS can be described by eight levels, as suggested by Arnold Amstutz:

1. Retrieval *The system can retrieve a record and display the information which it contains.*
2. Aggregation *Gathering numbers from one or more records and producing a total or subtotal.*
3. Arithmetic *Simple arithmetic operations are performed to develop averages or differences.*
4. Logical Analysis *Classification schemes are used to place data into categories, subsets, and segments.*
5. Statistical Analysis *Data are aggregated, extrapolated, and summarized, to develop trends, estimates of variance, and statistical best estimates.*
6. Macro-process models *These models relate factors in the decision environment to current and expected market conditions, and permit consideration of system performance over time.*
7. Behavioral simulation *This involves more sophisticated and detailed modelling of relationships between marketing decision variables and elements of the market system, with the objective of predicting response to marketing action.*

8. Adaptive heuristics   *Heuristics are decision rules for approaching an
optimum; adaptive heuristics permit the system to learn from
experience and proceed toward optimum system performance through
sequential decision making.*[3]

Related to these levels of system sophistication is the extent to
which decision-making authority is given to the information system
and models. Amstutz has suggested that there are seven stages of
system authority:

1. *retrieval*
2. *review and checking of data for errors*
3. *monitoring of performance and reporting of variances*
4. *recommending action*
5. *taking action*
6. *predicting outcomes from action (using behavioral models)*
7. *learning from experience by using adaptive heuristics to modify system
   parameters*[4]

The direct relationship between level of system authority and level of
analytic sophistication is illustrated in Figure 5–2.

THE EVOLUTION OF MIS

Based on his survey in 1968, Amstutz concluded that

*Although a few firms appear to use relatively sophisticated statistical
and modelling techniques, the vast majority is more concerned with
collecting and retrieving data and is unaware of or relatively unconcerned
with the development of frameworks or model structures designed to
aid management in assimilating and using information.*[5]

Reports by other observers confirm this state-of-the-art conclusion,
even at later dates. The relatively slow development of marketing
information systems and management science in marketing reflects a
variety of factors, including shortcomings in the available techniques
and, most important, communication difficulties between professional
analysts and the managers who must use such systems. A general
conclusion is warranted that successful MIS development is an evolutionary process that takes considerable time to progress from the
simplest to the most sophisticated applications of management science
and computing power. Attempts to speed up the process run the risk

[3] Arnold E. Amstutz, "Market-Oriented Management Systems: The Current
Status," *Journal of Marketing Research* 6 (November 1969): 481–496.
[4] Ibid.
[5] Ibid., p. 496.

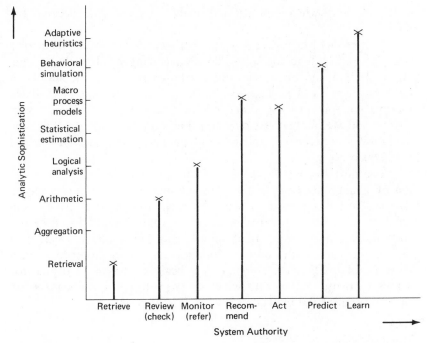

FIGURE 5-2
Relationship between system authority and analytic sophistication in marketing
information systems.

Source: From Arnold E. Amstutz, "Market-Oriented Management Systems: The
Current Status," *Journal of Marketing Research* 6 (November 1969): 483.

of destroying management confidence in the usefulness of the more
sophisticated scientific approaches to analysis and decision making.

The evolution of the MIS can be described by a series of stages:

1. *analysis of marketing results*
2. *research to measure results systematically*
3. *development of electronic data processing*
4. *building a data bank*
5. *creating a statistical analysis capability*
6. *developing a model bank*
7. *increasing MIS authority in decision making*[6]

These are not distinct activities but represent system evolution
toward increasing complexity; electronic data processing may come on
the scene at different points in time, for example, and only becomes

[6] This view and the remarks that follow are based on the concept of MIS
developed by David B. Montgomery and Glen L. Urban in *Management Science
in Marketing* (Englewood Cliffs, N. J.: Prentice-Hall, 1969), pp. 17–26.

really necessary when sophisticated analytical techniques become frequently used.

As illustrated in Figure 5–3, the first step in the development of a scientific approach to marketing decision making involves the systematic collection and analysis of information concerning the results of marketing actions. The stage can be thought of as the use of available information, provided by the company's sales reporting, order processing, and accounting systems, for purposes of understanding the relationship between controllable and uncontrollable variables in the marketplace.

The next step up the ladder of information sophistication is the use of market research, in the form of market surveys, experiments, and syndicated information services (such as consumer panels and retail store audits), to generate data. Of course, marketing decisions are still part of the system of inputs, and the results of marketing actions are part of the output from the market environment. With research information the company can begin to develop a data bank, a library of information with which to begin to study and understand the operation of the marketing system (Figure 5–4).

The data bank

What information should be stored in the data bank? This question is usually more difficult to answer than it first appears. What should be the unit of record keeping: individual customers, sales territories, salesmen, products, brands? In most computer-based MIS, the basic unit is the order line, identified by product, customer, day, and salesman. Data are typically stored in "disaggregated" form—in this case, the order line—and summarized according to the wishes of the

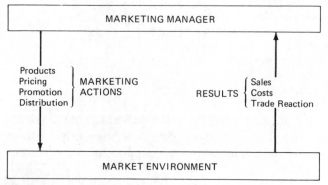

FIGURE 5-3
Marketing information systems: 1.

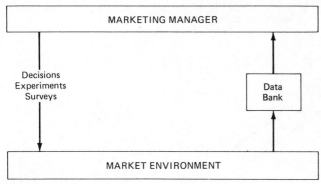

FIGURE 5-4
Marketing information systems: 2.

user in each instance. For example, the order lines can be summarized to get all sales to a given customer, all sales of a given salesman, all sales of a particular type of product, and so on. A disaggregated data file permits maximum flexibility and results in retaining the largest amount of information, but it obviously involves greater storage expense than retaining only summary measures. The whole concept of a disaggregated data bank has developed as a result of the availability of large computers.

Also in the data bank can be such information as market surveys, consumer panel data (for individual families, if desired), inventory records, information about each salesman, and so on. In addition to the actual data, the data bank may also have an information preprocessor (designed to code, clean, and summarize data) and an information-processing capability for retrieval, file organization, and updating.

Every information system requires some method of displaying the data to the information user (Figure 5–5). In computer-based systems, the display unit is either a printing device or some kind of visual display terminal—one using a cathode ray tube, for example. So-called time-shared computing systems, which have become increasingly popular in recent years, typically allow access from remote locations through a teletype device. The system user can initiate information requests and receive answers to his specific requirements, in printed form or perhaps in visual display, although the latter is less common.

The statistical bank

A large amount of disaggregated data has limited usefulness unless it can be easily, inexpensively, and flexibly processed using statistical techniques for summarizing, extrapolating, and otherwise analyzing the

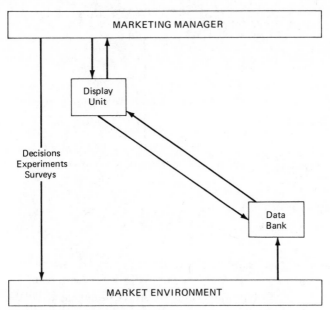

FIGURE 5-5
Marketing information systems: 3.

data (Figure 5–6). Output from the statistical bank can also be stored in the data bank in the form of summary measures. Modern computers make it quite straightforward to include a "library" of standard statistical routines in programs. Common statistical techniques used include analysis of variance and other methods for estimating the parameters of statistical distributions; regression analysis; time-series analysis; chi-squared and other "goodness of fit" tests; and multivariate procedures such as factor analysis, cluster analysis, and discriminant analysis. As noted in previous chapters, some of these multivariate procedures have become quite useful for analyzing consumer panel data and developing and testing alternative market segmentation strategies.

Putting the data bank, the statistical bank, and a display unit capability together produces a true computer-based marketing information system (Figure 5–7). The marketing manager can initiate requests for information either through a data-processing department representative or through his own terminal in the case of time-shared systems. The display unit permits him to both input and retrieve data as required, and the data flow between the statistical bank and the data bank as required for analysis. Continuous monitoring of market performance produces continuous updating of the data bank, often with delays of only a few days between an event and its incorporation into the data bank.

The model bank

Without a model bank, however, the MIS remains essentially unsophisticated and far removed from the potential values in the application of management science to marketing (Figure 5–8). Among the many kinds of models that could be developed and stored in the model bank are advertising budget-level models, sales force call allocation models, distribution system models, pricing decision models, new-product evaluation models, models of consumer behavior, and models of competitive response. Some of these models may be quite simple and others exceptionally complex. One determinant of complexity is the extent to which the probabilistic nature of market response is taken into account. This generally requires the statistical analysis of probability distributions for describing market response to marketing actions and other uncontrollable variables that are believed to influence market response.

Evaluation of alternatives and selection of courses of action represent only one of several ways in which management benefits from the use of models. Some models are much better suited for helping the manager develop his understanding of market processes than they are for actually making decisions. Both of these modeling benefits—better understanding of problems and actual solution of problems—serve to extend the decision maker's "bounds of rationality" and to push out the boundaries that have previously limited the effectiveness of his decision making and the degree of complexity he could deal with.

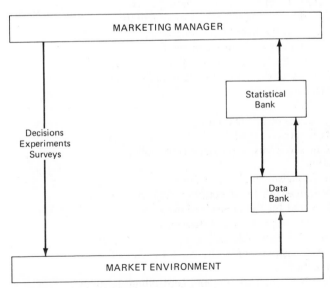

FIGURE 5-6
Marketing information systems: 4.

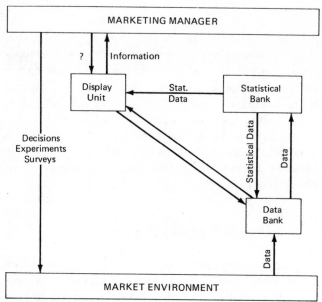

FIGURE 5-7
Marketing information systems: 5.

Montgomery and Urban have suggested the following sets of benefits from these two classes of models:

I. *Descriptive and Predictive Models—Understanding Problems*
   A. *Descriptive Models*
      1. transform data into more meaningful forms
      2. indicate areas for research and experimentation
      3. generate structural hypotheses for testing
      4. provide a framework for measurement
      5. aid in systematic thinking about problems
      6. provide basis for discussion that will lead to common understanding of problem
   B. *Predictive Models*
      1. make forecasts of future events
      2. validate descriptive models
      3. determine sensitivity of predictions to model parameters
   C. *Normative Models—Solving Problems*
      1. provide framework for structuring subjective feelings
      2. provide a tool for the analysis of decisions
      3. assess system implications of decisions
      4. yield solutions to problems
      5. determine sensitivity of decisions to the model's characteristics
      6. provide a basis for updating and controlling decisions[7]

[7] Ibid., p. 14.

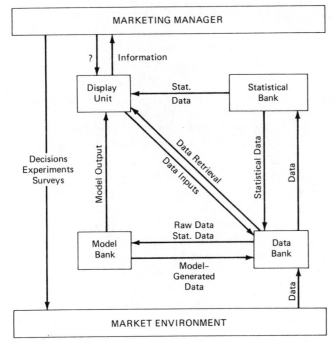

FIGURE 5-8
A complete marketing information system.

WHERE DO WE STAND?

In terms of the simple three-stage classification of MIS used earlier, *reporting systems* have been around for a long time. They are the easiest to develop. Computers have simply increased the ease and speed of getting out reports such as sales volume by district and the like. Computers have also increased the complexity of reporting systems, making them both more expensive and better able to provide more detailed information more quickly.

Information retrieval systems represent a significant extension of reporting systems. They can handle much more data, stored in disaggregated form, permitting greater flexibility in reporting. In the Amstutz survey, almost 90 percent of those reporting were using their information systems for information retrieval, and more than half were maintaining data in disaggregated form (i.e., at the invoice line level). It should be noted, however, that only 83 out of 500 firms (from the *Fortune* list of largest U.S. manufacturers) responded to this survey, and of the 83 only 39 were actually using computer-based marketing information systems. An additional 24 were planning such systems, and 20 neither had nor intended to develop such systems.[8]

[8] Amstutz, op. cit.

Decision systems are quite scarce. In the Amstutz survey, only 22 percent of the respondents who were systems users had given decision-making authority to their computers, and only 8 percent permitted computers to take such action as issuing an order or writing a letter.

In terms of analytical sophistication, 36 percent of the users had macroprocess models and 31 percent had microanalytic simulation capability. As Amstutz has noted, "generally management must gain substantial confidence in the quality of computer-based recommendations (advisory function) before it is willing to extend the authority granted the system."[9]

Models *are* available. Virtually every marketing decision area has received modeling attention from management scientists and researchers. Among the most commonly available are models for advertising media selection, new-product introduction, price level decisions, sales territory design, sales compensation plans, and whether to conduct a market survey and how much to spend for it. Many of the models are not very good, however, in terms of such criteria as understandability, availability of data required to make the model operational, the extent to which key relationships in the model can be measured rather than assumed, and distinction between the variables the manager can control and those he cannot. On such criteria as elegance and sophisticated mathematical reasoning and manipulation, the models often do much better.

Communication problems

The basic problem is one of communication. The manager is not comfortable with the kind of rigor and the jargon used by the management scientist, and the latter is not comfortable with the rules of thumb and intuitive judgment used by the manager. Several people have looked at these problems of implementation and have come to the same conclusion. For example, here are quotations from three different studies:

Management scientists are concerned with creation of new and more sophisticated techniques and give inadequate attention to questions of operational significance. As a result, sound approaches are often discarded because of unforseen implementation difficulties and, all too often, proposed techniques prove to be elegant solutions to irrelevant problems.[10]

. . . the scientist, whether academic or "real world," tends to

---

[9] Ibid., pp. 493–494.
[10] Henry Claycamp, "Letter from the Chairman," *TIMS College on Marketing Newsletter* 5 (November 1971): 3.

identify more with the technical side of his field, is turned on by nice elegant technical problems and solutions, and is rewarded psychologically and professionally by articles which need not involve implemented solutions. . . . The manager is often threatened by new techniques and responds by keeping them in the impractical window-dressing stage indefinitely.[11]

As the [manager] digs any study performed by human researchers in an ordinary OR group, he finds assumptions that are questionable, terminology that is confusing, and a certain tendency to ignore a variety of qualitative issues the manager feels are important. The manager feels that to get deep into the model and find out what is really going on is totally out of the question because he lacks the time and background. The solution to this predicament is often for him to pick on some seeming flaw in the model, usually a consideration left out, and make that the basis for postponing use into the indefinite future.

In this situation the operations researcher's response is often to conclude that his model is not complete enough. Therefore he goes back to work to make things more complicated and probably harder to understand. Meanwhile, the manager continues to use intuitive models that are much simpler than the one rejected.[12]

There is some basis for optimism that this situation may be changing as management ranks become increasingly staffed by well-trained people with graduate degrees in management and related fields. These managers are better able to understand the strengths and limitations of management science and to communicate with the operations researcher. At the same time, operations researchers may be becoming more sensitive to the communication problems and responsibilities involved in their profession. The grandiose schemes of earlier years, under which all marketing decisions would be made by a model bank in the computer-based information system, has given way to a more realistic view of what MIS can contribute and how a system should evolve over time.

SOME GUIDELINES FOR DEVELOPING MIS

Experienced information systems experts have analyzed the factors that discriminate between successful and unsuccessful attempts to develop

[11] David A. Aaker, "Management Science in Marketing: The State of the Art," paper presented at the Fall Conference of the American Marketing Assoc., Houston, Texas (August 1972): 20.

[12] John D. C. Little, *Models and Managers: The Concept of a Decision Calculus, Management Science* (April 1970): B–467.

an MIS. Their analyses can be summarized in a few guidelines:

1. Think small! Set reasonable goals that can be realized in a reasonable period and concentrate on getting usable results that can demonstrate to management the value of MIS.
2. Develop systems that are relevant for current operations and consistent with current practice. Start where the users are and build from there. Don't try to revolutionize the practice of management overnight.
3. Develop an internal systems design capability, but don't be afraid to go outside for help when it is needed. The internal capability is going to make communication much easier over the long run.
4. Involve the user in the design of the system, but don't ask him to list everything he wants in an information system. Let him choose among reasonable alternatives.
5. Think in terms of a flexible information-processing capability—criteria for evaluating information and some statistical capability that will help the manager with specific problems—and avoid developing a report- or printout-oriented system. The assumption that one more report, if anybody wants it, won't cost very much leads to an explosion of paper that eventually buries potential users and destroys interest in the system. People shouldn't be sent information they haven't asked for.
6. Along with a focus on general information capability, select one or a few decision areas where there is high management interest and involvement, and a high probability of demonstrable financial returns from investment in MIS development. New-product decisions are a good example. The best applications from the point of view of selling MIS to the rest of the organization are those in which there is an interaction between finance and marketing.
7. Canned programs (i.e., standardized routines in the program library) provide a starting point for developing useful systems. They can help define user needs but are seldom the ultimate answer. This is equally true for so-called service bureaus and computer utilities; their programs usually must be modified to fit the needs of specific users.
8. It is better to concentrate on maximizing the probability of success than to attempt to maximize the (conditional) value of the potential payoff. The more spectacular application is likely to have a lower probability of success.
9. Build the information system along the evolutionary sequence of development from information storage and retrieval through logical analysis and statistical analysis to modeling and, finally, adaptive control processes. Introduce modeling only when the data and statistical capabilities of the system require it and when management is ready for it. Even then, think small!

It is important to remember that the only good information system is one that will be used by management. Technical elegance is beside the point. A successful system is one that starts where management is, produces useful results early, and accommodates expansion and change in an evolutionary fashion.

SUMMARY

Management science and the computer have been slow in coming to marketing, compared with other fields, partly because of the complexity of marketing problems and partly because of serious communication problems between marketing managers and operations researchers. In general, the operations researchers have developed models and systems too sophisticated for their management users. In addition to technical problems such as the difficulty of parameter estimation, these sophisticated models also scare away the potential management user (who can be quite defensive about his inability to understand models and systems).

Because of its complexity, however, the marketing management field stands to receive major benefits from the development of more sophisticated approaches to decision making. Such approaches can extend the manager's bounds of rationality and strengthen his intuitive decision-making abilities.

MARKETING PLANNING AND FORECASTING

An insightful person has defined planning as the art of the possible. This definition has the virtue of capturing the idea that planning requires both creativity and analysis in the definition of market opportunities and constraints. More completely, planning can be defined as the process of guiding the business toward clearly stated objectives with the best possible view of the future. Planning involves both deciding what is desired and determining the actions required to realize it. It is the process of matching resources with opportunities.

Chapter 1 identified three types of decisions—strategic, administrative, and operational. Each kind of decision requires its own distinct kind of planning.

The planning process involves the use of concepts and information developed in each of the preceding five chapters. It includes definition of corporate and marketing objectives and strategy, analysis of buyer behavior, and determination of market segments. Information provided through market research and the company's marketing information system is a vital input to the planning process. The planning process performs three critical functions in the management of the business:

- It orients the business to the future and synchronizes decisions with changes expected to occur in the marketplace (customer preference, product technology, and competition).
- It coordinates and organizes the actions of the several parts of the business toward common goals and creates commonly shared expectations.
- It controls the operations of the firm by establishing standards against which to evaluate accomplishment and provides for systematic measurement and feedback of results.

TYPES OF PLANS

There are many different ways of characterizing and describing plans. For example, there are *functional* plans for different parts of the business—marketing, production, finance, research and development (R&D), personnel, purchasing, and so on. It is likewise common to describe plans on a time basis ranging from annual planning to long-range planning. Many authors distinguish between short-term *operational* or *tactical* planning ("planning to do things right") and long-term *strategic* planning ("planning the right things to do").

Differentiating among types of plans according to time horizon or type of decision produces the same result. Companies with well-developed planning systems usually have different types of plans, depending on both time period and kind of decision. For example, CPC Europe, a food products manufacturer for both consumer and industrial markets, has a "family" of three plans:

1. *The long-range strategic plan* has a time horizon extending ten or more years into the future. It sets long-range objectives and general strategy for sales volume, earnings, and return on investment; for products and markets (both existing and new); for company relationships with its total external environment; for company organization and structure; and for major resource requirements.
2. *The medium-term business plans* cover a five-year period and set objectives and specific programs for sales, operating expenses, earnings and return on investment for existing products and markets; for development of new products and markets; for capital expenditures, R&D, acquisitions, and financing; and for manpower, managerial, and organizational development. These plans are produced for both CPC Europe as a whole and each of more than twenty national affiliates.
3. *Short-term business and operational plans* cover a one-year period for the same areas as described for the five-year plan but with formal one-year goals that become the standards against which operations during

the year are monitored, evaluated, and controlled. Within the framework of the one-year plan, national affiliates are quite likely to develop quarterly or monthly operating plans in such areas as marketing, production, and purchasing.

At CPC Europe, the planning task itself is carefully planned by the corporate planning manager and his staff. The flow of necessary information is carefully coordinated, and there is a detailed timetable for the planning cycle.[1]

While the CPC Europe system may be somewhat too sophisticated for the needs of a smaller firm, it illustrates the different types of planning and how they fit together. According to the three decision types—strategic, administrative, and operating—the long-range plan is clearly strategic in nature and the short-term plan is clearly concerned with operating decisions. Administrative decisions are dealt with primarily in the medium-term plans, as these are oriented towards the affiliate companies.

Because Chapter 1 dealt primarily with long-range, strategic planning and the role of marketing management in that process, this chapter is concerned more with short- to medium-term planning of marketing operations. In other words, we will assume that the basic strategic choice of products to be offered and markets to be served has been made. This will enable us to concentrate on issues of determining the optimum level and mix of marketing effort to be allocated to those chosen products and markets.

THE MARKETING PLANNING PROCESS

The planning process can be conceptualized as a series of simple questions:

1. *Where are we and how did we get here?*
2. *Where are we headed?*
3. *Where do we want to go?*
4. *What is the best way to get there?*
5. *Who should do what? When?*
6. *How will we know where we are in the future?*[2]

More formally, the planning process is defined by the following stages, keyed to the questions just listed by the numbers in parentheses:

---

[1] J. R. Champion (corporate planning manager, CPC Europe), "Corporate Planning in CPC Europe," *Long-Range Planning* (December 1970): 8–17.

[2] Philip Kotler, *Marketing Management: Analysis, Planning, and Control*, 2d ed. (Englewood Cliffs, N.J.: Prentice-Hall, 1972), p. 366.

1. Situational Analysis
   a. Diagnosis   (1)
   b. Prognosis   (2)
2. Setting Objectives (3)
3. Programing
   a. Strategy   (4)
   b. Tactics   (5)
4. Control   (6)

Situational analysis

The first step in marketing planning is to determine the current state of affairs. This involves an audit of current operations and market position, and an analysis of the past strategic choices and tactical decisions that have led to this position. An appraisal of company strengths and weaknesses, strategic and organizational, and of available resources (financial, human, channels of distribution, products, etc.) is an essential part of this process. A careful assessment of environmental forces—economic, political, social, and technological—is necessary to develop an understanding of pressures on the business and its markets. Such analysis is often best done by outside experts on a consulting basis.

Diagnosis, the first part of situational analysis, is easier when the company has bench marks, in the form of previously established objectives, against which to measure performance and accomplishment. A variety of internal data (sales volume, market share, costs, margins, investment, etc.) and external data (industry sales figure, economic indicators, consultants' market studies, etc.) are required for thorough diagnosis. It should be a shared task rather than the responsibility of a single individual so that common perceptions can be developed as a basis for future planning and decision making, and so that all relevant viewpoints and important information are considered.

An attempt to position current products according to where they are in the product life cycle (a concept developed fully in Chapter 8) can be a very useful diagnostic exercise. Such analysis can also aid in prognosis as the future contributions of existing or identified new products are projected and the need for entirely new products is identified. The results of such analysis can be presented as shown in Figure 6–1.

The part of situational analysis labeled "prognosis" is actually a complicated process of looking into the many factors that will determine the future health of the business. A major part of prognosis is forecasting, but prognosis also involves qualitative analysis of the various forces influencing the business, their probable future development, and the complicated interactions among them. The several steps in developing a thorough prognosis for marketing planning can be described as follows:

1. Identify and evaluate all *major environmental trends* affecting industry and company (such as decreasing investment spending, increasing acceptance of specifically defined new technologies, inflation, increased antipollution forces, decreasing importance of industrial distributors, and so on).
2. *Make explicit all assumptions* necessary to project environmental trends into the future (e.g., a "surprise free" environment—no wars, no major political upheavals, etc.).
3. *Estimate market potential* (defined as the capacity of a defined market to absorb the product of a specified industry during a stated time period) and project industry sales volume as a function of expected trends in economic variables and other environmental factors.
4. *Forecast company sales* as a function of market potential and industry sales volume as well as marketing strategy and budget levels, which should be made as specific as possible at this stage.
5. *Forecast expected profit* as a function of sales volume, making explicit the necessary assumptions about prices, profit margins, costs of advertising, sales promotion, and distribution, as well as administrative expenses. It will be helpful at this stage for the marketing planner to work with financial planners to develop necessary estimates of required investments (both plant and equipment, and working-capital requirements) and calculate expected return on investment.
6. *Analyze estimates for sensitivity to basic assumptions* and to possible error in the estimates of key variables such as prices, margins, selling expenses, and market shares. (As explained in the previous chapter, computer simulation can be very helpful in asking these "What if?" questions.)

The situational analysis may indicate that the business is essentially "on course" toward predetermined objectives that are consistent with the threats and opportunities in the environment. Or it may indicate some serious problems such as major product deficiencies, danger-

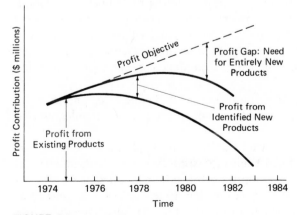

FIGURE 6-1
Product situation analysis.

ously low profit margins, or objectives that are incomplete, inconsistent, or out of phase.

Setting objectives

The central position of objectives in the planning process has already been established. But it is necessary to stress that objectives must be realistic and consistent with available market opportunities and company resources. Unattainable objectives not only serve no useful purpose but inevitably lead to bad decisions, wasted resources, and a demoralized management team. On the other hand, good objectives have a degree of imagination, and setting them requires creativity and some realistic enthusiasm for the company's ability to capture available opportunities. For example, a company objective of growth in profits at the rate of 12 to 15 percent per year can have no completely factual justification but must be defended on the basis of management's confidence and personal wishes.

Such general objectives as profit growth and return on investment need to be supported by a set of more specific objectives relating to sales growth, profit margins, new-product development, acquisitions, and market expansion.

Marketing programing

A marketing program is a plan for coordinated use of all marketing decision variables—product, price, promotion (advertising, personal selling, and sales promotion), and distribution—to attain marketing objectives. A critical part of the marketing program is the precise definition of market segments, their characteristics, size, and behavior. Related to the market segmentation strategy is the development of the generic product concept ("unique selling proposition"), of the benefits to be offered in each segment. Given this product concept, a detailed marketing program can be developed for implementing that concept, including the proper pricing and trade margins; the necessary channels of distribution and services; the correct mix of personal selling, advertising, and other promotional tools; and the right selling presentation and advertising messages to communicate the product concept to the intended market.

A major management problem in marketing programing is to recognize the interdependencies among the decision variables and to use these interactions to accomplish desired results. To illustrate, when Polaroid Corp. tried to introduce its Swinger camera in France, the marketing program suffered from inconsistency between dependence on camera shop dealers to demonstrate the product (since there was no commercial television in France at that time) and a low price and narrow profit margin, which made the product unattractive to the dealer.

A marketing program involves both strategy (a long-term plan for exploiting a product/market) and tactics (short-term plans for achieving specific results). *Tactical* plans (if they are sound) specifically recognize competitors and their probable actions and often involve *contingency* plans detailing steps to be taken if competitors behave differently than expected. Tactical planning is synonymous with operational planning in the marketing area.

Within the marketing program, the personal selling and advertising functions are most likely to have detailed tactical plans. The sales plan with its supporting budget includes sales goals (quotas) broken down by geographic area, new-account development goals, call frequencies for various types of accounts, specific products to be emphasized, key selling ideas for the period, and so on. The advertising plan (which may be nationwide or detailed for specific markets) will include total budget, a basic copy strategy, and media coverage, by time and by product.

If the company has product managers within the marketing organization, then a marketing program will be developed for each specific product. At the same time, a company-wide marketing program must still be developed to coordinate product marketing and direct total marketing effort to the accomplishment of long-term company objectives.

Control

Control of marketing operations is a major reason for marketing planning. The planning process is not complete until specific steps have been planned for evaluating and adjusting the marketing program on an ongoing basis. The central ideas in the concept of control are the continuous monitoring of system performance, comparison of actual accomplishment with predetermined standards, and adjustment of the system to bring it back into line with objectives when performance deviates from the standard. In designing the control dimension of the planning system, then, the planner must decide what to measure, to whom to report the results, and with what frequency.

Objectives, as previously established for guiding the development of the marketing program, now have the additional purpose of serving as standards against which performance is to be evaluated. Additional more detailed standards, such as specific quotas for individual salesmen, may be developed for controlling marketing operations at lower levels. The company's marketing information system can now provide the required information on a routine basis as needed by individual managers.

Experienced marketing managers typically report a preference for fewer rather than more measures as the basis for controlling their day-to-day operations. The trick seems to be to pick the right standards—those that truly reflect (hopefully on a lead rather than lagged basis) current marketing effectiveness and about which something can be done. Among the specific measures that marketing managers have reported using effectively are

- percentage of quota to date, by district
- actual sales compared to forecast, and trend to date
- orders booked to date compared to previous year (as a predictor of sales)
- backlog of orders, trend to date compared to earlier period
- period-to-period changes in market share
- number of distribution outlets as percentage of total available
- rates of awards to bids, correlated with prices and discounts offered
- trend in profit margin

One danger in selecting control measures is that of giving the line manager information that will lead him to act too soon and "second guess" his subordinates before they have had a chance to correct their own problems. For example, weekly or daily reports of order cancellations, by salesman and territory, can lead the sales manager to be critical of his salesman before any trend is established and before he has taken steps necessary to reinstate lost orders. In such situations the salesman might very well withhold information desired by the manager if he expects that it will be used unfairly against him.

MARKETING PLANNING
IN INDUSTRIAL COMPANIES

Before moving on to consider in greater detail the questions of market analysis and sales forecasting, it is appropriate to ask how the requirements for effective marketing planning differ for industrial companies as compared to consumer goods companies. Charles Ames of the consulting firm of McKinsey and Company has made some helpful observations.[3] His remarks are based on an analysis of the planning activities of fifty large, multidivision industrial companies. He traced their planning failures to three causes: (1) failure to fit the marketing planning concept to the industrial context, (2) overemphasis on planning systems at the expense of plan content, and (3) failure to recognize strategic alternatives available to the firm.

Failure to fit concept

Industrial marketing differs from consumer products marketing in several ways. In particular, most industrial marketers serve a variety of markets through a variety of distribution channels, and industrial mar-

---

[3] B. Charles Ames, "Marketing Planning for Industrial Products," *Harvard Business Review* (September-October 1968): 100–111.

keting effectiveness depends to a greater degree on other business functions (especially production, inventory control, engineering, and R&D) for its effectiveness in comparison with consumer products marketing. In Ames' words, "Rather than developing self-contained marketing plans, the industrial marketing planner must analyze and interpret market requirements so that top and operating management can decide how best to respond." Based on these considerations, Ames concluded that many companies had made a mistake of turning over the entire planning task to the marketing manager.

Overemphasis on system

Ames' finding that system was overemphasized at the expense of content has also been identified as a planning problem by many other students of planning and seems to be a common planning problem in all contexts, both consumer and industrial marketing.[4] Ames found the problem illustrated by the use of standardized formats for reports with little applicability to specific products and markets. It also led to a large amount of work for operating personnel and heavy demands on their time that made them less than enthusiastic about the planning process.

Failure to recognize alternatives

This problem is colorfully described as "tunnel vision"—too much straight-line projection of the past and a tendency to base current plans on past programs, to assume that the future will be like the past. Ames found that wishful thinking often dominated the planning process in the form of reluctance to admit that prices were too high, product quality inadequate, service poor, and so on. In his words, "insufficient or less-than-candid analysis is a prime cause of unimaginative planning." Likewise, another author has found that a major cause of planning failure is the development of "one-alternative plans" and failure to evaluate alternative courses of action.[5]

In contrast to these common elements of planning failures, Ames found three factors that characterized the successful marketing planning system: (1) better definition and direction from the top, (2) development of fact-founded product/market strategies, and (3) superior programing for strategy implementation.

Better definition and direction

Management involvement in the planning process must be there, but in a guiding role rather than one of interference. There are four ways

[4] For example, see Kjell-Arne Ringbakk, "Why Planning Fails," European Business (Spring 1971): 15–27.

[5] Ibid., p. 19.

in which management must participate in marketing planning to make it work: (1) specify corporate objectives, (2) determine organizational arrangements for planning and implementation, (3) provide for interfunctional coordination, and (4) contribute to marketing planning such specific information as required while avoiding an aggressive role that inhibits the exchange of ideas and opinions, especially about problems and alternative courses of action. Ames quoted an executive on this subject:

But so many considerations and options require a general management perspective that marketing can't be expected to come up with recommendations that make any sense from my point of view. Unless I set the basic direction for our business, specify who is to plan what, see to it that engineering and manufacturing really work with marketing to provide what is needed, and then challenge and contribute any ideas I can on how our business can be developed, the whole planning effort is nothing more than a paperwork exercise.[6]

Fact-founded product/market strategies

In Ames' opinion, "strategy development is an art few companies have mastered. Those that have this expertise stress the need for comprehensive knowledge of the economics of the business and the trends of the market." Experience suggests that poor planning often reflects inadequate market information combined with a limited conceptual understanding of what strategy is all about. Especially in industrial markets where several competitors are going after the same limited market potential (and where excess industry capacity is a chronic problem), sound knowledge of the economics of one's own business and that of competitors is a prerequisite for understanding the constraints within which pricing strategies, customer selection strategies, and long-term market development programs must be developed.

Superior programing

In companies with successful marketing planning, Ames found three ground rules that fostered superior marketing programing. First, management would approve no major program or project unless it was related to a product/market strategy that had been clearly defined. This requirement ensures that every product or project has a reasonable degree of success and relates it to the rest of the business so that they work together toward common purposes. Second, there is specific provision for follow-through on all major programs and projects, especially those that cut across functional lines. This is a particular kind of

---

[6] Ames, op. cit.

control, ensuring that the company actually does what someone says it will do. Third, successful companies used detailed programing techniques, indicating step by step what actions were required to reach a target; these techniques included PERT and other network techniques. They ensure that performance can be measured against specific bench marks and help signal potential problems soon after they have emerged.

Ames' comments are very helpful in identifying the requirements for effective marketing planning in industrial companies. They state clearly the need for good market analysis, close top management involvement in the planning process, and specific attention to problems of coordination among the various functional areas that share with marketing the responsibility for marketing success.

MARKET ANALYSIS

Good market data, intelligently analyzed, are the *sine qua non* of marketing planning. Among the most important informational inputs to the planning process are the following:

- a measure of market potential (industry sales) in each segment for a 5- to 10-year period
- identification of key buying decision influencers, their characteristics, and their buying patterns
- a company sales forecast
- an estimate of the marketing expense required to realize stated objectives

Definition of terms

Market potential, as defined earlier, is the capacity of a specified market to absorb the product of a particular industry in a stated period. Market, product, and period must be precisely defined for the concept of market potential to have meaning. Normally, industry sales volume is the same as market potential, assuming that there are no major deficiencies in marketing effort. For new or rapidly expanding markets (i.e., increasing primary demand) market potential is harder to define and takes on a more theoretical character. For example, what is the U.S. market potential of an electric, battery-powered automobile? It is possible to defend a variety of estimates, from near zero (there are no battery service stations, so how can there be a market for the car?) to very high numbers like 25 to 50 million units over a 5-year period (if one assumes that every urban household is a potential customer).

Market potential is best thought of as an upper limit that sales would reach if the company made an unlimited marketing effort (Figure 6–2). A monopolist in a stable market would approach 100 percent of market potential but probably never quite reach it because

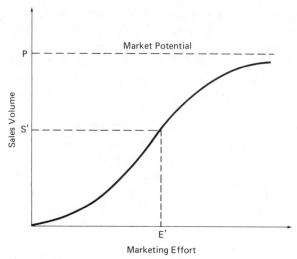

FIGURE 6-2
Relationship between market potential and sales forecast.

of the unjustified expense of selling to and servicing some potential customers.

A *demand schedule* is an estimate of the quantities of product demanded at various prices. There can be demand schedules for a company and for an industry. The demand schedule recognizes that demand for the product or service is determined in part by its price relative to competing products. Implicit in the estimate of market potential is an assumption about price, not just for similar products but for substitute products as well. An estimate of the market potential for fiberglass tire cord, for example, must make some assumptions about the prices of nylon, rayon, steel, and other tire cords relative to fiberglass. A demand schedule is useful in studying the relationship between price and sales volume. Estimating the demand schedule, especially for new products, is a difficult task requiring a large degree of experienced and hopefully unbiased managerial judgment. Interviews with key buyers, and perhaps a price experiment in a limited market test, can be helpful.

A *sales forecast* is a prediction of the sales volume actually expected by the company during the stated period, usually one year. It must be based on an assumed marketing program for exploiting available market potential (unless one is willing to assume that there is no relationship between sales volume and marketing effort!) The sales forecast can be thought of as a point estimate on the demand schedule. But since price is only one of several variables influencing sales volume, any attempt to use the demand schedule to forecast sales volume must also assume a marketing program (selling effort, advertising, etc.).

A *sales quota* is a part of the sales forecast assigned to some person or organizational unit (salesman, product manager, etc.) as his responsibility during the planning period. It is a goal and a standard against which performance will be evaluated. As such, it is part of the control system. Quotas can be developed for goals other than sales volume—for example, for new accounts, profit margin on sales, and number of displays set up in dealers' showrooms.

Figure 6–2 summarizes these basic concepts. Point E' is the assumed level of marketing effort, and S' is the sales forecast. P is the total market potential. The S-shaped curve would be a demand schedule if price were substituted for marketing effort on the horizontal axis. In a more general sense, the S-shaped curve is a *response function* relating market response (sales) to marketing effort.

The response function

Most marketing managers could significantly improve the quality of their decision making by thinking in terms of a response function. How does sales volume respond to

- number of salesmen and sales calls?
- advertising budget levels?
- customer service level (e.g., number of days between receiving an order and the customer's receiving shipment of it)?
- price discounts?

Obviously, the manager must make decisions every week based on assumed relationships between effort and response. Those decisions could be better if the response function was known with some degree of precision.

The response function can be estimated from correlation studies of the relationship between marketing effort in the past and sales results. Such studies are limited, of course, by the difficulty of sorting out the effects of various marketing variables and of establishing cause-and-effect relationships. More expensive but more accurate are experiments in which each marketing variable of interest is systematically varied under controlled conditions and market response is carefully monitored over time. As a company begins to add modeling and simulation capability to its marketing information system, estimates of response functions for each marketing variable should become a high-priority research task.

Models of buyer behavior

In a sense, the response function is a model of buyer behavior. If the response function is to be estimated through judgment rather than through empirical research, then a good knowledge of buyer behavior can help in estimating the shape of the curve.

Since Chapter 2 developed an overview of models of buyer behavior and stressed their importance in a professional, scientific approach to managerial decision making, here it is only necessary to point out their relationship to the planning process. First, such models can define the variables that management must measure and understand in detail as part of the planning process. Many companies' initial attempts to establish a marketing planning system have failed because there was little understanding of the factors that influence demand for their products. It therefore becomes exceedingly difficult to develop a meaningful data base for the planning effort. Attempts to forecast sales and develop coordinated estimates across products and markets become statistical fishing expeditions unenlightened by good theory.

Second, models of buyer behavior help make sense out of available data. By identifying key variables and suggesting possible relationships, they can bring structure into apparent chaos and begin to suggest the priorities to be assigned to the various elements of the marketing mix. How do buyers view the trade-off between price and quality? What is the role of the dealer in the buyer's decision process? Understanding the buyer's decision process is the first step in defining the best ways to influence that process.

Third, models of buyer behavior can aid predictions of response to marketing effort and thus contribute to more accurate forecasts. Since all forecasting involves prediction of the future consequences of marketing actions, a set of assumptions about buyer response must be used in forecasting. They should be made explicit and compared with available market information.

Estimating market potential

A company is fortunate if it is doing business in markets where governmental, industry association, and other data sources are available for estimating market potential. Industries and countries vary widely on this score. In industrial markets the United States, with its Standard Industrial Classification (SIC) code and regular reporting of industrial data by the Bureau of the Census, probably has the best market data in the world. Level of industrialization seems to be a poor indicator of the quality of data available. Germany, for example, has much less market data than many less developed Latin American countries. Likewise, the United States also offers the most complete and sophisticated range of syndicated consumer market data service such as consumer panels, retail-store audits, survey research firms, and computerized monitoring of product movements through the trade. The presence of such data sources can be tremendously helpful in estimating market potential.

At the risk of oversimplifying a very difficult and complex task, it is possible to indicate a logical sequence of steps to be taken in estimating the size of a market. The following sequence assumes that we are estimating the size of a market for a new product.

Define the market population

The market is defined by geographic limits and by the characteristics of potential buyers—age, income, occupation, and the like in the case of consumers and industry affiliation, size, technical expertise, and so forth in the case of industrial buyers. Definition of market population should include all relevant market segments, and the segments should be analyzed as distinct entities.

Estimate the number of consuming units

This entails a head count of the number of buyers in each of the segments. It is reasonably easy to do.

Estimate the spending
ability of consuming units

Ability to spend is a key determinant of demand. Much of the necessary analysis may already have been done in developing the segmentation strategy. But spending ability may vary widely among market segments in both consumer and industrial markets. Especially where the product requires substantial investment, ability to spend is of serious importance in market analysis.

Analyze buyer predispositions

Predispositions include existing loyalties to brands and suppliers, attitudes, needs, preferences, knowledge about the product, and so on. Predispositions reflect the strength of existing relationships with suppliers, the importance of the product to the buyer, and the marketing efforts of competitors.

Estimate willingness to spend as a
function of planned marketing effort

Willingness to spend reflects predispositions and the influence of marketing effort on them. The development of a market for a new product will occur faster or more slowly, depending on the level of marketing effort, although a variety of other factors will also determine the speed of the buyer's decision process.

Estimate rates of purchase and product usage

These estimates should be made for each segment, based on steps 3–5 in this list, with special attention to the importance of heavy users and especially large customers. This will yield a measure of market penetration for each segment and requires the most difficult of all judgments—the rate at which each customer or group of customers will buy and use the product.

Sum the estimates for all
segments to get total market potential
Multiplying total number of consuming units by rate of product usage leads to an estimate of total market potential.

So far, we have assumed that we are trying to estimate the potential market for a new product, of which the company is sole supplier. Thus, the estimate of market potential can lead directly to a sales forecast once decisions have been made concerning level of marketing effort. When considering market potential for new products entering competitive markets, specific judgments about market share (again, as a function of planned marketing effort) will be required in going from estimate of market potential to company sales forecast.

Sales forecasting

The process of sales forecasting can be a frustrating management exercise because, like all predictions, forecasts inevitably require judgment and almost always contain error, and because human factors always complicate the use of forecasts. Figure 6–3 presents a view of the factors to consider in thinking about the forecasting problem.

The starting point for any forecast is the nature and level of market demand. The more variability there is in demand, the more difficult it is to develop an accurate sales forecast. This important fact is often ignored. A good forecasting method can often yield inaccurate forecasts.

Next comes market data, which may also be incomplete, highly

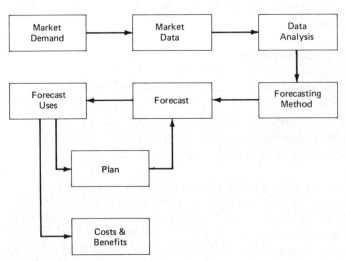

FIGURE 6-3
A view of the forecasting problem.

variable, and biased (if provided by dealers, salesmen, or customers themselves). Then the data must be analyzed—summarized, adjusted, and so on, often by an analyst who must add some of his own judgments (to correct for salesmen's bias, for example).

The analyzed data become inputs to a forecasting method, which also requires a number of assumptions about the form of the data and their accuracy. The forecast that results is used in a number of ways, one of which is in the development of the marketing plan. But the plan itself is one input to the forecast, and here we see that planning and forecasting constitute an iterative process requiring going through the plan⇌ forecast loop a number of times with increasing degrees of refinement.

Finally, the way the forecast is used leads to a set of benefits and costs that determine the true value of the forecasting process. Improvement in the set of costs and benefits can come from any step in the process—using marketing effort to reduce variability in market demand, obtaining better data, doing better data analysis, improving the forecasting method and the quality of the forecast, or changing the way the forecast is used in decision making.

Forecast uses

It is hard to separate the uses of a forecast from the uses of the plan itself. They are part of the same process that leads to common objectives for different parts of the business and to coordinated action. However, the specific estimate of sales revenue has a number of specific uses, including

- planning production, including size of labor force, and detailed production scheduling
- cash flow planning
- setting inventory levels
- planning purchases
- capital investment decisions
- setting dividend policy
- determining competitive bidding strategy
- setting prices
- planning advertising and sales promotion budgets
- deciding number of salesmen to be hired and trained
- setting sales quotas for salesmen and distributors

In short, the entire business is tuned to the forecasted revenue level and the pattern of expected sales. It should come as no surprise, then, when the business comes reasonably close to realizing its revenue forecast—all marketing efforts, production, and financial decisions were planned on that basis. A businessman friend remarked to me a short time ago with considerable pride, "Our business is running at 200 percent of plan!" When I asked whether this indicated a good result or a bad forecast, he had no answer. He did complain that he was working exceptionally hard as a result, and it was obvious that many of his problems could have been avoided by a more accurate forecast.

Developing the sales forecast calls for a systematic procedure and careful attention to the pervasive problem of making necessary assumptions explicit. The following sequence of steps indicates the relationship between forecasting and the rest of the planning process:

1. Gather data and make necessary assumptions about the external environment (economic, technological, social, political).
2. Estimate market potential (industry sales).
3. Input key managerial judgments about products, markets, and competitive policies as stated in the corporate strategic plan.
4. Appraise all available data on the market environment.
5. Develop the strategic marketing plan.
6. Develop the sales forecast.
7. Develop the tactical marketing plan and refine the marketing program.

The first five steps are continuous, long-range planning tasks, whereas the last two are recurring, short-term (annual, quarterly, and monthly) tasks.

Forecasting methods

The choice of forecasting methods should be based on consideration of several factors, including data availability, accuracy of available data, management sophistication, intended forecast use, and availability of electronic data processing. Sophistication in forecasting methods can easily run ahead of data quality and management ability to use the results. Well-established products pose a fundamentally different forecasting problem than new products, and forecasting methods should be chosen accordingly.[7]

The following brief review of forecasting methods is far from exhaustive and has the objective of suggesting the range of methods available. This review begins with the simpler methods and moves toward the more complex.

Executive judgment and its more formal-sounding cousin, the "jury of executive opinions," are simply methods for drawing on managerial

---

[7] For a good explanation of the influence of product life cycle on the selection of forecasting method, see J. C. Chambers, S. K. Mullick, and D. D. Smith, "How to Choose the Right Forecasting Technique," *Harvard Business Review* (July–August 1971): 45–74.

experience to develop a sales forecast. While all forecasting requires judgment, the problems of relying solely on this method were summarized well by the manager who observed, "It has never been clear to me whether we are pooling our knowledge or our ignorance."

Sales force estimates have the advantage of coming from those who are closest to the marketplace, but they are not without problems. If the estimates influence forecast, forecast determines quota, and quota determines compensation, then pessimistic estimates are to be expected. On the other hand, optimism may be expected if the salesman isn't penalized for it. For example, an optimistic estimate is likely if forecasts are used for production planning, and increased production and stocks lead to quicker delivery and lower prices, which make it easier for the salesman to obtain orders.

Surveys of customer buying intentions are helpful aids in sales forecasting if the customer is not afraid that he is committing himself to buy. Such surveys can be conducted by outside research agencies, by the internal research staff, or by the salesmen as part of their territory coverage. Salesmen must be trained and supervised properly in order to fulfill this additional responsibility, however. The information the salesmen are asked to provide should be of some value to them personally, and it must be clear that this is part of their responsibility for which they are compensated.[8]

A major problem with both sales force estimates and surveys of customer buying intentions is that neither salesmen nor customers are likely to be fully informed about the company's future marketing plans. As stated earlier, the plan must be an input to the forecast. In addition, neither salesmen nor their contacts in customer organizations are likely to be aware of all the environmental forces that are likely to influence the business during the coming period.

Projection of past sales into the future is a simple statistical procedure of finding a line of best fit through the plot of past sales and extrapolating it. The problem with this technique is that it is based on a questionable assumption that the future will be like the past. A slightly better technique is to first determine the trend line and then adjust it upward or downward to reflect plans and objectives. For example, one company has forecasted sales by plotting the trend line of its subsidiaries in each country and then adding an increment of 5, 10, or 20 percent above the trend each year, depending on its present degree of market penetration (making the questionable assumption that the

[8] F. E. Webster, Jr., "The Industrial Salesman as a Source of Market Information," *Business Horizons* (Spring 1965): 77–82.

weaker the present position the faster the company's sales should grow in the future, a forecast based more on wishful thinking than on analysis).

Regression analysis is a technique for analyzing the impact of many independent variables (say, advertising, previous period's sales, number of salesmen, and price) on a dependent variable (sales). The regression equation takes the form

$$Y = a + b_1X_1 + b_2X_2 + \ldots + b_nX_n$$

where n is the number of independent variables, the b_i's are measures of the impact of each independent variable on the dependent variable, Y is the dependent variable, and a is the intercept of the regression line on the sales axis (when all the X_i's equal zero). Projection can be thought of as a special case of regression analysis in which only one independent variable (time) is considered.

Regression analysis is a reasonably sophisticated statistical technique that can be performed much more efficiently with the aid of a computer. Many computer service bureaus offer regression analysis as one of their standard statistical packages. With the aid of the computer, literally hundreds of combinations of possible independent variables can be tested in developing a meaningful regression equation to be used in sales forecasting. Such analysis should be performed by someone knowledgeable in statistical analysis in order to avoid such technical problems as lack of independence among the "independent" variables, autocorrelation, and other ways in which data may fail to meet the requirements of the regression model, thus leading to serious forecast error.

It is important to realize that, to be helpful as an independent variable for forecasting sales, the variable should be easier to predict than the dependent variable. Regression thus takes on special value for forecasting where demand is quite highly variable but is influenced by several variables that are reasonably easy to predict. It can only be used where there are many years of past data to analyze (at least 5, with 10 or more highly preferable) and where it is reasonable to assume that the relationships between independent and dependent variables are changing very slowly, if at all. Any major "structural" changes in a market will destroy the validity of the regression model developed by analyzing past data.

Time-series analysis is another reasonably sophisticated statistical procedure for "decomposing" a sales history into four components: (1) a basic trend line; (2) cyclical variations, such as those caused by the business cycle; (3) seasonal (month-to-month) variations in demand; and (4) a "random" or "unexplained" component. When the basic trend line has been developed, it can be projected into the future, with necessary adjustments for the expected direction of the business cycle and seasonal variations. Time series analysis is also a standard feature of many computer service bureau libraries.

Seldom is the time series analysis adequate by itself for sales forecasting because it doesn't take marketing plans into account, except in the implicit assumption that they will not change. The so-called "random" component of the time series actually reflects changing marketing effectiveness and competitive conditions.

Of course there are a variety of other forecasting techniques, many of them refinements on these basic techniques. Computer simulation can be used to trace the consequences of different sets of assumptions.

Most actual sales forecasting procedures use a variety of statistical and judgmental methods that are subject to almost continual refinement (which makes it hard to study forecast accuracy over time). Whatever combination of methods is used, experience suggests several guidelines for intelligent forecasting:

1. The forecast should be put in writing, including all necessary assumptions and a brief description of the forecasting method used.
2. The forecast should not be worshiped but should be revised as conditions change and new information becomes available.
3. Management users should actively participate in the forecasting procedure, contributing facts, insights, and necessary assumptions, and not simply consume the forecast once it is prepared.
4. A new forecasting method should not be used until management understands it in detail.

SUMMARY

Planning is the process of matching resources to opportunities, as both change over time, and directing the business into the future in a coordinated fashion. Good planning is hard work. It requires an analysis of the environment within which the firm is operating and a careful appraisal of strengths and weaknesses. In this chapter we have focused on marketing planning for the medium to short term and have emphasized the problems of market analysis and sales forecasting, avoiding detailed discussion of analytical techniques in favor of general managerial guidelines for improved planning effectiveness.

MANAGING CREATIVITY IN MARKETING

In the words of Peter Drucker, every business has only two basic functions—marketing and innovation, the entrepreneurial functions. The basic purpose of any business is to create a satisfied customer, "for it is the customer, and he alone, who through being willing to pay for a good or a service, converts economic resources into wealth, things into goods."[1] As argued in Chapter 1, profit is the reward for creating a satisfied customer, and marketing is the process by which customer needs are defined and the resources of the firm are directed toward the objective of creating a satisfied customer. Marketing is broader than selling; it is the whole set of activities by which the firm responds to its market environment.

Innovation is the process of creating better goods and services that are determined to have value by the customer—not just more goods and services but better goods and services offering greater

[1] Peter F. Drucker, *The Practice of Management* (London: Mercury Books, 1961), p. 35.

economic value and leading to a more satisfied customer and more profit. Innovation goes well beyond research and development of products. It is a basic business function, extending across all activities and parts of the organization, for it is the efficiency and effectiveness of all parts of the business that ultimately determine the value offered to the customer.

H. B. Atwater, a General Mills executive, has stressed the importance of true marketing innovation in these words:

We feel that . . . strategic innovation is probably more likely to create major increases in profit than optimizing tactical operations. . . . We feel most strongly that only by creating major discontinuities in established marketing patterns are we going to be able to grow in profit at our projected rate.[2]

Note Mr. Atwater's equating of "innovation" and "major discontinuities." Here the point is that creativity must be at the heart of economic activity. How else can profit be realized except in creating new value by the judicious combination of new elements, which is really what creativity is all about. It therefore follows that the basic commitment and logic of the healthy firm must be to change, not to preserve the status quo.

You would have a hard time finding an observer of management who disagrees with these statements about the importance of innovation. Why is it, then, that lack of innovation is a major cause of company decline and failure? As noted by Peter Peterson, formerly U.S. Secretary of Commerce and before that president of Bell & Howell,

Most of us spend most of our time, money, and energy, not as creative marketers who build new markets and total consumption, but rather at what might be called "share of market" gadgeteering. We have become highly proficient at doing the same things a little bit better. . . . Much of what we euphemistically refer to as creativity is actually a kind of chrome-polished creativity, where we put a bit of polish on the same old products and selling techniques.[3]

Why do managers continually ask for new dedication to the task of innovation? Because it is perhaps the most difficult of all management functions. The source of the difficulty is the nature of the creative process and a basic inconsistency between the environment required for creativity and that created by most hierarchical, complex, formal organizations. In this chapter we will develop some observations about the nature of the creative process and offer some suggestions for improving the creative environment of the organization and stimulating its creative output. We will begin by considering the nature of

---

[2] H. B. Atwater, Jr., "Integrating Marketing and Other Information Systems," paper presented to the National Industrial Conference Board, 1967, p. 7.

[3] Peter T. Peterson, "Iconoclasm," in *Plotting Marketing Strategy*, Lee Adler, ed. (New York: Simon & Schuster, 1967), p. 309.

creativity and the creative process. Then we will look at the characteristics of the creative person and some implications for the organization and management of the creative process. After identifying some barriers to creativity, we can assess some of the best-known techniques for stimulating creativity and suggest some positive steps that a company can take to improve its creative output.

CREATIVITY

Creativity is the ability to develop new combinations of value to the individual or to society. Creative output has two characteristics: uniqueness and value. Creativity is a form of problem solving, and any problem solving can be said to be creative to the extent that it has one or more of the following characteristics:

1. *The solution has novelty and value.*
2. *The thinking is unconventional in the sense that it requires modification or rejection of previously accepted ideas.*
3. *The thinking requires high motivation and persistence taking place over a considerable span of time (continuously or intermittently) or at high intensity.*
4. *The problem as initially posed was vague and undefined so that part of the task was to formulate the problem itself.*[4]

Creativity is an individual capacity for identifying new relationships—the process of *bisociation.* Popular conceptions of creativity tend to focus on uniqueness but overlook the value component. "Creative" is often made synonymous with "far out," and we tend to think of creative people as different and even "weird." It is good, therefore, to have a clear definition of creativity in mind: *the individual ability to find new combinations that have value.* This definition clearly applies to the creative arts—music, painting, sculpture, literature, and so forth. It also applies to humor, where the essential element is the unexpected, the unique combination of two observations previously not seen as related.

Creativity has been defined in several ways that stress the importance of uniqueness and new combinations. All creativity is *metaphoric*—that is, it involves a statement of relationship among elements previously perceived as unrelated. It involves "making the familiar strange" as old ways of looking at things yield to new insights and new elements of beauty. Creative output is by definition unexpected and intellectually exciting. It contains the element of surprise.

---

[4] A. Newell, J. C. Shaw, and H. H. Simon, "The Process of Creative Thinking," in H. E. Gruber, G. Terrell, and M. Wertheimer, eds., *Contemporary Approaches to Creative Thinking* (New York: Atherton, 1962), pp. 65–66.

The essence of creativity is to ask, "What if?" to make the familiar strange, to reject (temporarily, at least) what has been "known" and accepted.

THE CREATIVE PROCESS

The creative process we will define as the mental stages involved in the generation of creative output—the method by which new combinations are identified. There are four stages: preparation, incubation, insight, and verification.

Preparation understand your product! _Research

It is appropriate to remind ourselves that creativity is problem solving. Gathering facts about the problem to be solved is absolutely essential to creative success. The advertising man will thoroughly understand his client's product and market before he attempts to write advertising. Michelangelo devoted tremendous energy and time to the study of anatomy. Hemingway's life style was dedicated to accumulating the rich variety of human experience necessary to portray characters, situations, and emotions truthfully and uniquely.

An important part of the preparation stage is the restructuring and restatement of the problem. It is quite unlikely that the original problem statement will prove to be adequate in the light of more complete information gathered during the preparation stage. It is important to note also that these four stages in the creative process do not occur in lock-step fashion. Rather, there is likely to be a great deal of repetition, backtracking, and iteration in the process.

Incubation Think about the problem

Seldom does a solution to a problem appear immediately. Recall our earlier definition of creativity in problem solving as involving at least one of four characteristics, one of which is that the thinking requires persistence and high motivation occurring over an extended time span, continuously or intermittently. In this incubation stage the problem is put on the shelf, so to speak; it is dropped from conscious thought into the subconscious, where it continues to be worked on, perhaps appearing from time to time in conscious attention, where it is dealt with for a while and then returned to the subconscious. Incubation is a reaction to the basic frustration of the creative process, a recognition that hard work is involved and the goal of a problem solution not readily achievable.

Insight

The solution to the problem - you were thinking about

Insight involves the sudden emergence into consciousness of a solution to the problem. It is the "Ahha!" or "Eureka!" phenomenon. It has been said that incubation and insight serve to differentiate true creativity from the more routine kind of problem solving that occurs when well-known principles are applied to familiar problem definitions. Some psychologists argue that insight is the best evidence there is for the existence of the incubation stage.

Suddenness is one of the characteristics of insight. People who regularly engage in creative activity know the importance of being able to catch the insight when it comes. Many report such practices as keeping a note pad and pencil beside one's bed because ideas often come in the evening, even waking the individual suddenly. Others report that the time immediately after waking—say, while shaving and showering—is one of the most productive, as if the mind were refreshed and renewed and ready to yield unique and fresh ideas.

Verification

The initial insight is often invalid; it proves not to be a true solution to the problem. The verification stage is the testing of the validity and reasonableness of the solution yielded through insight. It often reveals the inadequacy of the new combination and requires that the problem solver return to the incubation stage or even to the problem definition and fact-gathering stages. It is very important to note that original ideas do not always solve the problem, that the ideas the problem solver is most comfortable with are least likely to be unique, and that those that are truly unique are not likely to appear acceptable at first. As an advertisement for the J. Walter Thompson advertising agency has observed, "If you are comfortable with it right from the start, chances are it is not a new idea."

This is an exceptionally important point, for it gets at the basic difficulty of the creative process—few of us are really comfortable with a new idea. True creativity therefore requires a high degree of personal courage and a certain indifference to the opinions of other people.

CHARACTERISTICS OF THE CREATIVE PERSON

The nature of the creative process and the difficulty of true creativity suggest some of the characteristics of the creative person. Intelligence doesn't seem to be related to creativity except in areas of science requiring a large amount of education and specialized training. Among the characteristics of creative people that have been identified in research programs are the following: inherited sensitivity, early training, liberal education (creating openness to ideas and the ability to deal with questions rather than answers), asymmetrical ways of thought, personal courage, sustained curiosity, dedication, willingness to work, and freedom from time bonds. The latter is worth commenting on. It seems that the creative person does not work by the clock and may even have trouble making distinctions between morning, noon, and night in terms of the rhythms of his own life. Time has a personal, not a social, meaning for the creative person. Truly creative people seldom respond well to deadlines set by others. Creative people are more likely to be asocial than social, to care more for their own judgments of personal worth than those of others.

Other characteristics of creative people have special significance for the problem of managing them. They prefer situations that are less structured. As Henry Adams noted, "Chaos often breeds life, when order breeds habit." Here again we see the important relationship between the unconventional and creativity. At the Aspen International Design Conference in 1966, Ben Shahn was reported to have cried out "Give me more chaos!" in reaction against the excessive reliance on order and the logical world of reason as factors hindering true creativity in design. The creative person tends to be less dogmatic (and therefore more open to new ideas); he tends to view authority as relative rather than absolute. He tends to make fewer black-and-white distinctions and to show less conventional and conformist behavior. He shows more independence in both social and intellectual judgments. He has a better-developed sense of humor and shows a willingness to express whims and impulses, to be somewhat freer and less rigidly controlled. Other characteristics include flexibility of mind, tolerance of ambiguity, perserverance, discernment and sensitivity, self-confidence, and a preference for opportunity over personal security.

In summarizing his studies of creative persons, Abraham Maslow concluded:

It seemed to me that much boiled down to the relative absence of fear. They seemed to be less afraid of what other people would say or demand or laugh at. Perhaps more important, however, was their lack of fear of their own insides, of their own impulses, emotions, thoughts.[5]

The relationship between creativity and the individual is perhaps captured best by Carl Rogers in his comment: "The creative process is the emergence in action of a novel relational product, growing out of the uniqueness of the individual."[6]

[5] Quoted in "You and Creativity," *Kaiser Aluminium News* 25, no. 3 (1968): 25.

[6] Ibid., p. 3.

RELATIONSHIP TO THE ORGANIZATION

Some have argued that creative people cannot be managed, and some creative people argue that they should not be managed. Other observers believe that managing creative people is no more difficult than managing others. All three viewpoints are wrong. The truth is that creativity and creative people present unique management problems because they are somewhat unique phenomena. Creativity is different from routine problem solving, and truly creative people, regardless of where they are found within the organization, need certain conditions to be truly productive.

In some important respects, formal organizations conflict with the needs of the creative person. Formal organizations are best equipped to satisfy the individual's physical and security needs, whereas the creative person most needs the satisfaction of unique personal achievement. He is motivated by the need for achievement and the need for self-esteem, the highest-order needs in Maslow's need hierarchy. He has his own value system and operates from within. He substitutes his own thinking for orthodoxy and has a high regard for his own ability.

CHARACTERISTICS OF ORGANIZATIONS
THAT IMPEDE CREATIVITY

Formal organizations are best designed to do routine work. They are directed by authority and consensus rather than individual insight and initiative. They are much better at analysis and evaluation than at creativity, and they tend to punish failure as frequently as they reward accomplishment, with the magnitude of the punishment often being greater than the offsetting rewards. Organizations, and especially the formal planning process within organizations, tend to prefer low-risk to high-risk strategies; they would prefer a good chance of a small payoff to a small chance of a high payoff. They are averse to risk and prefer to deal with predictable situations, especially where there is public accountability and a trustee relationship to invested assets.

Within business organizations we see several barriers to creativity. At the top of the list is committees, which are much better at killing ideas than generating them. Committees are excellent devices for fact finding and for analysis and evaluation, but they are seldom creative. We frequently see a complete lack of understanding of the marketing environment on the part of R&D people, as well as a complete lack of understanding of the technical environment, and the problems and opportunities it presents, on the part of marketing people. There is inadequate communication between the two departments. Another barrier is created by poorly designed and executed market research, which cannot be trusted and is biased in favor of negative results for testing new-product ideas. There is the "majority fallacy" that every new product must appeal to the majority of the people surveyed. The assumption that all new products must have long lives is a similar fallacy. The well-known NIH factor ("not invented here") closes the mind of development people to new ideas from outside. The lack of a clear statement of product development objectives to guide the R&D group and general fear and uncertainty concerning management expectations for the development effort are also significant barriers. Organizations in general have little tolerance for the strange, new, or uncertain. Finally, there is the tendency to substitute personal value judgments ("I like it") for informed objective-related business judgments concerning the potential merit of a new idea.

Thus, there are several dimensions on which the basic characteristics of formal organization conflict with the requirements of the creative process and the creative person:

1. Creativity requires the freedom to generate ideas, many of which will not be successful, whereas organizations are much better at critically evaluating ideas and find it hard to accept failure.
2. Organizations value conformity and provide security, whereas the creative person prefers opportunity to security and tends to be unconventional and asocial.
3. Innovation by definition involves risk taking, whereas organizations prefer predictability.

STIMULATING ORGANIZATIONAL CREATIVITY

Because of this inherent conflict, innovation requires that management take special steps to stimulate, encourage, and reward creative activity within the organization. This is much easier said than done. It is something that cannot be decreed but that every member of the management team must strive to create and maintain, day after day. In appraising the characteristics of creative organizations and creative societies, social scientists have discovered that several factors are involved.

First, the time and material resources required for creativity must be available. The organization must have some "slack"—be able to use resources in ways that are not expected to be immediately productive. There must be an open communication system permitting a free exchange of ideas to stimulate and guide creativity. The system must provide social and economic incentives that reward creativity, and true creativity must be valued and accepted, not ridiculed, rejected, or punished. As we have seen, the creative person needs time and opportunity for privacy and meditation, and this is directly related to the need for organization "slack" so that not everybody has to be immediately productive. The creative organization needs effectively functioning peer groups within which the individual finds the stimulation of others' ideas, the freedom to express his own ideas, and a basic environment of acceptance and encouragement that will motivate and sustain his creativity. Finally, the educational system (including continuing education opportunities) must do more than transfer knowledge. It must encourage and reward free inquiry and stimulate the development of skills and attitudes appropriate to creativity.

It is within the context of these requirements for a creative organization that we must evaluate the potential contribution of several methods and techniques for stimulating creativity.

First, we must recognize that within each of us there is a psychological tendency that inhibits creativity: the tendency called *selective perception*. We do not pay attention to all of the potential information bombarding our senses, and what we do pay attention to we interpret in terms of our wishes, prejudices, and previous experience. Survival and sanity require this selectivity, and we strive for balance, to maintain the status quo.

An important step in stimulating creative output is to break through these perceptual defenses in order to let loose the basic creativity of every individual. Henri Poincare observed:

In the subliminal self reigns what I shall call liberty, if we might give this name to the absence of discipline and to the disorder born of chance. Only this disorder itself permits unexpected combinations.[7]

TECHNIQUES FOR STIMULATING CREATIVITY

Most of the techniques that have been developed for stimulating creativity make use of group processes. They recognize that the individual is to a certain extent trapped within the walls of his own perceptions. Groups can stimulate creativity by adding facts, contributing an important insight, refining the problem definition, and stimulating imagination. Several techniques have been developed, including brainstorming, synectics, morphological analysis, value engineering, bionics, hypothetical situations, attribute listing, scenario/alternative futures, and fundamental design method.[8]

Each of these methods shares certain common characteristics. First, note that there are three modes of thinking: analytical, judicial, and creative. These methods stimulate creative thinking by holding analytical and judicial thinking in abeyance. All encourage divergent

[7] Ibid., p. 14.

[8] Stanford Research Institute, *Structured Approaches to Creativity*, Long Range Planning Service Report, 1969.

thinking by placing value on the new, strange, and far out, as well as by encouraging individuals to play with each other's ideas.

Let us review several of these methods briefly.

Brainstorming

This method, developed by Alex Osborn[9] is perhaps the most famous of all structured techniques for stimulating creativity. Brainstorming groups usually consist of 6 to 10 people, and there is disagreement whether they should be given the problem statement ahead of time (in order to begin the preparation and incubation stages) or should come to the meeting with completely open minds. The usual procedure is to go around the group in a systematic fashion with the requirement that all participate. There are four rules to brainstorming:

1. Quantity of ideas is preferred—the more the better.
2. Free-wheeling, wild ideas are preferred.
3. Hitchhiking—building on and refining another person's ideas—is encouraged.
4. Evaluation is forbidden.

These rules apply to the second stage of brainstorming, which is the *idea-finding* stage. It is preceded by a *fact-finding* stage and followed by a *solution-finding* stage. Fact-finding can be an individual process or a group process and can be aided by such questions as

1. What changes in your organization are required to reach your goals?
2. What things take too long?
3. What is too complicated?
4. What bottlenecks exist?
5. In what ways are *you* inefficient?

There are two parts to the central, idea-finding stage: idea generation and refinement and reprocessing through modification and combination. The group leader tries to form the session accordingly but somewhat flexibly.

In the solution-finding stage there is also the need to generate the criteria by which alternative solutions will be judged. A brainstorming group can also be useful at this stage, both in generating criteria and in selecting a course of action; but the last step is often reserved for a management decision maker. Either the group or the individual must also develop a strategy of acceptance for each idea to be put forward in the organization, including a determination of who has to be influenced, a definition of the specific action required from him, and so on.

[9] Alex F. Osborn, *Applied Imagination*, 3d ed. (New York: Scribner, 1963).

Brainstorming has the advantages of being great fun and relatively simple. Group leaders should have some training in the technique, but it is not sophisticated. It fits best where the problems to be dealt with are not technically complex. It probably has a somewhat smaller chance of generating completely unique and revolutionary problem solutions than more sophisticated techniques.

Synectics

Synectics is a method developed by William J. J. Gordon,[10] who defines it as "an operational theory for the conscious use of the preconscious psychological mechanisms present in man's creative activity." Formal training is definitely required to use this method properly. It employs four mechanisms:

1. Personal analogy—*identifying oneself or someone else with an object or process: "If I were a _____, how would I feel about it?" This helps generate new viewpoints on the problem.*
2. Direct analogy—*comparison of parallel facts from different disciplines, again in order to develop a new understanding of the problem. For example, can we learn about desalinization by studying how seagulls live on sea water?*
3. Symbolic analogy—*using an image that is technically inaccurate but aesthetically pleasing: for example, a liquid wall coating that becomes hard after application and strong enough to be weight-bearing.*
4. Fantasy analogy—*developing improbable connections between the world as we know it and a world where anything is possible that can be imagined. If we could learn to communicate with porpoises in human terms, could they be used to deploy a military nuclear capability?*

These mechanisms are effective stimulants to creativity because they generate involvement, detachment, deferment, speculation, and autonomy of object or problem—the feeling that it has a life of its own. All techniques are metaphorical in nature, looking for new relationships between elements not previously perceived as related. The group leader's role is critical. He does not judge. There is a carefully defined sequence of nine steps in the synectics approach, and it is up to the group leader to see that the discussion follows that sequence. Which analogical route to take is a critical decision on his part, which he makes on the criterion of "maximum constructive psychological strain" that can be observed as the participant stretches out of familiar territory. The leader uses evocative questions to bring forth analogies.

Group leaders can be trained at Synectics, Inc., in Cambridge, Massachusetts. The usual procedure is to train group leaders from various areas of the company and then carefully reintegrate them into

10 William J. J. Gordon, *Synectics* (New York: Harper & Row, 1961).

the organization according to a strategy for maximizing their usefulness and impact.

In the interest of brevity, I will highlight only the essential features of the other techniques. The next two are structured techniques:

Morphological analysis—defines major variables of the problem and then develops a matrix using each of the variables as an axis. Then each of the matrix cells is examined to identify new combinations that could lead to invention or innovation.

Value engineering—an organized approach to identify unnecessary costs in engineering, manufacturing, and purchasing. It also follows a structured sequence of information gathering, speculation, planning, execution, and reporting.

Other methods are less structured:

Bionics—the art of applying knowledge of living systems to the solution of technical problems.

Hypothetical situations—a creation of artificial situations in order to free the analyst from routine thinking habits and the influence of the environment.

Attribute listing—defining peculiar characteristics of the product to be improved and systematically modifying each to see what the result would be.

Scenario and alternative futures—a description of how a hypothetical situation could come about as a result of combination of assumed and real factors.

Fundamental design method—uses 5 methods of thinking (parallel plane; concepts; 12 basic elements—e.g., factorize, assess risk, reverse decision, etc.; outline strategies; and different viewpoints).

It would of course be possible to suggest other ideas for stimulating creativity—use of decision trees, use of psychedelic drugs; spatial visualization through use of X-rays, holography, three-dimensional computer displays, and so forth.

All of these methods, whether essentially logical or spontaneous in nature, have an important characteristic: They permit group members to play with and explore apparent irrelevancies in order to evoke new insights—a luxury in the typical organization.

DEVELOPING ORGANIZATIONAL CREATIVITY

There is obviously a great deal more to developing organizational creativity than simply using a few techniques in which group members have been trained. Focusing on the area of product innovation, I would like to suggest the roles of top management, marketing management, and R&D management in the process.

The role of top management

At least one observer has laid the blame for lack of innovation at the door of top management. Top managements tend to underestimate the importance of their own contribution; they are preoccupied with day-to-day problems, and when they do become involved it is on a personal basis rather than in terms of the more important role of structuring and supporting the framework within which innovation can occur.[11] Top management's major role is twofold. First, it provides a statement of mission, a vision of what the business can be in the future, a carefully developed strategic plan and statement of objectives. This must be based on a thorough appraisal of the threats and opportunities presented by the ever-changing environment and of the resources available to the business to exploit those opportunities. Second, top management must, through plan and example, create an environment of open communication where ideas can grow without being nipped in the bud by early criticism and fear of failure. (In my experience, top management is often more open to risk taking than it is perceived to be within the organization. The problem here is often one of middle management prematurely killing ideas of subordinates based on erroneous assumptions about top-management expectations. There is a communication problem.)

The organizational climate must be conducive to sustained hard work, the possibility of failure accepted, and creativity explicitly acknowledged and rewarded. To tolerate the frustration and hard work involved in true creative effort, the individual must experience intensive job satisfaction.

The role of marketing management

As part of the top-management team, marketing management shares these responsibilities. In addition, marketing is responsible for tactical planning within the marketing area. Tactical planning involves the selection of market targets and the continuing expert analysis and feedback of information on customer needs and product benefits. A key tactical decision is the definition of market segments—homogeneous clusters of potential customers within the larger heterogeneous market. Here is where the "majority fallacy" can be a problem.

Marketing management is responsible for staying informed of the availability and merits of new analytical techniques. This is part of its responsibility for providing a continuous flow of current and correct information about the market. Such information has value not only in directing and evaluating marketing action but also in guiding and

---

[11] An interview with Dr. George Turfitt, chairman and managing director of R&D Management Advisory Ltd., in "Innovate or Perish," *Marketing* (March 1971).

assessing developmental activity. A routine (say, quarterly) report on market conditions would probably have great value for most R&D departments.

The role of research management

R&D management shares this responsibility for communication. It should not be afraid to ask marketing for information as required to find directions and test ideas. The direction for R&D must come from the markets the company wishes to serve, for, as we said at the beginning, only the customer can ultimately determine the value of a new product.

The R&D effort should, of course, be guided by a carefully developed research plan that defines key areas to explore, results desired, and development objectives. It should distinguish between areas where a specific result is needed at a specific time and those where technical parameters are to be explored without the need or expectation of immediate payoff. In other words, more "risky" areas should be explored in a planned but flexible fashion.

The single most important job of the research manager is that of supervision of people because motivation is the key to creativity. As we have seen, creativity is a uniquely demanding human task, and really creative people have some special needs and drives. We certainly need to beware of two traps—assuming that creative people can't be managed and assuming that the best researchers make the best managers. Rather, creative people require a somewhat unique organizational environment, and management, especially first-line supervision, requires some special sensitivity, attitudes, and skills. While the research supervisor must have technical competence if he is to be respected, he must also have empathy and sensitivity.[12]

Integrating creative techniques

If you wish to explore the use of some of the structured techniques we have reviewed, I would advocate the following steps as suggested in the SRI Report:

1. *Build a library of books on the total range of problem-solving methods.*
2. *Let it be known that you are interested in experimenting with these methods.*
3. *Find out what is already known about these methods by members of the organization.*
4. *Arrange to have members of the organization receive training in several of the methods.*

[12] John R. Hinrichs, *Creativity in Industrial Scientific Research*, AMA Management Bulletin, no. 12 (1961): 34.

5. *Be prepared to listen to members of the organization describe their experience and help them use their skills within the organization.*
6. *Maintain a sufficient acquaintance with the methods to generate questions that will stimulate.*[13]

Personal contribution to creativity

If you personally want to become more involved in creativity and to further its development in your company, here are some things you can do:

1. Study creativity: Be one of those who reads about it and perhaps attend one of the training sessions.
2. Stifle the urge to criticize.
3. Be patient and learn to tolerate ambiguity—the familiar is not new, and uniqueness must come from an initial state of confusion. Learning often involves unlearning as a first step.
4. Avoid overdetailed planning that can rule out real innovation. Learn to take risks in a planned fashion.
5. Don't be afraid to be different. Subtle changes in thought patterns often accompany small changes in dress and behavior. More important, creativity requires personal courage.
6. Have fun! Learn to play with ideas—fooling around with words, concepts, images, and thoughts is part of the excitement of creative work and absolutely essential to its success.

SUMMARY

Informed and sensitive management of the creative process is a critical requirement in the innovative firm. In this chapter creativity has been examined as a form of problem solving characterized by novelty and producing results that have social value. Truly creative people were seen to require special management that recognizes their unique needs. In addition, several techniques for stimulating organizational creativity were described and evaluated. Finally, some guidelines were offered for the individual wishing to improve his own contribution to organizational creativity.

[13] Stanford Research Institute, op. cit.

PRODUCT POLICY
AND NEW PRODUCTS

New-product decisions are the most important decisions made by a firm because they define the future course of the business. Product decisions commit the scarce resources of the firm to specific research and development and marketing tasks, and they are highly interdependent with decisions about markets to be served. From Chapter 1 it will be recalled that decisions about products and markets are the basic strategic decisions made by the firm.

From a marketing viewpoint, products are the basic building blocks of the marketing mix. All other marketing decisions—price, distribution, and promotion—logically come after the product decision. Product decisions thus place important constraints on decision making in all other areas of marketing.

To guide these product decisions, every company needs a clearly stated product policy and product strategy. Product decisions must be made in the light of clear company objectives, and care must be taken to ensure that product decisions are consistent with one another.

In other words, the total effect of a series of product decisions must be "synergistic," or greater than the sum of its parts, in its contribution to company objectives.

PRODUCT POLICY AND STRATEGY

To begin the discussion of new-product development, it is useful to define some basic concepts of product policy and strategy. A *policy* has been defined as a standing answer to a recurring problem. Policies serve to constrain the decision making of the organization and to aim it at common purposes. The major purpose of policies is to ensure consistency of decisions toward company objectives. A *product policy*, then, is a set of standing answers to recurring new-product proposals and a framework for evaluating a stream of new-product ideas.

Product policy is a relatively meaningless concept for the one-product firm. Rather, the concept of *product line* is integral to any discussion of product policy. A product line is all products marketed by the firm, and the concept of product line takes meaning from the fact that the products marketed by the firm depend on and influence one another in important ways.

The concept of product policy thus becomes operational when there is a stream of new-product ideas to evaluate. Examples of product policies include the following:

1. General Electric has an implicit policy of developing and marketing products that increase both the demand for and the efficient supply of electricity.
2. A European company has been highly successful through a policy of developing products and services to be sold through leased departments in large retailing establishments. These include hair care, key-making, and shoe repair services. A new product idea must be one that is not ordinarily sold through department stores and that the stores themselves are not likely to want to start.
3. A California-based electronics firm has a policy of developing only products requiring state-of-the-art technical developments, which capitalize on the firm's R&D skills and give a unique competitive advantage.

Product policies are in effect a statement of the common elements that bind products together into a product line. They identify the underlying logic of the product line, such as a basic technology, a production capability, a distribution strength, a focus on a well-defined subset of market needs, a common raw material, and so on. Thus, product policies can help in evaluating new-product ideas by comparing the new product with the existing product line in terms of

- interrelationship of demand characteristics
  —the competitive advantages of having a complete line in securing distribution outlets

—complementary products, where sales of one help generate sales of others
—balancing seasonal demand patterns
* use of company know-how by spreading a unique competence over multiple products
* use of common production facilities
* use of excess or idle production capacity
* use of common distribution channels
* improving salesmen's effectiveness and efficiency by giving them more products to sell on each call
* use of common raw materials

Relationship to generic product concept *descriptive of an entire group*

As we saw in Chapter 1, the definition of a generic product concept in terms of the basic human needs and wants to be served is a critical step in defining the nature and scope of the total business. Product policies should evolve naturally from the generic product concept. "What business are we in?" is the basic question, not "What is our current product line?" But the product concept must be specific enough to be operational, not so broad as to be useless in helping to make choices.

THE PRODUCT LIFE CYCLE

Given the difficulty of making new-product choices and the high rate of new-product failure, why is there so much new-product activity? Would it not be easier to avoid new products whenever possible? Of course it would be easier, but it is not a feasible alternative for most companies because of the inevitable influence of the product life cycle.

The life cycle is a fact of existence for every product. It should probably be called the product-market life cycle because it is specific to a given market. For example, the product life cycle would begin anew when an old product was introduced into a foreign market. The product life cycle is an inevitable influence on the product because of the influence of three factors over which the company has little or no control: changing market preferences, obsolescence of existing technology, and competition.

Stages in the life cycle

As illustrated in Figure 8–1, the product life cycle describes the sales *Introduction* and profit margin history of a product over time. This cycle can be *Growth* divided into five stages: introduction, growth, maturity, saturation, and *Maturity* decline. (Some authors prefer to combine maturity and saturation into *Saturation* a single stage called maturity). It is important to note that the life *Decline*

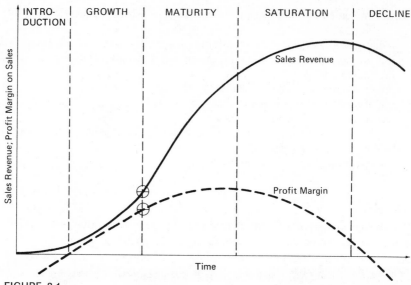

FIGURE 8-1
The product life cycle concept.

cycle concept describes a product in terms of its financial implications for the firm.

Introduction   In the introduction stage sales revenues begin to grow, but the rate of growth is initially very slow. Market acceptance will be cautious at first, reflecting the risk involved for customers in buying the new product and the problems of organizing and deploying marketing resources. Customers will initially buy on a trial basis, in limited quantity. Profits are nonexistent in the beginning, reflecting low sales volume, large product development cost, and heavy expenditure for market development. At the end of the introductory stage, however, sales are not only growing but growing at an increasing rate, and profit margins may become positive.

Growth   During the growth stage the rate of sales increase is most rapid and profits increase rapidly as well, perhaps reaching their highest level as a percentage of sales during this period. The end of the growth period is signaled by a decrease in the rate of sales growth—in mathematical terms, at the inflection point on the sales curve. During the growth stage competition is likely to appear, setting in motion a series of forces that will eventually reduce profitability.

Maturity   The maturity stage of the product life cycle sees a leveling of profit margins while sales revenues continue to grow. The advent of competition brings price pressures and may also require increased marketing expenditure in the battle for market share that must be waged even while effort continues to be aimed at attracting new users. Additional expense may be related to the need to modify the product and create product improvements, new models, a broader line, and so on. All of these expenses reflect increased competition and reduce profit margins.

Saturation Market saturation occurs when sales stabilize or at least do not grow faster than the growth in market population. All potential buyers are now using the product, and sales may be limited to replacement sales. Consumption is at a relatively constant rate, and the marketing task is exclusively a fight for market share, with the attendant higher marketing expenses. There will be an increasingly large number of competitors, many of whom come into the market solely on a price basis. Prices are likely to erode rapidly, and profit margins are likely to become very small, especially if no substantial production improvements and cost economies can be realized.

Decline In the decline stage sales decrease, slowly at first and then more rapidly. Entirely new products and services become a major source of competition, and customer preferences veer sharply away from the old product. Profit margins usually disappear long before the company decides to stop marketing the product. Substantial marketing expense may be incurred in an attempt to revitalize the product and reestablish it in the market, but the resuscitation attempt seldom restores life to the product. It is more likely only to prolong the inevitable and add to the losses.

From a strategic management viewpoint, the most essential feature of the product life cycle is the difference between the sales curve and the profit curve. Profit margins decrease long before sales. This has two critically important implications:

- First, a continuous stream of new products is required in order to hold profitability at acceptable levels.
- Second, strategic planning must specifically consider the changing relationship between sales volume and profitability in allocating marketing and other resources among parts of the product line.

The product life cycle concept is sufficiently broad to apply to a given brand, a group of products using a common technology, or an entire industry. It is most commonly used to refer to a specific product or brand in the company's product line. The time dimension involved may range from several months in the case of a fad or fashion item to many years for classes of products such as long-playing phonograph records. Of course, the product life cycle does not always develop as smoothly as this idealized model implies, but the general trend is always the same.

Strategic planning

There should be an explicit strategy for exploiting the product life cycle of each product or class of products in the company's line.[1] The marketing mix must be systematically altered to reflect the stage in the life cycle and its related profit opportunities. Inefficiency from wasted promotional resources and unwise pricing decisions is often the penalty for poor awareness of life cycle dynamics.

Analysis of the company's product line in terms of the life cycle stage of each product can be a significant aid in corporate strategic planning in general and planning a new-product development program in particular. The key diagnostic questions relate to the rates at which sales, profits, and the relationships between them are changing. For example, when the rate of growth of sales begins to slow, profit margins may begin to decline, although the absolute level of sales continues to increase.

There are at least three distinct classes of strategies for achieving growth by exploiting the product life cycle: (1) developing new products for existing markets, (2) developing new markets for existing products, and (3) developing new products and new markets simultaneously. These strategies can be called product development, market development, and diversification (Table 8–1). Within each class of strategy, further distinctions can be made according to degree of uniqueness and innovativeness. For example, product development can range from relatively simple product modifications of an evolutionary

[1] Theodore Levitt, "Exploit the Product Life Cycle," *Harvard Business Review* 43 (November–December 1965): 81–94.

TABLE 8-1
Alternative growth strategies

		Technical Requirements		
		Present Products	New Products	New Technology
Marketing Requirements	Present markets	Product modifications	Product development	
	Expanded markets	Market development	Market segmentation and product differentiation	
	New markets		diversification	

nature to much more risky research and development of basic technology. Likewise, markets can be expanded through relatively simple market extensions—say, into new geographic areas—or major moves such as into international markets. Increasingly refined and sophisticated methods of market segmentation are ways of expanding markets. If refined segmentation is combined with the development of products differentiated for the requirements of each segment, a kind of growth strategy close to diversification is the result.

The development of international markets has been a common strategy for exploiting the product life cycle. Transplanting an old product into a foreign market in effect regenerates the product life cycle. Such strategies have often led to the formation of a multinational corporation through a process that begins with export marketing, followed by local (i.e., foreign) production, followed eventually by development of full-scale corporate structures in host countries. Conversely, many product transplant attempts have failed because of a naive assumption that the new markets would respond to the same marketing strategies used at home.

Generally speaking, the most risky strategies have the highest potential payoffs. Development and exploitation of new technology has the possibility of much higher profits than more conservative strategies of product modification but also requires larger development investments and has a higher probability of failure. One strategic choice, for example, is whether to attempt to be consistently innovative in the chosen area of product competition or to follow a more conservative course and be an early follower. Levitt calls the latter a "used apple" strategy—"They are willing to eat off a used apple, but they try to be alert enough to make sure it is only slightly used—that they at least get the second big bite, not the tenth skimpy one."[2]

Skimming versus penetration

At the introduction stage in the life cycle, there are two distinctly different market development strategies available for exploiting the product life cycle. Which strategy is chosen depends on the nature of the product, especially how easily it can be copied, the size of the potential market, the expected difficulty of market development, and an estimate of the likelihood of new competitors at various times.

A *skimming* strategy aims at achieving high profit margins early in the life cycle. It focuses market effort on the customers and segments for whom the product yields the major benefits and who are willing to pay the most for it. It relies on high prices and concentrated promotional effort, systematically lowering prices to attract new market segments after the first segments have been captured, thus taking ad-

[2] Ibid, p. 82.

vantage of the inherent price elasticity differences among segments. The skimming strategy is likely to shorten the product life cycle, however, because of competitive forces, unless there is patent protection or the technology involved is hard to copy. Higher profit margins and concentrated marketing both attract new competitors early. Certain unexploited segments are left to competition, and the high price provides an umbrella for competitors' market and product development expenditures. To the extent that competition is attracted earlier rather than later, price pressures and the need to spend more for marketing and product improvements can reduce total profits over the entire product life cycle. In the short run, new competitive effort can help expand the size of the total market, but the effect on the innovator's profits may be either to increase them (if he has to spend relatively less for market development) or to decrease them if prices also erode rapidly.

Penetration strategies are the converse of skimming. In a penetration strategy prices are kept low in the hope of rapid market development. For the innovator this strategy can lengthen the product life cycle and enhance long-term profitability by increasing market share. Penetration can result in a rapidly gained toehold in the market and strong customer loyalty. Lower prices, of course, mean lower profit margins, and this may discourage some competitive entries. Lower prices go hand-in-hand with a broader marketing effort in search for large sales volumes. Penetration strategies are most attractive when the production process permits important economies of scale. If costs decrease rapidly with volume, it clearly makes sense to aim marketing strategy at securing a large sales volume as soon as possible.

Strategic choices made earlier in the life of the product clearly determine how the life cycle will evolve. Such decisions should therefore be made with a careful and explicitly stated view of future market and competitive conditions.

Extending the life cycle

Increased competition can cause an acceleration of the decline in profitability and can shorten product life. On the other hand, a series of product improvements and product modifications can extend the life cycle. Likewise, a series of market extensions can help keep an old product profitable. Such moves should be planned early in the product's life, even before it is launched commercially, as part of overall strategic planning and not from time to time as crises occur. Marketing strategies for extending the product life cycle include

- encouraging more frequent or more varied use
- industry-wide, cooperative promotional efforts to encourage product use
- frequent announcement of new, improved products

- extension of the product line through new sizes, flavors, models, product forms, etc.
- developing entirely new uses

Levitt summarizes his argument for having explicit strategies for product extension with these words:

For its own good, new product strategy should try to predict in some measure the likelihood, character and timing of competitive and market events. While prediction is always hazardous and seldom very accurate, it is undoubtedly far better than not trying to predict at all. . . . To be more systematically aware of the predictions one is making so that one acts on them in an offensive rather than a defensive or reactive fashion—this is the real virtue of pre-planning for market stretching and product life extension. The result will be a product strategy that includes some sort of plan for a timed sequence of conditional moves.[3]

Euthanasia for old products

One of the hardest decisions made by a management is to kill an old product. Deletion decisions are in many respects more difficult than addition decisions. One result is that many companies have in their product line old products that have long ago become unprofitable and are being retained only for "emotional" reasons. For example, salesmen may continue to resist a decision to drop an unprofitable product because of the difficulty of explaining to dealers or customers why the product they have been buying is no longer available. Likewise, top managers have often risen in the organization on the basis of technical or marketing accomplishments related to those old products. Furthermore, company accounting systems often do not permit clear identification of all the costs involved in maintaining an obsolete product, especially when joint costs (shared with other products) are involved. Most difficult of all costs to judge, of course, are the hidden *opportunity costs* represented by the earnings opportunities forgone because management, marketing, and production resources are being wasted on unprofitable products.

Periodic and systematic review of all products in the line according to preestablished criteria can be a major contributor to intelligent product deletion decisions. A review committee can meet every 6 or 12 months to evaluate product sales volume and profit trends. A committee working with a well-defined set of standards can attack the problem more thoroughly, rigorously, and unemotionally than the individual decision maker. Operating managers such as product managers and sales managers are unlikely either to find time to do the necessary analysis or to recommend deletion. Likewise, top management is unlikely to

[3] Ibid., p. 93.

do the necessary analysis until the evidence against the product is
overwhelmingly negative. Even then, there will be vocal opposition
from those with vested interests in the product. Yet for many companies product deletion may hold more profit opportunity than product
addition.[4]

MANAGING NEW-PRODUCT DEVELOPMENT

The inevitability of the product life cycle requires the development of
new products for new profit opportunities. New-product development
must be carefully planned and managed, or new products will not be
available when needed. Management systems must be installed that
stimulate, collect, screen, evaluate, develop, test, and commercialize
new-product ideas.

Idea generation

The first step in the new-product development process is the generation
of new-product ideas. New-product ideas come from a variety of sources,
including customers, salesmen, distributors, and engineering, production,
and other personnel. In the absence of a systematic collection procedure, such ideas are likely to be lost, and the stream of new product
ideas becomes highly unreliable. Simple procedures should be developed
to stimulate, collect, and respond to new-product ideas from all potential sources. If a salesman knows that a customer's suggestion for a
product modification is likely to be responded to, he is much more likely
to pass that idea on to the correct people in the marketing organization for more careful consideration. All ideas should be acknowledged,
both as a courtesy to the initiator and to motivate the sender to keep
supplying ideas as he uncovers them. It also helps if the initiator can
be given some indication of whether the idea will be developed further
and, if not, the reasons for this decision. In this manner he will
develop a better understanding of new-product decision criteria, and
this will help improve the quality of ideas coming forward.

Many new ideas are required to keep the product development
process functioning. According to one study, 58 new-product ideas were
necessary to yield one successful new product.[5] A much larger number
would be required in a company with no systematic procedure for
stimulating and collecting a stream of high-quality new-product ideas.

In companies with ongoing research and development activity, the
R&D operation of course carries a major part of the burden for the

---

[4] A specific system for such review is described by Philip Kotler in "Phasing
Out Weak Products," *Harvard Business Review* 43 (March–April 1965): 107–118.

[5] Booz-Allen & Hamilton, Inc., *Management of New Products*, 1968, p. 9.

stream of new-product ideas. Basic research exploration should be uncovering new-product ideas almost routinely. A formal product development group does not, however, relieve the rest of the organization from new-product responsibility. One of the greatest dangers in a company with a strong R&D capability is that the research process will provide its own imperatives—"research for the sake of research"—without adequate guidance from management and the marketplace. It is a misconception that researchers and product development engineers do not like to be "bothered" by marketing requirements. Nothing could be farther from the truth. There is nothing more demoralizing for a researcher than to find that he has wasted months or years on a project that will not have commercial feasibility. Like the rest of us, researchers need direction to make sure that their efforts are productive, and they want to know that their output will have value—in this case value in the marketplace.

Screening

Before effort is spent in developing a new-product idea, care must be taken to assess the probability of a successful result. The first step in this evaluation process is a simple screening of the new-product ideas against a predetermined set of criteria. The importance of a clearly stated product policy and product strategy was argued earlier in this chapter. The product policy and the related set of product development objectives provide the criteria against which this preliminary screening can take place. At this stage the evaluation is fast and simple; its purpose is to determine which ideas warrant more careful analysis, refinement, and development.

Screening can be conducted by asking a few simple questions about the new-product idea, such as

- Is the idea consistent with present and proposed business objectives?
- Is the idea compatible with present products?
- Does this company have, or can it be reasonably expected to develop, the technical resources necessary to develop the product?
- Is the idea within the financial capability of the firm?
- Does the company have, or could it develop, the necessary production competence?
- Is the idea consistent with the company's marketing capability, or could the necessary new competence be developed?

Responsibility for idea screening, as well as for other parts of the new-product development process, should be carefully assigned and not left to chance. If there is a new-product manager, then the entire process should come under his jurisdiction; but the responsibility should not be solely his. It is common to use a committee approach to the screening process, with the committee chaired by the person responsible for new products. Technical, production, financial, and marketing view-points should also be represented on the committee.[6] To aid the committee in its work, a simple checklist or printed form may be helpful. Each member of the committee can then indicate his judgments on the form. Rating scales—for example, a scale from 1 = excellent to 5 = poor, can be a simple device for combining judgments in a consistent scheme. New-product ideas can be evaluated on each of several dimensions, with the scores of each judge examined to determine the need for further action. If judges disagree significantly about the potential value of a new-product idea, this indicates a need for further discussion. If the scores are consistently low, no further action need be taken except to notify the source of the idea. A strong, positive evaluation indicates that the new-product idea should be subjected to more careful analysis concerning its feasibility and profit potential.

Business analysis

Business analysis is the stage in the new-product development process at which new-product ideas are carefully evaluated for their economic worth. Working with marketing, engineering, and production people to develop necessary estimates of required investment and of future revenues and costs, the analyst has the formidable task of defining and measuring the potential market, estimating required investments, and estimating profits over the life cycle of the product. This may require the conduct of market research to estimate the extent of the potential market and the conditions prevailing in the market with respect to pricing, distribution expenses, competition from other products, customer service requirements, costs of promotion, and related economic variables.

A key issue at the business analysis stage is to select the appropriate life span for the analysis. Awareness of the product life cycle can help generate realistic estimates. Care must be taken to appraise the time and financial investment required for market development (which usually tend to be underestimated), the time at which significant competition is likely to enter the market (it usually comes earlier than estimated), and when sales volume is likely to decline. It is a common mistake, reflecting the rampant optimism characterizing much new-product business analysis, to assume that products will go on generating sales in perpetuity. This rather silly assumption can be seen in any new-product analysis that gives figures in a format like Year 1, Year 2, Year 3 and After. The optimistic "and after" implies a stability that is

---

[6] For a good discussion of the organization question, see S. C. Johnson and C. Jones, "How to Organize for New Products," *Harvard Business Review* 35 (May–June 1957): 49–62.

virtually never found, and it can be the cause of basic misjudgments about rates of return on investment.

Business analysis should be conducted by a relatively disinterested analyst with the ability to work closely with those from whom essential estimates must be obtained. All too often, the analysis is done by the manager who has decided to champion the new-product idea. In such cases the analysis becomes a selling document for convincing top management and the board of directors of the wisdom of making the required investments in technical development and production capacity. Herein lies one of the major reasons why new products "fail"— they are developed on the basis of overly optimistic estimates, and this optimism is known by the people who make those estimates *at the time they are made.*

The business analysis should produce a report of the new-product study to be distributed to all interested decision makers, from the board of directors and president on down to top levels of functional management. It should not be regarded as a one-time study to be read and put on the shelf. Rather, it should be revised frequently as new information becomes available. It should be consulted regularly by those charged with the responsibility for developing the new product and marketing it.

Development

Based on the business analysis, a decision will be made whether to go ahead with the development of the new-product idea. Much uncertainty may still remain in the technical area, especially to the extent that product development will depend on achieving important technical breakthroughs. The time and cost required to achieve these results cannot be estimated with certainty, but a serious attempt must be made to assess them as part of the process of planning new-product development. The more basic the research required, the longer the time horizon in the new-product plan. Once again, undue optimism here can be the basis for future disappointment. The common tendency to overestimate the ease with which technical problems can be solved should be avoided.

During product development, the research and development effort should be guided by information from the marketplace and from the production department as required. As technical choices have to be made about the directions to take in new-product development, careful communication with marketing and production can improve the quality of those decisions. For these reasons, frequent (say, quarterly) review meetings can be very desirable, bringing together technical, marketing, production, and financial managers for a detailed review of product development progress and to provide guidance for future work. The danger of having research go ahead on its own initiative for as long as two years should be obvious—wasted developmental effort, uncoordinated activities by other departments, and failure to respond to a changing market environment. Two outcomes are especially likely in the absence of frequent communication: development of products significantly different from what the market requires, and a reluctant conclusion that the new-product idea is not technically feasible, with the high probability that investments will have been made in other areas on the assumption that the new product was forthcoming.

Testing

Once a new-product idea has been developed to the point where there is a product concept, a physical product, or several potential versions of a final product, a variety of testing procedures must be employed. These include product concept testing, laboratory testing, production testing, and market testing.

Product concept testing is conducted with potential customers for the product and has the objective of refining the definition of the basic product idea and determining its acceptability before proceeding into more expensive development phases. Potential customers can be asked to state their preferences for alternative product types and to react to the basic idea. As an example of product concept testing, it is reported that in November 1968, Ford Motor, among several other tests, conducted a clinic in Seattle, Washington, to obtain customer reaction to alternative product features for its proposed subcompact automobile, the Pinto, which at that time was called the Tucson. The Tucson was compared with six other automobiles on display.

Respondents were asked to rank various attributes of each model on a 1 to 10 scale. Different aspects of appearance such as looks, fast versus slow, expensive versus cheap, and modern versus old were used to learn how consumers viewed each model. An over-all measurement of acceptance was taken by asking respondents to pick the model they liked best and the one they liked least.[7]

Product concept testing is intended to guide the research and development effort. It may also provide guidance for advertising copy writers, who must begin developing a promotional strategy while the product is still being developed.

Laboratory testing is intended to test the performance of the product as measured against technical criteria and to simulate conditions of actual consumer use. For example, a new packaging material might require testing for strength under a variety of conditions of stress, humidity, heat, and twisting. Panels of consumers may be used

---

[7] *Ford Motor Company,* case in Kenneth R. Davis, *Marketing Management,* 3d ed. (New York: Ronald, 1972), pp. 547–568, at pp. 561–562.

to test new consumer products when there is uncertainty about consumer understanding of the methods of using the product or consumer preference data must be obtained before it can be determined whether the development has been successfully concluded or needs to go further. Strictly speaking, when the test moves into the consumer's household, it is no longer a laboratory test but has become a household test or a consumer preference test.

Production testing involves the making of the product under simulated actual production conditions, as in the case of "pilot plant" production runs. A pilot plant is usually a small-scale version of the actual production process intended. In production testing the objective is to determine if the product as designed can actually be produced according to specifications and within estimated cost limitations. It is often the case that production requirements are more difficult than marketing requirements in product development. Design of the production process may be a much more demanding task technically than design of the product itself. So production testing is a critical step in the development process, making sure that the product as designed can be produced economically, to quality standards, within acceptable limits of scrap rates, with minimum breakage, and so on.

Market testing has two purposes—to determine customer acceptance of the product and to determine the final marketing program to be used to develop the market for the product. In the market situation, the product does not stand alone but is part of the total marketing program of price, packaging, distribution, display, advertising, sales promotion, and personal selling. Each of these factors influences the sales volume realized on the product, and care must be taken to isolate analytically the effects of each of the important variables—the product itself, trade acceptance, level of advertising and sales promotion, quality of promotional appeals, and so on.

The important variables to be estimated in a market test are the sales volume and the market share to be expected in a national marketing program. In addition, special surveys and consumer panels may be conducted to determine consumer attitudes and levels of acceptance. Finally, competitive reaction must be carefully noted.

Ideally, the market test would take the form of an experiment, carefully conducted to permit accurate statistical inferences about sales volume and market shares, based on the test market sample. More commonly, the nature of the test market falls short of the ideal experimental situation in that all variables are not systematically manipulated or controlled. Nonetheless, it is possible to estimate with a reasonable degree of accuracy the sales volume and market share to be expected on a national basis, given certain assumptions about the nature of competitive response, if the test market itself is reasonably representative and the market test has been done with care. The subject of test marketing is quite complex, but there are a variety of good textbooks and handbooks that explain all aspects of test marketing in considerable detail.[8]

Test market data can be used to make a final go/no go decision on whether to market the product nationally. A decision to gather additional information in another test market or to continue this test may also be made, but competitive conditions usually make this difficult. Estimates of sales volume, derived from the results of the test market, should be compared with the original projections in the product plan developed during the business analysis stage of the development process. Any substantial variation from those estimates should be very carefully considered for its effect on estimated payout period, return on investment, required investment in market development, plant investment, and so on.

Commercialization

Commercialization, the last stage in the product development process, involves the launching of the product with a full-scale marketing program. New products require very special marketing effort to establish them in their intended market segments. Definition of the market target is an important part of the total decision process, one that should be made during the business analysis stage and subsequently refined as the product is tested.

To launch a new product, channels of distribution must be filled with the product and all selling agencies—salesmen, distributors, wholesalers, and retailers—fully informed about the new product, the planned marketing program, and their roles in it. Salesmen need special sales presentations. Special incentives for agent middlemen may be an important requirement for securing full distribution of the product. Special customer incentives may be required to stimulate trial and overcome existing product preferences and brand loyalties.

Scheduling of promotional events, especially the timing of media advertising, must be carefully coordinated with distribution and with other elements of the promotional program. It is absolutely essential, for example, that full-scale product distribution be achieved before national advertising is launched.

Commercialization of industrial products raises some problems quite distinct from those of consumer product marketing. For one thing, development of markets for new industrial products often requires the conduct of joint technical development programs with

[8] A good brief review is presented in F. Ladik, L. Kent, and P. C. Nahl, "Test Marketing of New Consumer Products," *Journal of Marketing* 24 (April 1960): 29–34. For a more thorough treatment, see Harper W. Boyd and Ralph Westfall, *Marketing Research: Text and Cases*, 3d ed. (Homewood, Ill.: Irwin, 1971).

potential customers. A new raw material, for example, would require working closely with the technical personnel in potential customer organizations to help them develop the necessary product formulations and production processes. In other cases the major requirement is to work with potential customers in joint marketing efforts to develop *their* markets. A chemical manufacturer who developed a new coating material for packaging applications found it necessary to work with manufacturers of fiberboard packaging materials, with their customers the package manufacturers, and even with *their* customers, the food packagers. In some cases this required going all the way to the food retailers, where the important customers were major food-retailing chains.

All of this joint technical and marketing effort takes time, and it is important to build realistic estimates of the time required for customer decision making into the new-product marketing plans. Failure to do so can cause substantial error in forecasting sales volumes, cash flows, and return on investment.

Inadequate and poorly managed marketing effort is often the cause of market failure for basically sound new products. Especially for industrial products, where the level of marketing management competence may be somewhat below that found in the typical consumer products company, preoccupation with technical and production problems may cloud management's view of the marketing requirements. A common error is to ask the same group of people who developed the product to assume responsibility for marketing it. Thus, a special-products department composed primarily of scientists and engineers may be assigned to go into the field to talk with potential customers and stimulate interest in the product. While such arrangements can help during the product development stage, they are no substitute for professional, carefully planned and executed marketing effort during the commercialization stage. Clearly stated marketing objectives, market segments, customer (account) strategies, and sales volume objectives should guide the market planning for new products and the subsequent execution of those plans by experienced, trained, and carefully managed marketing professionals.

DIFFUSION OF NEW PRODUCTS

The development of markets for new products follows a somewhat predictable pattern, which, if understood by the marketing team, can provide some important clues for the development of effective new-product marketing strategies. This market development process is technically called *diffusion of innovations* and is defined as the spread of a new idea through a social system over time. This definition identifies the four elements of the diffusion process: a new idea (or product), a social system (or market), communication and influence processes among members of that social system, and time.

The diffusion process is in a sense the same as the product life cycle concept, except that the diffusion process looks at what is happening in the market (as a "social system"), whereas the product life cycle describes the flows of revenues and profits to the firm as a result of the diffusion process. Graphically, the diffusion process is described by the cumulative normal distribution shown in Figure 8-2. The diffusion process is a social process that reflects another process called the *adoption* process, an individual decision process consisting of five mental stages: awareness, interest, evaluation, trial, and full-scale adoption of the new product. Individuals differ in the speed with which they move through the stages of the adoption process as well as in the time at which they characteristically become aware of new products.

Customers in both consumer and industrial markets can be characterized according to the time at which they appear in the diffusion process. For purposes of consistency and comparison, these adopter categories are defined according to standard deviations around the mean time of adoption in the diffusion process, which is described by the bell-shaped normal distribution illustrated in Figure 8-3. Statistically, this curve is the first derivative of the S-shaped curve in Figure 8-2. These are somewhat arbitrary dividing lines, but these are the now-accepted definitions used in well over a thousand studies of the diffusion process in such fields as agriculture, pharmaceuticals, politics, and marketing. Once customers are placed in these categories, it is possible to develop some generalizations about their characteristics and their behavior that are useful in developing marketing strategies.[9]

[9] The most up-to-date review of these studies and the general theory of diffusion is presented by E. M. Rogers and F. F. Shoemaker, *Communication of Innovations: A Cross Cultural Approach* (New York: Free Press, 1971).

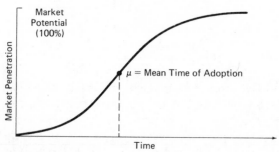

FIGURE 8-2
The diffusion process, described by the cumulative normal distribution.

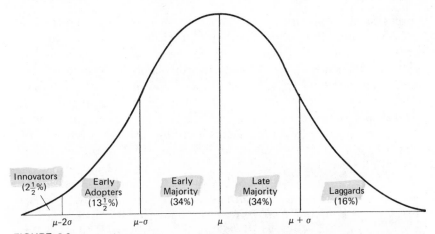

FIGURE 8-3
Adopter categories defined by standard deviations around mean time of adoption.

Innovators

The innovators are the first 2½ percent of the market to adopt the product. The key characteristic of the innovators is their venturesomeness. They are both more willing and more able to take the risks inherent in being the first to use a new product. They tend to be better off financially; in the case of farms, firms, and doctors, their operations are likely to be somewhat larger than average—although the influence of size of operation is quite complex, as we shall see. They also tend to have more specialized operations. Innovators are also distinguished by their cosmopolitan orientation—that is, outside of the local community. They are more likely to identify with other people in their professions than with local townspeople, for example. In the case of physicians, to illustrate, the innovators are likely to be research scientists, frequently presenting research papers at national and international meetings of their specialties; if they practice medicine at all, it is a limited and specialized practice. Their important social contacts are likely to be with others who are working in the same areas of inquiry. Innovative firms are characterized by technical orientation, more specialized operations, and better-informed personnel in terms of current use of business and technical media. They tend to have younger and more aggressive managements, and they are more likely to have a recent record of rapid growth in sales volume and profitability.

For individual innovators, there appears to be no particular relationship with age. At one time the evidence seemed to suggest that innovators were somewhat younger than average, but later studies have suggested the opposite. Other variables such as the technical field involved (and, thus, the importance of recent education) and the amount of investment required by the innovation probably interact with the influence of age. Studies are consistent, however, in finding that innovators tend to be better educated and much better informed. Their major sources of information are technical literature, the mass media, and other innovators, as well as certain so-called professional change agents such as county agents and farm products dealers in the case of agricultural innovators, or pharmaceutical detailmen in the case of physician innovators.

Socially, innovators tend to be isolated, a characteristic consistent with their cosmopolitan orientation. They are not well integrated into the local community, and this means that they are more likely to influence the diffusion process by making the new product visible— that is, by "demonstration," rather than by personal interaction or by the force of their social position in the community. Innovators have been characterized as "in tune with a different drummer," but to complete the metaphor it should be noted that this drummer is the one leading the parade.

Early adopters

The early adopters, the next 13½ percent to adopt a new product, are the opinion leaders in the community. They bring social pressure and word-of-mouth communication into the decision process. Opinion leadership is a terribly important force in the development of most markets, and the early adopters are the key to this process. They are the social leaders in the community, holding elected and appointed positions in local professional groups, churches, service clubs, and local government. They tend to be better-educated, wealthier, and more successful than average. Mobility is another key to understanding these people because they tend to be more mobile in all respects— physically, they tend to move more; educationally and occupationally, they have gone farther than their parents; socially, they are moving up the status ladder.

Another important characteristic of the early adopters is that they have substantially more exposure to information from all sources, especially the mass media but also other opinion leaders, than other adopter categories. This fact has led to the development of the so-called "two-step flow of communication" hypothesis, which states that mass media influence public opinion by influencing the opinion leaders, who then influence the rest of the population, rather than by influencing the mass of the population directly.[10]

---

[10] The best review of this theory and of the data supporting it will be found in Elihu Katz, "The Two-Step Flow of Communication: An Up-to-Date Report on an Hypothesis," *Public Opinion Quarterly* 21 (Spring 1957): 61–78.

It is not clear, however, whether opinion leaders are better informed because they are aware of their opinion leadership and attempt to keep up for this reason or whether they are sought out because they are better informed. Chances are that both sets of forces are at work and tend to reinforce one another.

Social integration is an important characteristic of the opinion leaders. This helps explain a somewhat confusing research finding: that the most important source of information for opinion leaders is often other opinion leaders. It has been found that opinion leaders are somewhat specialized in their spheres of influences, both in their influence on certain products or areas of social concern and in terms of social class. Thus, an upper-middle-class woman who is an opinion leader in matters of fashion may influence only other upper-middle-class women and may have almost no influence in such areas as politics or child-rearing practices. On the other hand, there is some limited evidence that certain individuals do tend to be influential in several product areas, and the possibility of generalized opinion leadership would seem to be strong when one considers that the important individual and social characteristics leading to opinion leadership exist relatively independently of particular products and services.

As in the case of innovators, the relationship with age is not clear. Many studies have found that early adopters tend to be somewhat younger than average, but this relationship has not been found in all studies. Again, the influence of age probably depends on other factors.

Application of the concept of opinion leadership to industrial markets presents some special problems because we do not have a good theoretical and conceptual vocabulary for talking about how one firm influences another. In most industries, however, there do appear to be a small number of firms that are consistently watched by other members of the industry for their use of new products and services. Information about their practices may come from a variety of sources, including industrial salesmen, trade journals, and social contacts among the employees of firms in the industry.

As noted earlier, the relationship between innovativeness and size of firm is complex. The most important variable in unraveling the puzzle is the amount of investment required to adopt the innovation. If the required investment is small, then relatively smaller firms tend to be the innovators and early adopters. Their innovativeness seems to be related to the fact that they can make decisions quicker, given less organizational bulk and complexity, as well as to their aggressive growth orientation. The larger firms, conversely, are already leading the industry and do not need the competitive advantage of the innovation as much. Likewise, the larger and more established firms are likely to have a somewhat stronger commitment to existing technology. Finally, the larger firms may regard themselves as the "experts" in a given area and be unwilling to accept the technical and economic arguments being used by the seller of the innovation. This has been called the "not invented here" or "NIH" factor and is a major source of resistance in selling new technology to large, established firms in an industry.

When the innovation requires major investments, however, only the larger firms may be able to afford the financial risks and to tolerate the possibility of failure of the innovation. In these cases marketing effort is probably most effectively concentrated on the larger firms, with secondary attention to smaller firms in the hope of putting some competitive pressures on the larger organizations but recognizing that this means market development is going to take a long time.[11]

The early adopters, then, tend to be more mobile, better informed, and socially integrated. They influence through the force of their social position—that is, by who they are. Industrial firms that are early adopters tend to be smaller, somewhat more technically oriented and specialized in their operations than the average in the industry, but growing rapidly and noted for aggressive managements. These managers also tend to be younger and more aggressive personally than the industry average.

Early majority

The early majority are the next 34 percent to adopt the innovation and bring the total adoption rate up to 50 percent. The early majority have earned the respect of the community and approach the average in such areas as income, occupation, education, and age, though with somewhat favorable variations. That is, they are somewhat better educated, wealthier, and somewhat above average in social status. They influence the diffusion process by making the innovation "legitimate," removing it from the status of novelty or luxury. They begin to put social pressure on the nonadopters.

The key characteristic of the early majority is deliberateness. Compared with earlier adopters, they are more cautious and thorough in their decision making. Like the early adopters, the early majority are well integrated into the local community, but they are not as likely to hold leadership positions. They need evidence of successful adoption by others before they will commit their own resources.

Late majority

The next 34 percent to adopt the innovation are the late majority. They tend to be somewhat older, less well educated, less well off financially,

---

[11] The special case of the diffusion of innovations in industrial markets has been discussed in more detail in F. E. Webster, Jr., "Communication and Diffusion Processes in Industrial Markets," *European Journal of Marketing* 5, no. 4 (Winter 1971/72): 178–188.

and less well integrated into the community. They might be best characterized by the word "skeptical," since they are suspicious of new products and new ideas. These people influence the diffusion process by making the innovation a clear necessity. Only when public opinion clearly favors the innovation do these people finally succumb.

Compared with earlier adopter categories, the late majority are much more dependent on word of mouth, and personal sources of influence are more important for them. These people are significantly less exposed to mass media than the early adopters.

Laggards

The last 16 percent to adopt the innovation are the laggards. Laggards tend to be older, with less education, poorer, and less well integrated into the local community. They emphasize tradition in their orientation to life, and most of their social contacts tend to be familial. These people have little exposure to mass communication media, especially the print media. They are very local in their orientation and have very few contacts outside of the local community. They may rely most heavily on television for their information, with radio and perhaps local newspapers having some influence as well. Magazines and other media with limited and specialized appeals seldom reach them.

The term *laggard* is not to be regarded as one of derision or opprobrium. It is not meant to be critical of life style or orientation but simply to describe the traditional and local orientation of this class of adopters. Their roots tend to go deep; they value such things as permanence and family relationships and favor simplicity over complexity. Rural dwellers, for example, generally tend to exhibit these tendencies. As targets for marketing effort, laggards are difficult, if not impossible, to reach and require considerable expense that may not be justified.

In industrial markets, the laggards are the small, marginal firms that have limited growth potential. Many of them have already seen their best days. They probably compete in a limited market area and on the basis of price and standardized products. They may be quite profitable because of their carefully defined market niches, but their managements are likely to be uninterested in, and even incapable of, substantially improving sales volume, operating efficiency, or profit.

Strategic implications

As targets for marketing effort, the adopter categories clearly represent quite distinct challenges and opportunities. A major variable to consider is their unique patterns of reliance on various sources of information. In general, the innovators must be reached through technical and specialized media aimed specifically at them. In industrial markets, personal selling and limited media advertising can be used effectively. Early adopters can be reached through the mass media, although personal selling may also be used efficiently in industrial markets if the early adopters can be identified. Mass media information is also used by the early adopters as they influence the early majority through opinion leadership. The early majority are thus reached both through the opinion leaders and through the mass media, as are the late majority. The laggards are generally hard to reach, although they may be exposed to some general-appeal mass media. Social pressure and social visibility for the product are the major influences on laggards.

Most firms find it impractical and unnecessary to have five distinct market development strategies, one for each adopter category. Every firm can probably develop two distinct marketing programs, however, one for the earlier adopters (innovators and early adopters) and one for the later adopters (early majority, late majority, and laggards). The key differences between these two strategies are the selection of market targets and the use of communication media. The preceding comments on the characteristics of adopter categories should be helpful to most marketing managers in defining the characteristics of the customers most likely to be among the first to adopt new products, and these should be the targets of early promotional effort. Specialized media can be used efficiently to reach the earlier adopters, with mass, general-appeal media being more appropriate for later adopters.

In industrial markets, the innovators take on special significance in the development of markets for new products. In many markets it is possible and desirable to isolate the innovators as a special class of customer for early sales effort. Here the emphasis should be on technical-development programs. In medical instrumentation and pharmaceuticals, for example, it is common practice to contact the leading authorities in a given field and ask them to do laboratory and clinical investigations with new products. The results of their research can contribute to the development of both the research field in which the authority is working and the market for the new product through publication of papers on the research results, papers presented at professional meetings, and other professional channels of communication.

Generalizations like these have limited value, however, until they are tested and made specific in the context of particular markets through the conduct of market research. The diffusion of innovations is a specific example of the generalization offered in Chapter 2 to the effect that models of buyer behavior can be useful both in planning marketing research and in predicting response to marketing strategy. In this case, the theory suggests the characteristics to be sought in adopter categories, but specific dimensions require the verification of good market research data. Likewise, these generalizations make possible some limited predictions about responses to strategies for developing markets for new products, but major investments in market development programs should be protected with the insurance of market research studies, not dependent upon crude generalizations.

SUMMARY

New products are the lifeblood of any dynamic and growing business. Competition, changing customer preferences, and evolving technology work to bring about the eventual obsolescence of every product. Profit margins generally decrease faster than sales volume. To remain healthy and grow, therefore, every company needs a continual stream of new products. New products don't just happen but require carefully planned and guided programs for stimulating, collecting, evaluating, developing, testing, and commercializing new-product ideas. When this is done well, the chances of new-product success increase substantially—there is almost a 90 percent chance of developing a product that meets the profit and return-on-investment objectives established for it. When done poorly, product development is a negative force on the business, draining its financial and technical resources and demoralizing the R&D and marketing personnel.

Development of markets for new products is a distinctly complex task requiring careful planning and deployment of marketing resources. This task can be aided substantially by awareness of the theory of diffusion of innovations, which suggests the characteristics of the customers most likely to respond favorably to a new-product idea and offers guidelines on how to reach them most efficiently.

PRICING DECISIONS

Pricing decisions link marketing actions with the financial objectives of the firm. They are a major influence on the size of the firm's sales potential, and they are a major factor determining the rate at which the market for a new product develops. Pricing strategy determines the positioning of the firm in the market vis-à-vis its competitors. Among the most important marketing variables influenced by pricing decisions are trade margins, profit margins, rate of return on investments such as new-product development and advertising, and the image of the product.

Pricing decisions therefore have a central role to play in the design of the marketing mix. Yet, with few exceptions, responsibility for pricing decisions is seldom clearly defined within the firm. If one looks at a marketing organization chart, one is likely to see managers of advertising and sales promotion, sales, market research, products, new products, and distribution, but no manager of pricing. Where there is a pricing manager, his responsibility is likely to be at quite a low level, for small adjustments of prices in response to market con-ditions, constrained by policies and strategy decided at a higher level.

This lack of clearly defined responsibility is a problem because it often means inadequate attention to pricing strategy and usually leads to slowness in responding to pricing problems and opportunities. It is a reflection of the fact that pricing decisions are a concern of all functional areas, including financial and production management as well as marketing management. It is not uncommon for cost and financial criteria to dominate pricing and for the marketing effectiveness of pricing strategy to suffer as a result.

PRICE THEORY

From economics we have the well-known demonstration that profits are maximized by a price at which the slope of the demand curve is equal to that of the cost curve. This is illustrated in Figure 9–1. The slope of the cost curve is determined by production technology and reflects accounting judgments about the allocation of overhead and fixed costs to specific products. The slope of the demand curve shows how demand changes as a function of price—the lower the price, the more demanded. This relationship can also be presented in tabular form as a *demand schedule* showing the quantities demanded at various prices. From a marketing manager's viewpoint, estimating the demand schedule or

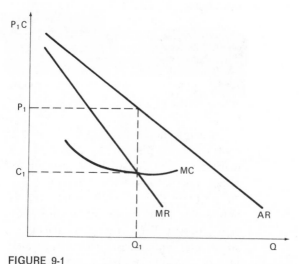

FIGURE 9-1
Cost-price relationships. According to price theory, the most profitable quantity to produce and sell is the quantity at which marginal cost (the incremental cost involved in producing another unit) is equal to marginal revenue (the incremental revenue to be realized from sale of that unit).

the demand curve is one of the most difficult tasks in making pricing decisions. It is more often guessed at than estimated on the basis of careful market research.

Elasticity

Underlying the demand schedule is the concept of *demand elasticity*— a measure of the percentage change in quantity demanded in relation to the percentage change in price given by the formula

$$E = \frac{(Q_2 - Q_1)/Q_1}{(P_2 - P_1)/P_1}$$

where Q_2 is the new quantity demanded, Q_1 is the old demand level, P_2 is the new price, and P_1 is the old price. This is the formula for *price elasticity* of demand. Demand is said to be elastic if revenue changes faster than demand in response to price changes, and it is said to be inelastic if a percentage change in price results in a smaller percentage change in revenue. If the percentages are the same, this condition is called *unitary elasticity*—that is, when $E = 1$. A similar concept can be developed for *income elasticity*, a measure of changes in revenue attributable to percentage changes in market income levels. Sales of liquor, for example, are known to be "income elastic."

Price elasticity of demand may be difficult to estimate for two reasons. First, it is likely to vary at different points on the demand curve. Second, if the marketer tries to use research to estimate price elasticity, it is hard to control factors other than price that influence demand levels. Similar problems come up when an attempt is made to estimate elasticity using historical sales records.

Pricing in an oligopoly

An oligopoly is a market condition in which there are relatively few sellers, too few to meet the economist's criterion of "perfect" competition in which no individual seller can influence the price of the product. One of the distinctive features of an oligopoly is the fact that each firm sets its own prices (rather than "the market" setting the price) and each firm's pricing influences and is influenced by the pricing behavior of competitors. This interdependence of competitors' pricing strategies constrains the individual firm's pricing options. If it prices below competitors, then any advantage realized is likely to be short-lived as competitors meet the lower price. But if prices are set above competitive levels, then demand is likely to drop off rapidly.

These features of pricing in an oligopolistic market are presented graphically in the familiar "kinked demand curve" shown in Figure 9–2. Of course, as is often the case, things are not quite as simple as

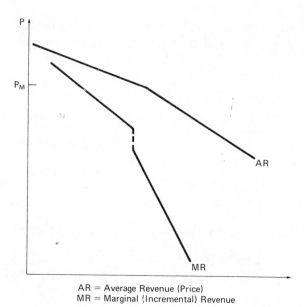

AR = Average Revenue (Price)
MR = Marginal (Incremental) Revenue

FIGURE 9-2
The "kinked demand curve" is an oligopolistic market.

presented there. Instead of the discrete point of discontinuity, P_M, shown, the market may actually have a range of "acceptable" prices, probably related to moderate differences in product features and product quality. But the basic notion is sound—there is a level of price above which sales fall off rapidly.

"Psychological" pricing

The economic theory of price makes a number of simplifying assumptions concerning products and buyer behavior. It is assumed, for example, that buyers' tastes and preferences are "given" and that the buyer is essentially "rational," meaning that he will consider alternative product offerings in terms of the price he must pay for a given level of quality. Such marketing nuances as brand image, brand loyalty, and benefit segmentation lie outside the scope of the economic theory of price.

It is clear that psychological reactions to price, especially for consumer products, are terribly important considerations in pricing strategy. Perhaps most significant in this realm is the consumer's tendency to use price as an index of quality for certain classes of products such as cosmetics, jewelry, and clothing. Such products often have hidden benefits and values that the consumer cannot judge on a rational, objective basis. In the absence of physical cues of product quality and where psychological product dimensions predominate, price may be the best available indicator of product quality and value, at least for certain customers. Implicit in this judgmental process may be a degree of faith in the market mechanism—"If it costs more, it must be better."

Another psychological dimension of pricing has been called "charm pricing," the use of standard, accepted pricing conventions that seem to have a certain charm for the consumer. Prices like $9.99 or $2.98 or 29¢ are examples; $9.99 sounds like a better value than $10.00, and there is also a tendency for an uneven price, once established, to become a kind of norm expected by the consumer.

A third psychological dimension of pricing is seen in "price lining," the common marketing practice of offering several price lines for a given class of product—television sets, kitchen appliances, automobiles, cameras, and the like. This dimension is related to the first, the tendency to use price as an indicator of quality. A common retail selling strategy is to "trade up" the customer from a basic, low-price model to a higher-price model with better features. Many manufacturers have a product strategy that offers low-price models primarily to attract potential customers into the retail outlet, where it is hoped that retail salesmen can sell a higher-priced, more profitable product. The basic product and its price become a frame of reference for the customer, a standard against which to assess the values offered by higher-priced products.

Thus, pricing decisions require consideration of a variety of economic and psychological factors, including demand elasticity, competitive response, and buyer habits and preferences.

ENVIRONMENTAL FACTORS

Each firm faces a unique array of environmental influences on its pricing actions. These influences most often operate as constraints, limiting the strategic choices available to the firm. At the same time they reduce uncertainty and give the manager a more predictable decision-making environment. Environmental influences are exerted on the firm by a variety of institutions, including government, trade associations, and the press. Among the most important environmental constraints are governmental pricing regulations, industry agreements, distribution channel conventions, and likely competitive response.

Governmental pricing regulation

Many countries impose rather strict regulations on a firm's pricing activities. These regulations have the overriding purpose of protecting the public welfare and are aimed in one of two directions—preserving competition in the marketplace or controlling inflation.

In the first area, antitrust legislation is usually heavily concerned

monopoly pricing

with pricing practices, especially pricing that could tend to create a monopoly by driving out small competitors. So-called "predatory pricing" involves large firms' offering low prices until competitors' operations become so unprofitable as to force them out of business, at which time the larger firm increases its prices. A related problem is "discriminatory pricing," which favors certain customers (usually the larger ones) and in turn gives them a competitive advantage, forcing their competitors out of business and tending to create a monopoly in customers' industries. In the United States a large body of legislation has been developed to deal with such practices, including

- *The Sherman Act (1890)*—aimed at collusive practices, including pricing practices, that tended to create monopoly.
- *The Clayton Act (1914)*—an amendment to the Sherman Act that made it unlawful to discriminate in price among purchasers of like products where the effect of such discrimination is likely to be the reduction of competition.
- *The Federal Trade Commission Act (1914)*—created the FTC and empowered it to act as necessary to prohibit unfair methods of competition and, with the U.S. Department of Justice, to enforce the Clayton Act. Among the laws that have subsequently come under the FTC's enforcement powers is the Automobile Information Disclosure Act (1958) requiring automobile dealers to display the manufacturer's suggested retail price on new cars. The FTC's major thrust, however, has been to regulate deceptive practices in the areas of labeling, packaging, advertising and personal selling.
- *The Robinson-Patman Act (1936)*—an amendment to the Clayton Act that had the purpose of extending the coverage of the act to preservation of competition in buying industries and to situations in which competition was not "substantially lessen(ed)" but merely "injured." This law also made specific practices illegal, such as brokerage payments to firms not truly operating as brokers and the demanding of discriminatory prices by customers. It also required that not only prices but also promotional assistance (displays, catalogues, etc.) must be offered to all customers on an equitable basis.
- *The Miller-Tydings Act (1937)*—an amendment to the Sherman Act that made resale price maintenance legal (i.e., not in violation of Sherman Act provisions against collusive practices) in states having resale price maintenance statutes, the so-called "fair trade acts."

This very brief summary of the nature of various pieces of legislation affecting pricing decisions is obviously incomplete. No body of law can be understood without reference to the large number of court decisions that interpret the law, set precedents, and over time contribute substance to the law in the changing business environment.[1]

[1] For an excellent review of this body of legislation and of court decisions affecting price strategy, see M. C. Howard, *Legal Aspects of Marketing* (New York: McGraw-Hill, 1964), esp. chs. 2 & 3, pp. 23–75.

Only recently has the U.S. government attempted to regulate prices in an effort to control inflation. Under President Nixon, a variety of price restrictions have been tried, including guidelines as to permissible price increases in percentage terms, selective restrictions on such industries as meat packing, and the need to justify price increases with cost data. Changing regulations and the difficulties associated with implementation of new administrative procedures have led to a good deal of confusion as American business tries to learn how to operate under these new constraints.

Each country presents a unique environment of legislative and regulatory constraints on pricing decisions. Not only is there the influence of government but there may also be varying degrees of intra-industry cooperation. It is quite common in European countries, for example, for competitors to discuss pricing practices, and such discussion may become routine and carefully planned, a practice that would be illegal in the United States. Likewise, pricing practices vary significantly from industry to industry within a country.

Price leadership

In many industries there is an acknowledged price leader, a firm whose pricing practices lead and are followed by the rest of the firms in the industry. Such price leaders are the first to announce price changes and can be reasonably certain that their competitors will follow suit. The price leaders are often but not necessarily the largest firms in the industry. They are, of course, aware of the role they play. With that role comes not only a degree of pricing freedom but also a kind of responsibility for the health of the industry. Price leaders are found in banking, basic metals, and the chemicals industry, to cite a few examples.

It is generally true that a price leader can be confident that his price increases will be followed by his competitors, but it is of course also possible that they will elect to behave differently at any given time. Some smaller competitors may hope to obtain a temporary price advantage by holding back, at least briefly, on meeting the price leader's increases. If the price leader is a very large firm, then any price decreases are even more likely than price increases to be followed by smaller competitors.

Basing-point pricing

Another pricing practice that is common in certain industries needs to be mentioned briefly here. This is the practice of basing-point pricing. In this pricing approach, all sellers in an industry agree to price their products as if they were being shipped from one or a few key cities, even if plants are not located in those cities. Thus the basing point may not be the actual shipping point but is nonetheless used for quoting shipping charges in order to put competitors on an equal footing independent of their actual plant locations. Use of basing-point pricing leads to so-called "phantom freight," when freight charges result in revenues in excess of actual freight costs incurred by the shipper, and to "freight absorption," when the freight charges quoted as part of the price from the basing point are less than the shipper's actual freight costs. The objective of such systems is to offer uniform delivered prices and to eliminate differences in freight charges as a basis for selecting suppliers. Ideally, this practice both increases the number of options available to the buyer and increases the geographic scope of the seller's market. But such systems can come very close to a form of price collusion, and the courts have ruled against them in certain cases in which there are both uniform prices and uniform transportation charges.[2]

PRICING OBJECTIVES

A variety of objectives may guide decision making in pricing, including the following:

1. to maximize sales volume and share of market
2. to maximize profit, either in total dollars or as a percentage of sales
3. to maximize return on investment
4. to enhance the quality image of the product
5. to secure dealer support
6. to provide necessary profit margins to support the promotional program

These different objectives are not necessarily mutually exclusive, and several of them may be involved in a specific decision. It is usually true, however, that there is a conflict between a sales maximization objective and a return-on-investment objective, except where it is believed that maximum market penetration in the short run (as in the early stages of the product life cycle) is the key to maximum return on investment in the long run.

Relationship to other marketing decisions

The appropriateness of certain pricing objectives depends, of course, on the overall marketing strategy of the company and the specific marketing program for the products involved. A strategy stressing high product quality clearly calls for relatively high prices. Heavy use of consumer advertising and sales promotion indicates the need for reasonably high gross profit margins and relatively low trade margins. Use of selective

---

[2] *Federal Trade Commission v. Cement Institute*, 68 C. Ct. 793 (1948).

distribution, on the other hand, often dictates the need for relatively high trade margins. The relationship of price to other elements of the marketing mix is developed more completely in Chapter 11, where the difference between "push" and "pull" strategies is set forth in considerable detail.

As we saw in Chapter 8, pricing strategy for new products is a major determinant of the length of the product life cycle. To summarize that discussion, relatively low prices and a penetration strategy are likely to discourage early entry by competitors but will yield lower profit margins per unit while, perhaps, extending the product life cycle. Conversely, a skimming strategy that involves high prices and profit margins may attract competitors into the market earlier and can shorten the product life cycle.

Financial considerations

Especially as the trend continues toward stressing financial criteria in marketing decision making, pricing strategy is likely to be increasingly guided by return-on-investment criteria. This variant of cost-plus pricing is called "rate of return" or "target" pricing, where the objective is a target rate of return on investment. In implementing this approach, there are three key investment elements to consider:

1. investment in research and development expenses to create the new product
2. investment in plant and equipment required to produce the product
3. investment in advertising, personal selling, and sales promotion required to develop the market for the product

After developing these estimates of investment, the pricing analyst must next estimate the expected life of the product and the pattern of additional investment and expenses required over the life of the product. It is common practice today to use discounted cash flow analysis and present-value analysis in evaluating alternative product investment opportunities. The implications of several different sets of assumptions about product life, promotional expenses, prices, and so on can be readily assessed using computer simulation and the present-value model. A major judgmental problem in using such models is to estimate the market response to alternative levels of marketing investment in promotional expenditure.

ALTERNATIVE APPROACHES TO PRICING

The pricing problem is complicated enough so that it is optimistic to the point of foolishness to expect that a mechanical, checklist approach to pricing can be developed that will tell the manager exactly what price to charge for a product. But this does not mean that it is impossible to develop a reasonably orderly and logical approach to the pricing problem that has general applicability and can significantly narrow the range of prices that the pricing decision maker must consider. In this section we will first examine briefly several commonly used approaches to the pricing problem and then develop a somewhat more complete and general approach.

Cost-plus pricing

A very common pricing practice is to base the selling price on the cost associated with producing and selling the product. The standard approach is to add up all costs, including materials, direct and indirect labor, administrative and overhead expense, and selling expense and to add to that total a standard percentage for profit. This approach is formalized in cost-plus contracts for sales to the U.S. federal government, in which allowable costs are defined by relevant government purchasing regulations. The distribution trades usually follow a cost-plus practice as well, marking up by a standard percentage merchandise that they purchase for resale.

There are two major shortcomings to cost-plus pricing: It is relatively insensitive to the influence of price on demand and there is no particularly logical basis for choosing a profit percentage to be added to costs. In cost-plus pricing, demand is estimated independent of price, and cost estimates are based on the forecast sales volume. Such an approach largely overlooks the possibility that price will determine sales volume and thereby also determine actual production and selling costs.

Should profit be calculated at 10 percent, 15 percent, or 100 percent? The defense of a particular percentage usually depends on past practices, industry tradition, and so on. Today it is increasingly common to find an add-on related to the company's return-on-investment criterion.

The cost-plus approach to pricing is so popular because it is relatively easy to justify compared with other approaches. Accounting estimates of various costs are reasonably easy to develop and justify, and talking about profit as a given percentage of costs gives a sense of security compared with the uncertainties involved in talking about profit as a variable to be determined by the influence of price on demand. This is a false sense of security, however, because the vagaries of the demand schedule are still present even though they haven't been considered in the pricing decision.

Incremental-cost pricing

In certain industries where there are high fixed costs as a portion of total costs, incremental- or marginal-cost pricing may be found. Simply stated, the pricing objective becomes one of covering variable, out-of-pocket costs and, hopefully, making some contribution to fixed overhead. It is assumed that business that would not otherwise be available to the firm can be obtained through low prices. Such is the logic behind so-called "promotional" airline fares, for example, and in the development of special commodity rates by the railroads. Some usage of incremental-cost pricing is quite likely in any industry characterized by large investments in plant and equipment, especially if there is excess production capacity. The railroad, airline, agricultural chemicals, and synthetic fibers industries are good examples of this situation.

The practice of incremental-cost pricing is always dangerous for a firm because it can lead to destructive price competition within the industry and, over the long run, to failure to recover total costs. If some products are not expected to cover full costs, including a fair allocation of fixed costs, it becomes increasingly difficult to justify full cost allocation on other products. Likewise, it is unfair to ask certain products to carry more than their share of the cost burden. Incremental-cost pricing is certainly one of the reasons for the sorry state of the American railroads today. Among other consequences, there is the obvious result that adequate profit margins were not available to support necessary improvements in capital equipment.

Competitive-parity pricing

In many market situations, standard industry practice indicates what the price for the product should be. There are three somewhat different types of conditions in which this is found:

1. in nearly perfectly competitive markets, where there is a market price established independent of the decisions of individual sellers, such as markets for agricultural markets.
2. in markets dominated by a strong price leader.
3. in markets where traditional practice has favored certain popular prices —such as the 10¢ candy bar (which used to be 5¢!) and many consumer packaged goods, including beer, cigarettes, potato chips, and toothpaste.

Competitive parity pricing says, in effect, that the individual firm has little ability to control price and price becomes a passive element in the marketing mix. It is found in situations in which actual physical differences among products are quite small.

A variation on competitive parity pricing is to set prices at a specified amount either above or below the going price. This is a strategy of premium or discount pricing in a situation where there is a traditional, established market price. Such a strategy still uses the going market price as a standard. Premium pricing is followed by certain brands of beer, for example, and can also be found in such diverse industries as air freight forwarding and grinding wheels. Discount pricing is popular for certain brands of household appliances, paint, and rented cars.

What the market will bear

your going to buy it n

A strategy of charging as much as possible has often been advocated for certain classes of products for which demand is somewhat inelastic with respect to price. Sophisticated instruments of various kinds can often be priced in this fashion, as can certain raw materials that have a critical function to perform in manufacturing and of which there is limited supply.

By charging as much as the market will bear, the firm may be encouraging early entry by new competitors, as in the use of a skimming pricing strategy. In addition, the firm using this approach is insensitive to the influence of price on demand and may, in fact, be overlooking opportunities for improved profitability. Obviously, what the market will bear is not a precise concept and can only be estimated subjectively and through trial and error. Finally, in these days of increased buyer activism, there is the strong possibility that what-the-market-will-bear pricing will incur active and vocal buyer opposition if buyers feel that they are at the mercy of a monopolistic seller who is charging unfair prices. The current heated debate over branded versus generic drug prices is a case in point.

Nonetheless, there are some situations in which this form of pricing makes sense—especially when costs are hard to estimate and it is known that demand is relatively inelastic over a wide range of prices. These conditions are found, for example, in the repair of certain types of heavy industrial equipment, which is done on a job shop basis and where the repair shop may have little comparable previous experience with which to estimate costs. In this case, one possible guideline (an upper limit) is provided by the cost of a new replacement unit, with what the market will bear being something below that level. Similar pricing situations are found in the sale of other repair services, reconditioned furniture and appliances, recapped tires, and custom-made products of various kinds, including boats, flower arrangements, and houses.

Isn't this like what the market will bear

Demand schedule pricing

From an ideal standpoint, the firm facing a major pricing decision should take the time necessary to estimate the influence of prices on the level of demand—that is, to estimate the demand schedule. Such estimates could be developed through the use of experimentation in test market situations, where the level of price is systematically varied and market response carefully noted. Assuming that the results of such tests are reasonably accurate and reliable, the pricing analyst could then estimate the price at which marginal revenue would be equal to marginal cost, the profit-maximizing point in the demand schedule.

There are a variety of reasons why this ideal approach is seldom followed. First, the necessary research is expensive, time-consuming, and subject to error. Second, there are a large number of constraints on the pricing decisions in the typical firm, as we have seen—constraints such as leader-follower relationships, customary industry prices, governmental regulations, and so on. Third, there are many products for which demand is relatively insensitive to price and more sensitive to other variables such as product quality, retailer support, and level of sales promotional effort.

The multistage approach to pricing

A somewhat more complicated but logical and straightforward approach to pricing decisions has been proposed by Professor Oxenfeldt.[3] The multistage approach presents a long-run view of pricing strategy and specifically relates pricing to other elements of the marketing mix in the following sequence of steps:

1. Select market targets.
2. Choose a brand image.
3. Compose a marketing mix.
4. Select a pricing policy.
5. Determine a pricing strategy.
6. Arrive at a specific price.

Selection of market targets defines the competitive niche of the firm, suggesting the product quality and brand image strategy that must be pursued in the product positioning. Brand image clearly dictates a relatively narrow range of price alternatives and the marketing mix that is required to compete most effectively in that market. Likewise, the marketing mix chosen narrows still further the range of prices that can be considered and leads to a pricing policy to guide such decisions as how prices should compare with industry averages, whether to use price promotions and, if so, how frequently, the margins to be offered to various types of middlemen, and whether to use resale price maintenance, i.e. "fair-trade" pricing. As Oxenfeldt points out, it is hard to draw a precise distinction between pricing policy and pricing strategy, but policy can be thought of as constraining pricing de-

[3] A. R. Oxenfeldt, "Multi-Stage Approach to Pricing," *Harvard Business Review* 38 (July–August 1960): 125–133.

cisions—"standing answers to recurring pricing problems"—whereas a pricing strategy is a plan for responding to a specific market and competitive situation. Finally, the specific price is determined, based on cost and demand considerations but only after the many qualitative factors influencing pricing have been taken into account in the first five stages. Oxenfeldt sees this approach as having four benefits:

1. It breaks the pricing decision into six more easily manageable stages.
2. It reduces the risk of destroying corporate and brand image investments.
3. It facilitates delegation of pricing responsibility by providing necessary guidelines.
4. It helps the analyst deal with the qualitative factors in the pricing decision, especially the influence of price on the total impression of the seller and his product.

The Oxenfeldt model has special relevance for consumer products in cases where brand image and company image are key marketing variables, although it can also be applied to virtually all pricing situations because the qualitative factors that it helps analyze are always present to a degree. A somewhat more generalized approach can be suggested, however.

A GENERAL PRICING DECISION MODEL

A complete and logical approach to the pricing decision must recognize the relationship of pricing to overall marketing strategy and the impact of price on both demand and cost factors. The following sequence of steps would meet these analytical requirements:

1. *Define market targets.* All marketing decision making should begin with a definition of segmentation strategy and the identification of potential customers.
2. *Estimate market potential.* The maximum size of the available market determines what is possible and helps define competitive opportunities.
3. *Develop product positioning.* The brand image and the desired niche in the competitive marketplace provide important constraints on the pricing decision as the firm attempts to obtain a unique competitive advantage by differentiating its product offering from that of competitors.
4. *Design the marketing mix.* Design of the marketing mix defines the role to be played by pricing in relation to and in support of other marketing variables, especially distribution and promotional policies.
5. *Estimate price elasticity of demand.* The sensitivity of the level of demand to differences in price can be estimated either from past experience or through market tests.
6. *Estimate all relevant costs.* While straight cost-plus pricing is to be avoided because it is insensitive to demand, pricing decisions must take

into account necessary plant investment, investment in R&D, and investment in market development, as well as variable costs of production and marketing.

7. *Analyze environmental factors.* Pricing decisions are further constrained by industry practices, likely competitive response to alternative pricing strategies, and legal requirements.

8. *Set pricing objectives.* Pricing decisions must be guided by a clear statement of objectives that recognizes environmental constraints and defines the role of pricing in the marketing strategy while at the same time relating pricing to the firm's financial objectives.

9. *Develop the price structure.* The price structure for a given product can now be determined and will define selling prices for the product (perhaps in a variety of styles and sizes) and the discounts from list price to be offered to various kinds of middlemen and various types of buyers.

As noted before, the pricing decision is too complicated to permit the development of a mechanical, checklist approach. But the general procedure just outlined provides a logical guideline for the development of pricing strategy and the determination of specific prices.

COMPETITIVE BIDDING

The final topic to be considered in this chapter is the use of competitive bidding, a common buying practice in industrial and institutional markets. Organizational buyers depend on competitive bidding to obtain the best possible price in markets characterized by relatively few sellers and reasonably standardized products. Part of the difficulty of competitive bidding from the buyer's viewpoint is to develop a set of product specifications that will be attractive to and feasible for several potential suppliers but specific and complete enough to ensure that bidders are offering comparable products.

From the seller's viewpoint competitive bidding poses three major challenges: (1) estimating the likely bids of competitors, (2) estimating costs carefully enough to know the profitability of various bid prices, and (3) knowing the criteria by which the buyer will evaluate alternative bids. It is generally but by no means always true that the business will be awarded to the lowest bidder. If bids are not directly comparable (e.g., the products differ in important respects or some include service and others do not) or some bids are not completely responsive to the requirements and information requests of the buyer or the buyer has substantial doubt about the supplier's ability to perform under the terms of the contract, then the low-price bidder may not get the business.

It is a common selling practice in markets where competitive bidding is substantially used to try to get specifications developed that favor the seller's product, thus removing him to a certain extent from strict price competition. New product features are often developed with this objective in mind.

The competitive-bidding situation can be quite complicated for subcontractors who are submitting bids to contractors who are in turn submitting bids to a potential buyer. This is a common situation in defense procurement and in the construction business. Subcontractors may have to select among potential contractors as part of their bidding strategy. The subcontractors' bids determine the contractors' ability to compete for the business.

The general approach to the pricing decision presented earlier applies as well to the competitive-bidding situation. But the competitive-bidding problem is complicated by the need to find a price as low as possible consistent with overall marketing objectives. This requirement puts special emphasis on the need to estimate costs carefully. At the same time, the firm must be careful not to respond to a particular bidding situation in a way that hinders its future competitiveness and profitability. Bids that are too high can result in lost opportunities to bid on future business, whereas bids that are too low can lead to reduced profits on a stream of future business from this customer and perhaps from other customers as well. Obviously, the firm should not be so anxious to obtain a given piece of business that it destroys its profitability in order to win the award. In the competitive battle for a major award, it is easy for undue optimism to enter into cost estimates.

A simple application of the expected value method illustrates the difficulty, as shown in Table 9–1. As the firm lowers its bid price, it increases the probability of winning the award but reduces the value of the award. Simple estimates of the kind shown in the example can be useful in the systematic analysis of bidding alternatives. It is of course a moot question whether expected profit should be the decision criterion. Somewhat more complicated decision models are possible that

TABLE 9-1
Relationship of expected profit and bid price

Bid Price	Company Cost	Profit at This Price	Estimated Probability of Winning Award	Expected Profit
$100,000	$75,000	$ 25,000	0.05	$ 1,250
90,000	75,000	15,000	0.25	3,750
85,000	75,000	10,000	0.35	3,500
80,000	75,000	5,000	0.50	2,500
75,000	75,000	—	0.75	0
50,000	75,000	−25,000	0.95	−23,750

use other criteria such as avoiding the worst possible outcomes, minimizing "regret" (the difference between possible and actual profit), and so on.[4]

SUMMARY

Despite its inherent complexity, the pricing decision can be approached systematically, rigorously, and logically. Pricing decisions relate marketing decisions to the financial objectives of the firm and must therefore be based on careful analysis of the impact of prices on both revenue and cost. Estimation of the demand schedule is a difficult task, but this is not adequate justification for basing prices solely on cost considerations.

Pricing decisions cannot be made intelligently unless pricing is distinctly analyzed in relation to the other elements of the marketing strategy, including segmentation and the strategy of differential advantage, product quality and image, reseller strategy, and promotional strategy. For these reasons, pricing must be part of the top marketing executive's responsibility if its strategic implications are to be adequately assessed.

[4] For an extended example of the application of Bayesian analysis to pricing strategy, see W. Alderson and P. Green, *Planning and Problem-Solving in Marketing* (Homewood, Ill.: Irwin, 1964), pp. 261–265.

DISTRIBUTOR AND PHYSICAL-DISTRIBUTION MANAGEMENT

Some management authors have described distribution as the last frontier of marketing. The metaphor is justified because it is true in most companies that distribution efficiency could be dramatically improved. There may be no other area of marketing management where practice lags so far behind what is possible in terms of improved management techniques, increased efficiency, and greater effectiveness.

Distribution really includes two rather distinct problem areas: the physical distribution of products, or the activities involved in physically moving and storing products, and the management of a distribution organization of agent middlemen and other forms of resellers. The former is usually called *physical-distribution management*, although a variety of more poetic terms, such as *logistics* and *rhocrematics*, have recently been offered. The latter is often referred to as *channel management* or *channel-of-distribution management* in marketing literature. The two areas overlap to the extent that middlemen perform some of the physical-distribution function (most notably, storage and inventory management). But a variety of functions other than physical distribution are also performed by middlemen, including promoting the company's products and adjusting them to the needs of individual customers, providing market information, and so on.

Distribution is a "management frontier" for three reasons. First, it has traditionally received inadequate management attention. Second, a variety of new analytical and decision-making techniques, often associated with the field of management science or operations research, have been developed in recent years to aid these decisions, but these have been underexploited. Third, several technical developments in the field of distribution have created important new profit opportunities —developments in such fields as containerization, air freight, order-processing systems, and communication.

THE TOTAL DISTRIBUTION COST CONCEPT

An important development in the field of distribution management occurred with the articulation of the total distribution cost concept. The origin of the concept appears to have been Professor Cherington's 1954 study entitled *The Role of Air Freight in Physical Distribution*,[1] which was developed as a result of a sponsored study to define opportunities for intelligent use of air freight. The ideas incorporated into the total distribution cost concept came from the general area called systems theory, which can be summarized by three simple propositions:

1. All systems are composed of interdependent subsystems, and these subsystems interact in a synergistic fashion—the whole is greater than the sum of its parts.
2. Attempting to maximize the performance of any subsystem can block optimization of the total system.
3. The objective of the system manager should be to optimize total system performance.

Different experts have offered somewhat different views of the elements of a distribution system, reflecting the obvious fact that the elements of distribution cost are subject to definition in a variety of ways. Most authorities would be willing to accept the following breakdown of total distribution cost:

[1] Paul Cherington, *The Role of Air Freight in Physical Distribution* (Boston: Graduate School of Business Administration, Harvard University, Division of Research, 1954).

1. transportation
2. order processing
3. cost of lost business (an "opportunity" cost due to inability to meet customer demand)
4. inventory carrying costs, including
   a. storage-space charges
   b. cost of capital invested
   c. taxes
   d. insurance
   e. obsolescence and deterioration
5. packaging
6. materials handling

To illustrate the logic of systems analysis, it is only necessary to consider how decisions in one of these areas are likely to influence costs in the others. For example, the company that spends more for protective packaging may reduce its storage costs (losses due to mishandling) and may be able to use lower-cost forms of transportation. Or, use of air freight as part of the distribution plan may permit substantial reduction in field inventory investments.

New interest in distribution cost

Several forces have combined to stimulate management interest in the total distribution cost concept in recent years. Among the most important considerations is heightened management attention to the related areas of cost of capital and return on investment. It is probably fair to assert that there has been a general heightening of interest in the financial implications of marketing decisions as a result. Of course, the fact that management consultants and academic experts in the field of distribution have been writing and talking about total distribution cost has also been an important influence. In addition, the transportation industry and most notably the suppliers of air freight services have been using this concept as part of their marketing approach. (Without the total distribution cost concept, it is obviously difficult to sell the planned use of "more expensive" air freight in a distribution system.) These two factors—financial considerations and transportation marketing—have combined to cause customers (industrial buyers, distributors, and other organizational decision makers) to push suppliers to hold inventories for them and to absorb other costs of distribution. As a result, suppliers have had to become more interested in finding means of controlling and lowering their distribution costs.

Another factor encouraging this new interest in the distribution area is product and service innovation by the transportation industry itself. Such developments as containerization, better schedules, new equipment, new order-expediting and communication systems, and new warehousing arrangements have all stimulated thinking about what is possible. The jumbo jets, double-bottom trucks, supertankers, and a variety of new railroad cars were all innovations of the 1960s bringing new opportunities for lower transportation costs and lower total distribution costs as a result.

DIFFICULTIES OF IMPLEMENTATION

The total distribution cost concept has direct implications for distribution management, implications for coordinated decision making with respect to all elements of distribution. It seems to call for a distribution "czar" who can coordinate, if not actually make, all decisions affecting total distribution cost in order to avoid suboptimization. In addition, the total distribution cost concept requires accurate information about each element of distribution cost and about the relationship between each element of cost and demand for the company's products.

There are four major areas of difficulty to be encountered in implementing the total distribution cost concept:

1. specifying the desired level of customer service
2. estimating each element of distribution cost, and the relationships among them, as a function of volume
3. organizational arrangements for coordinating distribution decision making
4. managing relationships with suppliers of distribution services and the reliability of these services

Each of these problems will be discussed briefly.

Defining the level of customer service

Experts in the field of distribution management report that defining the desired level of customer service is often the most difficult, yet most important, step in developing a rational, objective-oriented approach to distribution decision making. To understand the nature of this difficulty, one must first realize that every distribution system is less than 100 percent reliable. Transportation delays, inventory shortages, order-processing errors, and so on mean that no system can perform with 100 percent efficiency at reasonable cost. Furthermore, costs rise at an increasing rate as reliability and efficiency are increased. The managerial issue is to define the trade-off between increased reliability and increased cost. That determination in turn requires some knowledge of how level of service influences demand for the company's products.

Level of service can be defined in terms of percentage of orders to be shipped and received by customers within x days after receipt by the selling company. Most companies have only a vague notion of how distribution performance influences demand. It is a hard question to research, but experimentation with various levels of service can be helpful. Generally, the issue is resolved by reference to current industry practice and competitive conditions. In some industries, ability to deliver fast is the most important competitive variable.

It is often true that reliability of distribution system performance is more important than average level of service. In other words, the percentage of orders shipped and received within a stated period is more important than the length of the period itself. This is because customers' planning is dependent on reliability of system performance. For example, a manufacturer needs to know that components promised for delivery in x days will be received in x days plus or minus some small deviation. He can adjust his inventory levels and ordering procedures accordingly as long as he has a reliable estimate of x, regardless of whether x equals 7 days or 30 or 60.

Example

Nonetheless, because each element of distribution cost tends to increase at an increasing rate as a function of reliability, it is virtually impossible to design an economical distribution system that offers 100 percent reliability. A commonly used figure is 95 percent reliability. The possibility for error and delay must be recognized and planned for, typically with special distribution subsystems. Procedures for expediting delayed orders must be designed in order to avoid customer dissatisfaction. The main distribution system must be backstopped. It is often more economical to maintain special subsystems (e.g., selective use of air freight) than to build increased reliability into the main system.

Estimating distribution costs

Various studies have shown that it is not uncommon for distribution costs to approach 50 percent of total cost of goods sold. Yet traditional accounting methods (oriented as they are to public accountability more than to managerial decision making) often do not provide adequate information with which to estimate distribution cost on either a per-unit or per-order basis. The problem is often one of allocating total costs (e.g., warehousing cost or transportation cost) among different products and customers, different order sizes, and different facilities. The problem is not so much the level of costs as their behavior and interactions.

Each element of distribution cost is likely to behave differently, some being essentially linear, others growing rapidly as a function of volume, and others being quadratic (or U-shaped). The interactions among them are often so complex that they can only be analyzed by using computers and sophisticated simulation models. This is one major reason why management science has opened up some new frontiers in the distribution area. Even with such approaches, however, some important distribution costs such as product obsolescence and the cost of lost orders may defy precise estimation.

Organizational arrangements

The typical company has suboptimal distribution decision making built into its organization structure. For example, manufacturing departments are usually responsible for inventory policies, marketing departments usually manage the order-processing function, and transportation decisions may be the responsibility of an independent traffic department. The latter may be interested mainly in obtaining the lowest transportation cost per unit per mile and may be relatively insensitive to customer service requirements and the impact of transportation decisions on other distribution costs. Likewise, the traffic department is usually responsible only for outbound shipments, whereas the purchasing department is responsible for inbound shipments, another potential source of inefficiency and higher costs.

Within the organization you have to work together

An often-advocated solution to this problem is to have a distribution "czar," a high-level executive responsible for all distribution decisions from packaging to inventory control, from transportation to materials handling. Such a position is consistent with the very notion of total distribution cost. One could further argue that the distribution czar should report to the top marketing executive because of the importance of distribution decisions in creating a satisfied customer at a profit, as advocated by the marketing concept. There are clearly some strong arguments in favor of centralized distribution decision making.

But there are also reasons to distrust the argument in favor of a distribution czar. First, there are benefits from having countervailing viewpoints—financial, marketing, manufacturing, purchasing, etc.—represented in distribution decisions. Having only one of these viewpoints represented in distribution decisions would almost certainly lead to suboptimization and inefficiency—financial concern for inventory investments, marketing concern for customer service, and so on. On the other hand, the distribution czar could develop policies that were likewise biased. He could very easily develop his own decision criteria, in favor of lower warehousing and transportation costs, for example; but his authority would give these undue weight while ignoring other important criteria.

Second, the earlier analysis of difficulties in estimating distribution costs suggested that in many companies data would not be available to manage a centralized distribution function on a purely scientific and rational basis.

Distribution decisions are really made throughout the organization. The fact that they are so important and pervasive does not necessarily lead to the conclusion that they should be the responsibility of one man. Furthermore, a manager with the necessary experience, training, and other qualifications necessary to be a distribution czar is very hard to find.

Arguments against a distribution czar are not arguments against coordinated distribution decision making. Centralization is only one method of coordination. Although some companies have in fact moved toward the distribution czar idea (typically withholding some distribution decisions from his responsibility), more have moved toward the use of distribution committees to coordinate decisions. These committees usually meet frequently—say, weekly or semimonthly—and have the dual function of setting distribution policy to guide decisions in the various areas of total distribution cost and of reviewing and deciding about major distribution problems such as warehouse location and major changes in transportation. Committee representation usually comes from marketing, manufacturing, and finance, and it is common for the chairman to be the top distribution executive in the company, with the title Manager or Vice President of Distribution, Transportation, or Traffic.

The committee approach has major benefits, including the recognition that distribution problems are often too complex to be the responsibility of one man and the maintenance of healthy competition among different viewpoints and criteria concerning distribution decisions, a creative conflict if properly managed. The committee approach also avoids the addition to administrative costs and organization complexity implied by having a distribution czar and department.

Distribution services suppliers

A fourth problem area in implementing the total distribution cost concept is that of managing relationships with suppliers of distribution services. These difficulties reflect lack of control over these services and lack of reliability (or "quality") in the services themselves.

Distribution services are performed by a variety of specialized companies, including railroads, truckers, barge lines, airlines, ocean transporters, public warehousemen, freight forwarders, and so on. Level of service varies markedly among them. For example, public warehouses are generally recognized as providing a very high level of service, while railroads (in the United States) are noted for low reliability.

When a distribution company is contracted to perform a service, the shipper (or hiring company) loses control to some degree over the performance of that service. A decision to use such outside suppliers reflects a judgment that the loss of control is more than offset by the specialized knowledge and operations of the supplier and the economies and greater effectiveness that should result. To illustrate, most manufacturers find it more efficient not to worry about the problems of running their own trucking operations. But the resulting loss of control creates an added dimension of uncertainty and risk.

Likewise, lack of reliability in distribution suppliers' operations is a major difficulty. For example, the time required for shipment between New York and Chicago via railroad may vary between two days and two weeks. Such variation can obviously complicate inventory decision making, warehousing requirements, insurance costs, and so on. The overall effect is to increase total distribution costs and to make true optimization a very distant goal.

Field research has shown that these issues of control and reliability are very important to distribution managers. One private survey revealed, for example, that manufacturers were generally not interested in a new, fully integrated distribution service (including multiple-mode transportation, warehousing, and inventory management) because this would require giving control over too much of the total distribution function to one supplier. Another study revealed that lack of reliability was a major management problem, especially at connecting points in a distribution system where a shipment is transferred from one carrier to another.

To summarize, four difficulties in implementing the total distribution concept have been discussed—determining service level, estimating cost, organizing the distribution function, and managing relationships with distribution service suppliers. Because of these difficulties, surveys find that no company has gone all the way to implementing the total distribution cost concept, although several have applied total distribution cost analysis to particular products or groups of products. As in some other areas of "systems analysis," the total distribution cost concept implies an approach that is almost too grand to manage. Furthermore, most companies' accounting and operations research staffs are not up to the challenge of working with this management approach in its sophisticated detail.

Nonetheless, it is a valuable aid to management thinking and decision making, for it sensitizes the manager to the complexities of this important area and to the opportunities for improved system design. It makes him aware of the impact of decisions about one element of distribution cost on all other areas. By doing so, it helps him evaluate new distribution alternatives, such as use of air freight, that might seem uneconomical if one used a simpler analytical scheme. Gradual improvements in distribution cost accounting and distribution service supplier performance are bringing the ideal concept closer to being a managerial reality, creating new opportunities for competitive advantage for the firm willing to be innovative in its distribution.

THE DISTRIBUTION CHANNEL

A distribution channel is defined by a set of contractual arrangements linking manufacturers and various types of middlemen with end-user markets. Figures 10–1 and 10–2 define simple distribution channels for consumer and industrial markets. There is a tremendous variety of middlemen capable of performing a range of distribution functions; we could spend the next several pages defining terms that describe these various types of middlemen. Instead, a briefer listing of major types will be developed:

Middleman—any intermediary between manufacturer and end-user markets; synonymous with *reseller.*

Agent— any middleman with legal authority to act on behalf of the manufacturer.

Manufacturer's representative—a middleman who sells the product but usually does not take legal title to or physical possession of the merchandise.

Wholesaler—a middleman who sells to other middlemen, usually to retailers. This term usually applies to consumer markets.

Retailer—a middleman who sells to consumers.

Broker—a middleman who performs limited selling functions, usually only writing orders to be turned over to the manufacturer for delivery, and usually specializes in sales to a particular kind of customer such as grocery stores.

Sales agent— a middleman who agrees to sell all of the output of a manufacturer, at a stated commission rate or for a stated fee, but who usually does not take physical possession of or legal title to the merchandise.

Distributor—an imprecise term, usually used to describe a middleman who performs a variety of distribution functions, including selling, maintaining inventories, extending credit, and so on. It is a more common term in industrial markets but may also be used to refer to wholesalers.

Dealer— an even more imprecise term that can mean the same as distributor, retailer, wholesaler, etc. It is virtually synonymous with *middleman.*

Jobber—usually used in an industrial marketing context to refer to distributors, or in certain fields such as paper and hardware to refer to wholesalers characterized by broad lines and reasonably complete service offerings.

There are a variety of other middlemen, but few of these terms are mutually exclusive. The various types are usually defined by the particular set of distribution functions—or, more generally, marketing functions—performed by the middleman.

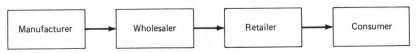

FIGURE 10-1
A typical consumer market distribution channel.

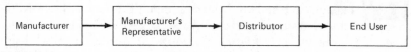

FIGURE 10-2
A typical industrial market distribution channel.

Functions performed

Marketing scholars have defined a variety of functions that are involved in the performance of marketing. Again, different scholars have developed somewhat different lists, but most would find the following acceptable:

Selling—promoting the product to potential customers.
Buying—purchasing a variety of products from various sellers, usually for resale.
Assorting—providing an assortment of items (often inter-related) for potential customers.
Financing—offering credit to potential customers, to facilitate the transaction; also, providing funds to sellers to help them finance their affairs.
Storage—protecting the product and maintaining inventories to offer better customer service.
Sorting—buying a quantity and breaking bulk items into amounts desired by customers.
Grading—judging products and labelling them as to quality.
Transportation—physically moving the product between manufacturer and end-user.
Market information—providing information to manufacturers about market conditions including expected sales volume, fashion trends, and pricing conditions.
Risk taking—absorbing business risks, especially risks of maintaining inventories, product obsolescence, etc.

Other terms that have been used include the *contactual function*— buying and selling, merchandising (including sorting, assorting, and adjusting the product to the buyer's needs), and the propaganda function (promotion). Some middlemen perform only one or two functions (e.g., transportation companies or sales agents), whereas others perform the full range. The importance of each function to a particular manufacturer reflects the nature of his products and markets. For example, some depend heavily on middlemen for market information and others not at all.

The important point to remember is that all of these functions must be performed somewhere in the channel, by either the end-user, the middleman, or the manufacturer. In other words, one can "eliminate the middleman" but not his functions.

Designing the channel

The problem of designing the distribution channel, then, is one of finding the most efficient and effective way of performing the necessary distribution functions. The manufacturer must decide which functions to perform himself, which to contract with middlemen to perform, and which to leave to the end-user. For example, a firm may decide to market its products through mass-merchandise retailers. This implies that the manufacturer will take major responsibility for selling (using advertising to create consumer pull) and for market information. Consumers may have to finance the transaction themselves, since such stores typically do not offer credit (or delivery). The retailer will perform buying, assorting, storage (and display), and risk-taking functions. Other firms must be contracted with for the transportation function.

An important aspect of the design of the distribution channel concerns the availability of middlemen. New firms entering markets often find that the competition already controls the most attractive distribution alternatives. The search for unique competitive advantage sometimes requires that the firm develop entirely new distribution arrangements. Likewise, an established firm may work hard to maintain competitive advantage by "tying up" the best middlemen. In retailing, for example, the best stores in such areas as men's and women's fashions, jewelry, and photographic equipment may be able to exercise great selectivity in determining the lines they will carry. Another example is major food chains, which offer very valuable distribution arrangements to the companies whose lines they agree to carry.

Selecting distributors

The selection of distributors must be based on a clear statement of marketing strategy and of the distributor's role in that strategy. This statement should indicate the critical functions to be performed by the distributor and the criteria by which performance will be judged.

Finding acceptable dealers in a given area can be a very difficult task, especially where strongly entrenched competition has tied up the strongest dealers. Perhaps the most important factor to assess in appraising a possible distributor is the quality of his relationships with potential customers. Does he know the market and is he known as a reputable and qualified supplier? Can he perform the necessary services —especially repair and maintenance—where required?

Two other major factors to evaluate are the strength of his organization and his financing. Does he have well-trained salesmen in adequate numbers to cover the market thoroughly? Are they adequately compensated? Is the field sales management function well staffed and directed? Similar questions must be asked about other areas of the organization, including warehousing, applications engineering (where it exists), repair service, order processing, and accounting and control.

Since many distributors operate on a rather thin financial base, the financing questions should receive special attention. Will the dealer be able to pay us for merchandise shipped and to maintain necessary levels of inventory? Many dealers expect the manufacturer to finance their inventories, and some will let their financial obligations to the manufacturer "slide" long after they have sold the merchandise and received payment for it. It is absolutely essential to check banking references very carefully in evaluating a potential dealer. Also, a recent financial statement should be obtained, checked for accuracy, and carefully reviewed with the management of the dealer organization.

A characteristic of most dealerships is that they are usually privately owned, often controlled by one man and his immediate family. What happens if he dies or loses interest in the business or retires? Is there a son or daughter or a trusted business associate with the necessary interest and ability to fill his shoes?

DISTRIBUTOR MANAGEMENT

Marketers who depend heavily on distributors for the execution of the marketing strategy should have specific programs for managing these critically important relationships. The entire marketing program, including product, pricing, and promotion strategies, should be consistent with the needs of the distribution channel. Among the most important requirements are full product lines, adequate price margins to compensate dealers for required effort, and effective promotional programs to help the dealer sell the product to his customers. The relationships among the elements of the marketing mix, developed more fully in the discussion of push and pull strategies in Chapter 11, depend heavily on whether the distributor organization has an active role of aggressively seeking buyers or a passive role of stocking the product.

Profit orientation

It pays to remember that the distributor is a profit-oriented businessman who will evaluate products and programs in quite selfish terms—"what's in it for me?" The answers must be reasonably specific: higher sales volume, better profit margins, more repeat business, increased customer loyalty, and benefits forthcoming in the reasonably near term, not in the distant future. Specific promotional programs such as consumer deals, sales contests for distributors' salesmen, special product models or packaging, counter displays, cooperative advertising programs, and all the rest should always be presented in terms of specific profit opportunities for the dealer.

Dealer profitability can also be improved in areas other than marketing practices; efforts to help dealers in the management area not only make them better dealers but also strengthen the relationship. Among the most promising areas in which dealers can be given help are accounting practices, record keeping, and office management. Some marketers have developed consulting teams to work with dealers in these areas. Another practice that often produces improved distributor profits is that of working with the principal of the firm to help him plan and use his own time more effectively as a manager.

Improving distributor performance

Because distributors almost always handle the lines of many manufacturers, each firm must develop plans for improving distributor performance on its products. There is usually the joint desire to obtain more time and attention for its own products and to improve the quality of the effort received. Four different types of activities may be used to achieve these ends, all of which also meet the criterion of enhancing the potential profitability of the dealer:

1. reducing competition with other distributors
2. improving the demand-generating power of the company's marketing program
3. increasing the monetary incentives for the distributor
4. improving the distributor's marketing practices[2]

The opportunities for reducing competition with other distributors are well defined and constrained by laws at both the state and federal levels. These include granting exclusive territories, refusing to sell to certain types of resellers, and enforcing a policy of resale price maintenance. The common objective of all such actions is to make the product line more attractive and more profitable for selected dealers by protecting them from destructive competition with other middlemen.[3] The granting of selective or exclusive franchises gives the distributor a unique competitive advantage in his marketing, and resale price maintenance protects the profitability of each sale.

Special trade and consumer incentives as well as improved advertising and sales promotion programs can be used to increase demand for the company's products and therefore increase the dealer's sales volume. Virtually every element in the company's marketing communi-

[2] Louis P. Bucklin, "A Theory of Channel Control," *Journal of Marketing* 37 (January 1973): 39–47.

[3] For a discussion of some of the issues and recent legal rulings in this area, see M. C. Howard, *Legal Aspects of Marketing* (New York: McGraw-Hill, 1964).

cation program can be designed to benefit the reseller organization. A common practice is to use "missionary salesmen," salesmen employed by the company who call on retail stores or end-users to stimulate demand and goodwill but turn any orders written over to the usual distributor.

Raising monetary incentives to the distributor can be done on a general basis through increased profit margins and commission rates, or it can be done more selectively through special promotions. Commonly used tactics include special quantity discounts, free merchandise offers ("buy six, get one free"), delayed billing, cooperative advertising allowances, and sales contests for dealers' salesmen. If used excessively, such special deals come to be expected by the trade and lose their effectiveness. Generally, their use also requires special consumer and end-user incentives as well; otherwise the effect may be to build dealer inventories without building greater sales volume. Such special incentives should be carefully planned to be consistent with the overall marketing program.

The greatest opportunities for improving the distributor's performance often lie in the area of helping him improve his marketing practices. This can be done by training his salesmen in product knowledge, selling technique, and management of time and territory. Or it can be done by giving distributors better selling aids, including catalogues, samples, promotional materials, audio-visual sales aids, suggested advertising formats, and demonstration devices. Distributors often need help in identifying and qualifying prospective customers, and this can be done by providing them with the results of market studies and by using advertising to generate sales leads for them.

The issue of control and conflict

In one sense the interests of the distributor and the manufacturer are congruent—both want to sell more goods more efficiently and more profitably. But there is also an inherent conflict in the relationship. This conflict has two dimensions. First, there is a "joint payoff function," which means that both contribute to and benefit from a sales result that must be shared between them. Second, there is the issue of who controls the relationship with the ultimate customer.

Profit margins and commission rates are based on some assessment of the fair distribution of rewards, supposedly as a function of effective selling effort. The higher the margin or commission rate, the more the distributor is expected to contribute to the final sales results. Obviously, it is not uncommon for a company to judge that its trade margins are too high, while distributors judge they are too low. The distributor's claims are often muted, however, by the realization that the higher his margins, the more quickly it becomes economically attractive for the manufacturer to take over the functions performed by the distributor. Furthermore, distributors often depend for their survival on the lines of one or a few manufacturers.

Conflict between a marketer and his dealers may be greatest when the marketer maintains both a direct sales organization and a distributor organization and the distribtuors perceive that the direct customers could just as well be their customers. Often the direct customers are the largest accounts. Such segmentation is frequently justified on the basis that larger customers have unique service requirements that can be most thoroughly and efficiently performed directly, whereas the distributors' capabilities are best suited to servicing smaller accounts with their special needs. The underlying analysis must be the basic one of what distribution functions must be performed most efficiently in each segment.

The issue of channel control is a complicated one. In a "pull" strategy heavily dependent on consumer advertising, the manufacturer has more control over his marketing activities. In a "push" strategy relying on personal selling through several kinds of middlemen, the manufacturer may lose virtually all control over relationships with end-users. His welfare is determined solely by how well the middlemen perform their appointed marketing tasks.

In such cases special care must be taken to direct and control resellers' efforts. Market analysis, quotas based on market potentials, and programs for improved distributor performance become relatively more important as the manufacturer's dependence on the distributor increases because distributor quality becomes increasingly important. Especially where channels are complex and consist of many types of potentially competing resellers, attempts to strengthen channel control and to direct resellers' marketing efforts to ensure a consistent and optimal program may be thwarted by the fact that a dealer's profitability will be reduced if he cooperates. Such conflict often occurs, for example, when products are distributed through both specialty shops and mass merchandisers ("discount houses").

Such conflict can never be completely eliminated; the marketing manager must learn to live with it and manage it creatively.

BARRIERS TO INNOVATION

As markets evolve under the pressures of changing customer preferences and habits, dynamic competition, and advancing technologies, distribution strategy must be changed accordingly. Particular distribution institutions themselves may become more or less effective over time. One need only consider how the retailing sector has changed in the past two decades to grasp this fact. And, of course, individual distributor firms grow and become strong while others wither and die, often because of the interests and abilities of one man. As a firm's overall product/market strategy develops, so does the optimum distribution structure change. Entirely new market segments and new types of buyers and buyer behavior may make existing distribution arrangements obsolete. The emergence of large buyers requiring direct marketing may further complicate the distribution picture.

But there are a variety of barriers to innovation in the channel of distribution, some practical and some more emotional.[4] Over the years, a firm and its management develop a strong commitment to existing distribution channels, a commitment to individual distributors and their managements as well as to the existing structure itself. Furthermore, the distributors themselves, especially those that have become very well established, will be resistant to change. These two factors combine to make management reluctant to consider alternatives that could produce conflict with present distributors and thereby threaten existing market positions. Furthermore, the nature of distribution channels is such that it is often impossible to evaluate alternative arrangements systematically and rigorously except by actually going ahead on an experimental basis. A final factor leading to a favoring of the status quo is the fear that competitors will take over existing channels of distribution if the company allows conflict to emerge or its own relationships to weaken.

Eventually, however, new distribution strategies emerge as the forces of a changing market and a changing product line build up to the point at which the barriers to innovation are overcome. Nonetheless, distribution strategy is likely to be the most permanent part of the marketing mix, largely because of the institutional relationships involved and the difficulty of changing them.

SUMMARY

Distribution decisions are a management frontier partly because of new analytical techniques and distribution innovations and partly because of management inattention. But change comes to the distribution area slowly because it is complex, probably too complex to manage operationally as a single entity, because good data often are not available, and because of institutional arrangements. The total distribution cost concept provides an important analytical tool for thinking about opportunities for innovation in physical distribution. Likewise, analysis of distribution channel alternatives is aided by awareness of the important marketing functions that must be performed, the task being to find the optimum combination of middlemen and direct coverage to perform them most efficiently.

[4] For many of the following ideas I am indebted to Professor E. Raymond Corey of the Harvard Business School.

MARKETING COMMUNICATION STRATEGY

11

Sophisticated marketing managers have adopted a "communication" view of their firms' promotional activities. The two essential features of this view are, first, the notion that the receiver (potential customer) is an active participant in the process of communication and, second, that all marketing communications must be planned as part of a total system, not as independent pieces. The communications mix includes personal selling, advertising, publicity, and all forms of sales promotion.

In developing marketing communication strategy, there are six major areas for management analysis and decision:

1. setting objectives for communication
2. selecting target audiences
3. defining the roles of various communication modes
4. determining the level of effort
5. developing the message strategy
6. planning campaign evaluation

The quality of management decisions in these areas can be enhanced by an understanding of the social and psychological dimensions of the communication process and by careful consideration of the role of communication in the total marketing mix.

THE COMMUNICATION PROCESS

Communication is most simply defined as the *sharing of meaning*. It involves transfering a concept, idea, fact, impression, or other "cognition" from a communication *source* to a *receiver*. *Messages* are combinations of symbols selected by the source to convey the intended meaning. Messages are sent through *channels* such as radio, television, magazines, newspapers, and face-to-face interaction. The source *encodes* the message by choosing symbols to convey the desired meaning, and the receiver *decodes* the message by assigning meanings to the symbols. Communication actually takes place only to the extent that the meanings the receiver assigns to the symbols are the same as those intended by the source when he selected the symbols. Communication is likely to be most complete when source and receiver share a common background of experience—a common culture and language, for example— so that symbols have the same real-world referents in experience. These concepts serve to define the communication process as diagramed as Figure 11–1.

All communication is motivated or goal-oriented because it is developed in order to influence the receiver in some way desired by the source. If the source did not have some objective relating to the receiver, there would be no reason for communication. As the receiver responds to the decoded message, the source is provided with *feedback* that he can evaluate to determine whether his communication is realizing his objectives. Based on this feedback he can modify messages and, perhaps, channels to better achieve his objectives. Because feedback occurs almost instantly in face-to-face communication, personal interaction is the most efficient form of communication. In contrast, mass communication takes months and years to evaluate because feedback can only be obtained through complex research procedures that contain a large measure of variability and error.

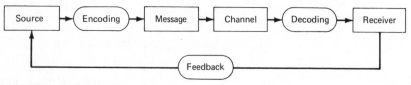

FIGURE 11-1
The communication process.

Kinds of response

The purpose of any communication is to achieve some response from the receiver. In marketing the desired response is often, but not always, a buying decision—a behavioral response. In simplest terms, we can think of three distinct kinds of response: (1) awareness, (2) changed attitudes, or (3) new behavior. Communications that change what a person knows can be said to produce a *cognitive response* (awareness and knowledge), whereas those that change how he feels can be said to produce an *affective response.*

It is possible to describe responses to marketing communications in terms of hypothetical stages in the potential buyer's decision-making process. Three of the most popular models in the marketing literature are the following:

Steps in the Sale	Adoption Process	Hierarchy of Effects
Attention	Awareness	Awareness
Interest	Interest	Knowledge
Desire	Evaluation	Liking
Action	Trial	Preference
	Adoption	Conviction
		Action

It is not important to decide which model is best. The important thing is to recognize that communication accomplishes its objectives in a series of mental stages as the receiver moves from unawareness through to actual purchase. For most products, several messages through several modes of communication (channels) are required in order to complete the process. Recognition of this important fact is essential in setting marketing communication objectives. Before one can decide which messages and media are most desirable, the specific purpose of the communication must be made very clear.

Predispositions

The receiver is an active participant in the communication process. The meaning of a message is not inherent in the symbols used in the message but is assigned to the symbols by the receiver. The concept of predispositions is useful in understanding this process.

Predispositions can be thought of as categories of meaning stored in the mind of the receiver. The concept of predispositions includes such familiar concepts as attitudes, goals, beliefs, and values. Predispositions are learned from experience and involve a tendency to act toward a particular object in the environment in a particular way. Thus, predispositions toward a company or a brand determine the potential customer's buying actions.

The purpose of all marketing communication can therefore be restated as "to influence predispositions toward the company and its products." This restatement serves the useful function of reminding the marketing communicator that predispositions already exist. No communicator writes on a clean slate. Even if the company and its products are unknown to potential customers, predispositions toward competing companies and products must be considered, as well as relevant predispositions toward communication modes, toward the product class, and relating to such variables as family and life style, in setting marketing communication objectives. Simply stated, the first rule of communication is "Know your audience." It is impossible to intelligently plan marketing communication without knowing something about existing predispositions.

Sources of predispositions

There are three major sources of predispositions: the culture of which the individual is a part; the social groups with which he identifies; and the socioeconomic, demographic, and personality characteristics of the individual himself. Some inferences can therefore be made about an individual's predispositions if something is known about these factors, but such inference is not an entirely adequate substitute for information about the predispositions themselves. Culture, for example, defines shared values toward such things as work, leisure, religion, family, achievement, security, life style, and so on. Social influences range from the specific influence of family to the general influence of reference groups, social roles (lawyers or Irish-Americans), or specific groups (a church or a political party) from which the individual derives standards for his own behavior. Individual characteristics such as personality, income, occupation, education, and age also shape predispositions in important ways.

The selective processes

Response to communication is "subjective" as each receiver finds his own meanings. Predispositions can also be thought of as filters through which messages pass in influencing the receiver's response tendencies. There are three related processes involved: selective attention, selective perception, and selective retention. The selective processes were discussed briefly in Chapter 2. In each of these, predispositions operate essentially as mechanisms to preserve the mental status quo, to maintain a steady state, and to make life as pleasant as possible. Predispositions change very slowly. Habits, ideas, attitudes, and so on, once acquired, become valued for their own sake.

Selective attention is the process by which the receiver selects the messages he will expose himself to and become aware of. For example, people are much more likely to listen to political candidates whose views they agree with. Consumers are more likely to read advertisements for their favorite brands. Individuals are more likely to search out and pay attention to messages that are consistent with their existing predispositions.

Selective perception is the tendency to select meanings for messages that are consistent with predispositions. We hear what we want to hear and see what we want to see. To illustrate this, ask two football fans cheering for opposite sides to evaluate a referee's call. In a sense, all advertising, except for one's favorite brands, is "unbelievable."

Two mechanisms contribute to selective perception. *Sharpening* is the tendency to add meanings to a message in order to make it consistent with predispositions. Thus, the tendency to view General Electric as an appliance company can interfere with advertising for General Electric time-sharing computers. *Leveling* is the tendency to ignore parts of a message that are inconsistent with predispositions. For example, a buyer who is dealing with supplier A is likely to overlook many of the sales presentation points being made by a salesman for competing supplier B who wants part of the business. The tendency to perceive selectively can therefore interfere with communication objectives. The dangers are minimized when the communicator is aware of his receiver's predispositions.

Selective retention is simply the tendency to remember communication in a manner that reinforces predispositions. Again, the basic principle of consistency applies. It is much easier to "play back" commercials for favorite brands because they are obviously more favorable to existing predispositions. This fact is one reason why "recall" measures of advertising effectiveness must be used with care—if loyal customers are overrepresented in the sample, the data will overstate advertising effectiveness.

The impact of the selective processes underscores the importance of information on predispositions as the basis for planning marketing communication strategy. The concept of predispositions also provides substance to the idea of the "active audience." In a sense, predispositions rather than people should be the target of marketing communications. This view helps the communicator focus on the specific behavioral response desired from the receiver.

So far the discussion has considered primarily how the characteristics of the audience influence response to communication. Characteristics of the source and of the message also exert a substantial influence, but this always occurs in interaction with the characteristics of the audience.

Message effects

The effects of message characteristics depend on the nature of the receiver, including his intellectual ability, whether his predispositions are basically in agreement with the message, and his self-confidence. Perhaps the most efficient way to illustrate this is to cite several research findings related to message effects:

1. One-sided arguments are most effective with people who are initially in agreement with the communicator, with people of below-average intellectual ability (as measured by amount of education), and when the receiver is not subsequently exposed to the opposing viewpoint. Conversely, two-sided arguments are more effective when the receiver is initially opposed, with people of above-average intellectual ability, and when the receiver is subsequently exposed to counterargument.
2. Emotional appeals are more effective with receivers of less intellectual ability, whereas rational appeals are generally more effective with receivers of high intelligence.
3. In general it is better to arouse needs first and then present information rather than to present information followed by need arousal.
4. Emotional appeals help arouse interest and can motivate the receiver, but emotional appeals, especially fear appeals, can create too much emotional involvement and anxiety when overdone, causing the receiver to block out the intended meanings.
5. Drawing conclusions can be helpful because it precludes the receiver's missing the point, but it must be done with care, especially when the receiver is an expert, to avoid an impression of assumed superiority.
6. Although there are important exceptions, the items presented first in a communication tend to dominate the impression received.
7. Obtaining early commitment from the receiver, especially when it is publicly stated, enhances the effectiveness of subsequent arguments.
8. Active participation by the audience enhances message effectiveness.
9. Repetition, especially with some variation in presentation, improves message effectiveness provided it does not become boring or annoying.

Source effect

A communicator is more effective to the extent that he is believable to the receiver as a source of communication. Source credibility is a function of perceived trustworthiness and expertise. Notice that credibility refers to the receiver's perceptions of the source and not to objective characteristics of the source. It has been found repeatedly that high-credibility sources always obtain a more favorable response to communications than low-credibility sources using the exact same message. This is called the *source effect*. However, these differences in effectiveness attributable to differences in source credibility tend to disappear over time. This tendency is called the *sleeper effect*, since response to low-credibility sources tends to improve over time and response to high-credibility sources tends to diminish. Sleeper effect is explained by a tendency for the receiver to dissociate the message from the source—to retain the information but to forget where he heard it. When the receiver is reminded of the source, initial source effects reappear. Because sources tend to be highly visible and memorable in marketing communications, sleeper effects may not occur so readily and source effect may be somewhat more permanent.

Source credibility becomes more important as the amount of perceived risk in the action requested by the source increases. From Chapter 2, where the perceived-risk model was introduced, it will be remembered that perceived risk is a function of uncertainty and the seriousness of outcomes. High-credibility sources are better able to reduce uncertainty because they are perceived as more trustworthy and more expert. For example, it has been found that physicians tend to favor the products of well-known pharmaceutical firms over those of companies with less strong reputations as the seriousness of the illness being treated increases.

Implications

In these few pages it has not been possible to do more than outline the ways in which the findings of communication research contribute to the development of effective marketing communications. The main themes of this review of the communication process can be summarized with these implications for management decision making:

1. Communication objectives should be formulated as precisely as possible in terms of specific responses desired.
2. Each mode of marketing communication should be used in such a way as to maximize its particular effectiveness at specific stages in the receiver's hierarchy of responses and to maximize the positive effects of interaction among communication modes.
3. Data on target audience predispositions, scientifically gathered and analyzed, are the *sine qua non* of effective marketing communications.
4. Long-term investment in developing company reputation (source credibility) can have payoffs in terms of enhanced effectiveness of other communications.
5. It is always easier to show how the product or service being offered fits existing predispositions (needs, goals, attitudes, etc.) than it is to change predispositions.
6. Message effectiveness depends on audience predispositions, so
   a. Salesmen must be taught to ask probing questions and to analyze predispositions (i.e., to listen) as the basis for their presentations.
   b. Effective mass communication cannot be developed without good information about existing levels of awareness, attitudes, and preferences.

AN INTEGRATED COMMUNICATION MIX

Not all communication modes are equally effective for all buyers or for all stages in the hierarchy of responses to communication. Personal selling, advertising, catalogues, direct mail, free samples, display, promotional deals, publicity, trade shows—each has strengths and weaknesses as a communication mode, depending on the nature of the products, characteristics of the market, stage of market development, and stage of the buyer's decision making. These unique strengths and weaknesses should be explicitly considered in designing the communications mix, as should the interactions among the various modes in determining total communication effectiveness.

Determining the role
of communication in the marketing mix

There are three components in the marketing mix: the goods and services mix, the distribution mix, and the communications mix. Decisions in each area constrain the range of choices available in the others. In very general terms, the goods and services mix should be determined first, followed by design of the distribution mix, and the communications mix should be tailored to products, service, and distribution. Of course, it is not that simple. Communication decisions for some consumer products take precedence over product and distribution decisions, for example. Nevertheless, most communication strategy issues must be resolved within the boundaries established by prior product and distribution decisions.

What tasks will be assigned to communication? The answers depend on at least the following factors:

- the number and distribution of potential customers
- the nature of competition
- the functions performed by resellers in the channel of distribution
- the nature of the product, especially the extent to which demand can be "created" by communication (as in the case of life insurance) and the importance of emotional appeals and hidden product benefits (as with cosmetics)
- the stage of market development and the relative importance of such marketing objectives as
  —creating awareness
  —obtaining trial
  —differentiation from competitive offerings
  —keeping the customer sold

The interdependence of communications with other marketing decisions should be clearly recognized. One way of thinking about these interdependencies is provided by the distinction between "push" and "pull" strategies.

"Push" and "pull" strategies

Push strategies rely heavily on personal selling, while pull strategies depend on mass communications, especially advertising and consumer promotions. Industrial marketing strategies are most likely to be push strategies, whereas pull strategies characterize the marketing of consumer products, especially packaged goods. The terms *push* and *pull* refer to the direction of influence in the marketing channel, as illustrated in Figure 11-2. Although the illustration uses industrial market terms in describing a push strategy and consumer market terms for the pull strategy, either strategy could be found in both markets.

In a pull strategy, the idea is to pull the product through the channel by creating end-user demand. Customers go to retail dealers and ask for the product, forcing them to stock it. In turn, the retailers demand the product from wholesalers, who must then place orders on the manufacturer. Of course personal selling also plays a role, but it is largely a facilitating, passive role—essentially "order taking"—except that the manufacturer's salesman may have a major role to play in convincing retailers to stock a particular consumer deal, for example, and in explaining the profit opportunities for cooperation in the manufacturer's promotional programs.

The importance of advertising and sales promotion in a pull strategy are reflected in the low rates of personal-selling expense to total marketing costs. Dealer margins are lower than in a push strategy, reflecting both the manufacturer's need for the profit margins to support mass communications and the essentially passive role of

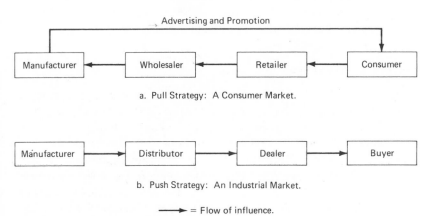

a. Pull Strategy: A Consumer Market.

b. Push Strategy: An Industrial Market.

⟶ = Flow of influence.

FIGURE 11-2
Illustration of push and pull strategies.

the dealer. Pull strategies are generally found where the amount of product adjustment and after-sale service is small, where the product has relatively low unit value, and where distribution is broad rather than selective.

The converse is true for push strategies. They tend to be found where products have high unit value and require adjustment and specific application to customer needs. Obviously, personal selling is critical here. Push strategies usually require relatively high dealer margins to compensate them for their efforts in actively promoting the product. Distribution tends to be selective owing to the need to make the product line attractive to the dealer so he will promote it more aggressively and also because demand is often limited and segmented. Push strategies are usually found for products with relatively high unit value. These differences are summarized in Table 11-1.

Every pull strategy has a little bit of push in it and vice versa, but consistency among strategic elements is an essential part of effective marketing strategy. For example, a push strategy can be ruined by inadequate dealer margins or a low retail price. Likewise, major inefficiency can result from combining selective distribution with extensive advertising.

Small companies often find a pull strategy impossible because they do not have the financial resources required to launch extensive advertising campaigns, especially where this requires a toe-to-toe promotional battle with larger national competitors. Push strategies may be more consistent with a segmented, concentrated marketing approach. The company that has elected to compete on the basis of technical capability, product quality, and customer service has implicitly opted for a push strategy. Although advertising may have an important role to play in supporting salesmen and dealers (and in creating source credibility), it is not as important as personal selling.

The concept of push and pull strategies is a useful way of defining the role of communication in the marketing mix, in reference to the goods and services mix and the distribution mix.

Selecting communication targets

Implicit in the company's market segmentation strategy is the selection of the targets for marketing communications. If inadequate attention has been devoted to the question of segmentation strategy, this weakness will be revealed forcefully as management begins to design communication strategy. But there is a very important difference between basic segmentation and the selection of targets for communication: Market segments are usually defined in demographic terms—age, income, education, family size, size of company, SIC classification, etc.— whereas communication targets must be defined by predispositions as well as by demographics.

TABLE 11-1
Major dimensions of difference between push and pull strategies

	Push	Pull
Communication	Personal selling	Advertising & promotion
Price	High	Low
Margins	High	Low
Product adjustment and service	High	Low
Distribution	Selective	Broad

For a variety of reasons, different market segments may receive quite different emphasis in communications, so not all segments will necessarily be market targets. Communication opportunity, again distinguished from marketing opportunity, is defined by existing predispositions. An industrial-equipment marketer, for example, might elect to focus his limited promotional resources for the year on a particular class of potential buyer such as those in a specific industry, those with equipment more than ten years old, or those in a given location. Selection of marketing communication targets might be based on data from a study of existing levels of awareness or attitudes as well as on estimates of customer buying potential.

Without careful analysis of market segments, all potential customers will be assumed to have the same value as targets for communication. Seldom is that assumption correct. For a seller of minicomputers, for example, increased awareness among bankers may not be as valuable as increased awareness among engineers. Judgments of the potential value of market targets are necessary before alternative communication channels can be evaluated. Never is this problem as simple as obtaining the maximum number of sales calls or advertising exposures for a given expenditure. Some delivered messages will be worthless and others worth a great deal.

In industrial markets, selection of target audiences requires a special understanding of the organizational buying process, especially the composition of the buying center. Chapter 2 presented some useful concepts for analyzing organizational buying behavior. Industrial marketing communications should be aimed at specific individual decision influencers and tailored to their needs and attitudes, not aimed at the organization at large.

Setting communication objectives

Communication objectives are distinct from marketing objectives, but they must be consistent with those marketing objectives and contribute to their realization. A marketing objective of increasing market share may translate into a communication objective of changing attitudes and securing increased product trial. A marketing objective of gaining new accounts may require communication objectives of increased awareness and increased selling activity in specific segments.

Consideration of objectives takes us back to the concept of the hierarchy of effects and is directly related as well to the problem of evaluation. The essential point to remember is that an actual sale to a customer can almost never be attributed to a specific communication. (The closest we can come to this "ideal" is advertising or direct mail that invites readers to fill in a coupon or order form, but even here the response may result from many prior exposures.) Measurement of communication effects is easiest at the earliest stages of the hierarchy— changed levels of awareness and altered patterns of attitudes. Assume that an advertiser knows that 37 percent of his potential customers are aware of his product at the beginning of the campaign and that 86 percent are aware at the end. Such shifts can almost certainly be attributed to the advertising, assuming that no other marketing variables were substantially altered. But suppose sales also increased 12 percent. Can this also be attributed to advertising? Chances are that advertising contributed to this result, but the relationship will always be obscure. What happened to prices during the period? Did competitors do anything differently? Were salesmen more effective because the advertising excited them? Did our product line change in any way? How fast did our customers' sales increase? Did our increase simply reflect greater demand for their products? The point is undoubtedly obvious— it is impossible to say that communications in a given period caused sales results in that period unless very careful experimentation is done (at considerable expense) to control the influence of all other variables. Furthermore, different parts of the communications mix may have quite different effects, and these should be considered separately.

The logical conclusion would seem to be, then, that the marketing communicator who wishes to systematically evaluate his promotional efforts should set objectives in the more easily measurable terms of changes in awareness and attitudes rather than sales measures. Right? Not necessarily. The problem is that the marketer can't cover his payroll or declare dividends based on increased awareness and improved attitudes. The ultimate payoff in profitable sales must be there or communications are ineffective.

The debate is not academic but a practical issue in the effective planning and management of marketing communications. Herein lies a major reason for thinking specifically about what each element of the communications mix can do best and what its contribution should be to an overall sales result. For example, advertising may be best for creating awareness, direct mail for securing serious evaluation, and personal selling for getting product trial. Such objectives should be made as specific and distinct as possible. In general, communication objectives (i.e., changes in awareness and attitudes) should be favored for mass communications because they can most realistically be held accountable in this way. Sales volume objectives are best for personal selling and for various sales promotion devices designed to get specific buying action.

Determining the role of each mode

The specific objectives and relative importance of each mode of communication depend first on the basic strategic choice of push or pull strategy. A second factor is the stage of market development. In Chapter 8 the diffusion process was introduced as a way of thinking about market development. It was noted that different adopter categories— innovators, early adopters, early majority, late majority, and laggards— have different preferences and patterns in the use of various sources of product information. Here we can look at those differences more carefully and consider their implications for design of marketing communication strategy.

Innovators have above-average contact with professional change agents such as county agricultural agents (in the case of farmer innovators) and dealers. Technical and professional literature are used heavily by these people. In many technical fields and industrial markets, they are well known both to one another and to marketers. They are sought out to test and evaluate new products, to publish the results of their research with or on the product, and to participate in conferences of various kinds. They rely on and can best be reached through rather specialized media, and these media are quite likely to be marketer-dominated and commercial in nature. Highly tailored personal selling and selective use of technical and professional journals are efficient ways of reaching innovators in the early stages of market development.

The early adopters are distinguished by a very heavy exposure to media of all kinds. They are the opinion leaders and have significant influence on the buying decisions of other people. It has been said that the influence of the mass media is exerted on the population through the opinion leaders in a kind of "two-step" flow of information and influence:

Mass ⟶ Opinion ⟶ Mass
Media   Leaders   Population

It is also true that opinion leaders tend to be heavily influenced by other opinion leaders—that is, they also talk with one another. The implications for marketing communication are straightforward enough— advertising, publicity, and special promotions have an essential role to play early in the product life cycle in attracting the attention of the opinion leaders and developing their preferences. Market growth will not "take off" until the opinion leaders have been reached and valuable word of mouth started. A promotional broadside will not be as efficient, however, as communications aimed specifically at the opinion leaders. Who are they? It depends partly on the product, and research is required to find out, although Chapter 8 suggested some general characteristics that may help identify them.

The early majority is also influenced by the mass media, especially as a source of awareness information, but they may rely heavily on personal, noncommercial sources of information (word of mouth from opinion leaders) in their actual decision making. In general, both the early majority and the late majority require some personal source of information to convince them to buy a new product, even if mass communications have created awareness.

Laggards are hard to reach with any mode of communication because they are simply less exposed to information from all sources. From a marketing standpoint they may not be worth the effort. In general, personal sources are more important to them, especially members of the family.

Certainly specific marketing conditions can make this kind of generalization about the role of modes of communication quite meaningless. These comments are not intended to provide definitive answers but rather to suggest an analytical framework within which to think about formulation of communication objectives and strategy. The recommended framework, summarized in Table 11–2, is based on three dimensions: (1) adopter categories and stage of market development, (2) stage of buyer's decision making, (3) type of communication— mass versus personal and commercial versus noncommercial.

Synergistic effects

The effectiveness of each mode of communication is determined in part by the impact of all other modes on the buyer's decision making.

TABLE 11-2
Information use by stages of market development and buyer decision making

Stage of Market Development	Stage of Buyer Decision	
	Awareness (Knowledge)	Conviction (Action)
Innovators	Technical-professional; salesmen	Technical-professional; salesmen
Early Adopters	Advertising; word of mouth salesmen & dealers	Word of mouth salesmen & dealers advertising
Later Adopters[a]	Advertising; word of mouth salesmen & dealers	Word of mouth salesmen & dealers

[a] Early majority and late majority in diffusion process terms

They are all interdependent to some extent—a synergism in which the whole is greater than the sum of the parts. The basic idea of an integrated approach to marketing communication strategy depends very heavily on the explicit recognition of these interdependencies. We have already begun to develop this point by stressing how different types of communication may be more or less effective at various stages of the buyer's decision-making process. That is one aspect of interdependence. The concept of source effect, developed earlier, is another aspect of interdependence—for example, company reputation developed through advertising can increase personal selling effectiveness.

Other aspects of interdependence can be easily identified:

- Advertising can solicit inquiries to provide leads for salesmen's calls.
- Salesmen's efforts to secure shelf display will determine the effectiveness of consumer promotion.
- Trade incentives to obtain dealer stocking are essential to the success of a consumer promotion.
- Advertising that features a consumer deal can make or break the success of the special promotion.
- The effectiveness of a sales call can be enhanced by literature or samples left behind by the salesmen.
- (Free) publicity can give an important boost to an advertising campaign.
- Corporate advertising and public relations have long-term effects that enhance the effectiveness of current communications.
- Salesman follow-up is often essential to the success of a direct-mail campaign.
- Consumer recognition of the product is enhanced by showing the package in advertising.

To summarize this section dealing with the development of an integrated communication strategy, several central themes have been presented. First, the push-pull framework provides a useful device for thinking about the role of communication in the marketing mix. Second, communication objectives should be developed in terms of stages in the buyer's decision-making process and predispositions in various market segments. Third, stage of market development influences the effectiveness of the various modes of communication. Fourth, communication objectives should be set in a way that enhances effective evaluation. Fifth and finally, interactions among campaign elements should be explicitly considered in designing communication strategy.

DETERMINING LEVEL OF EFFORT

An appraisal of predispositions and evaluation of communication opportunities in various market segments leads to the establishment of specific communication objectives. In that analytical process, the manager develops some feeling for the magnitude of the task facing marketing communication. This general awareness must be translated into specific estimates of planned expenditures for personal selling, advertising, sales promotion, and so on—not an easy task.

Profit-maximizing conditions

Economic theory provides a definition of the ideal conditions under which the profitability of marketing communication expenditures can be maximized. Although this ideal is somewhat difficult to apply, given problems of measuring the relationship between communication effort and sales results, it does provide some useful guidelines.

Assuming that the incremental sales response to additional promotional effort is positive but decreases as effort increases, additional money should be spent until the gross profit margin (sales price less cost of goods sold and distribution expenses) on the incremental sales volume is equal to the incremental promotional cost. These conditions are diagrammed in Figure 11–3, where $P* is the optimum promotional expenditure. In mathematical terms, this occurs where the slopes of the two curves are equal—that is, the curves are changing at the same rate. Stated differently, the first derivatives of the functions describing the profit margin curve and the promotional cost curve are equal. Spending beyond that point will increase sales but decrease total profit as promotional costs increase faster than profit margins.

Talking about total promotional effort presents an "apples and oranges" problem. Units of advertising are different from units of personal selling, and the two cannot be added together in any meaningful way except in dollar terms. How should a total promotional budget be allocated among communication modes?

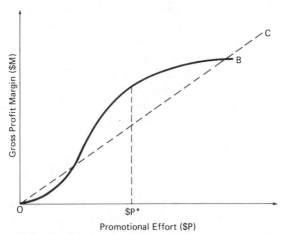

FIGURE 11-3
Relationship between level of promotional effort and gross profit margin.

Again economics can suggest the ideal profit-maximizing con-ditions—namely, so that the marginal returns to a dollar invested in each communication mode are the same. Once again the assumption is that the rate of return is decreasing but still positive. If an incre-mental dollar in advertising will produce more than an incremental dollar in selling, funds should be shifted from selling into advertising (or new funds invested in advertising) until the rates of return are the same. To use mathematical terms again, the profit-maximizing alloca-tion occurs when the first derivatives of all functions describing the relationship between effort and response are the same for all pro-motional modes. If the total promotional expenditure is at the optimum level, these incremental returns will be just equal to the incremental cost of promotion.

The response function

To make this line of reasoning operational, the manager needs to know rather precisely the nature of the relationship between promotional effort and sales results. This relationship is described by a *response function* of the kind illustrated by the line O-B in Figure 11–3.

While promotional response functions certainly differ for different products and services and for the same product in different markets, it is reasonable to assume that most are S-shaped. The reasons are that the initial units of promotional effort are likely to have little impact until some "critical mass" is reached. Then additional units have increasingly positive impact up to a point at which diminishing returns set in because of a kind of saturation effect. These diminishing returns may still be positive and additional spending worthwhile, al-though each incremental unit has somewhat less impact until the point is reached at which further spending is not justified.

A precise estimate of the response function is practically impossible but ideally could be derived from a perfectly controlled experiment in which many levels of effort were tested in markets of known potential and the subsequent sales response carefully noted. Somewhat more reasonable would be an attempt to estimate a portion of the response function by testing a few, reasonable levels of promotional effort and attempting to relate increments in sales results to differences in pro-motional effort. Some firms have done so successfully. Through such experiments, one brewer found convincing evidence of overspending for advertising and was able to save large amounts of money by selectively and cautiously reducing advertising expenditure.

Without experimentation, the next best approach is to analyze past sales and promotional expenses (both personal and mass com-munications), both over time and across markets, to estimate relation-ships. It is also possible and desirable, of course, to analyze current expenditures in the same fashion and even to plan small variations in promotional spending in order to estimate sensitivity but not with the detailed controls required for full experimentation.

The reason for wanting to know the response function is to permit more accurate prediction of the results to be expected from alternative levels of promotional effort. It is then possible to estimate where the profit-maximizing points are, as explained earlier.

Relating effort to objectives

Few companies have actually developed estimates of their promotional response functions. The usual approaches to promotional budget setting are primitive by comparison. Among the most commonly used methods are percentage of sales (last year or forecasted), competitive parity (at least as much as competition), and all-we-can-afford. The notion that there is an optimum level of spending seldom seems to enter the decision-making process. Nor is there usually a careful consideration of the relationship between promotional effort and marketing objectives except for the casual assumption that increased sales volume or increased market share will require more expenditures for advertising, sales promotion, and personal selling. How much more is decided by hunch, intuition, and the politics of the budget-setting process.

There is a middle ground between these naive approaches and the sophistication of response functions and marginal analysis. Usually referred to as "objective and task" methods, these somewhat rigorous approaches still rely on a heavy dose of managerial judgment. The steps in an objective-and-task approach can be outlined as follows:

1. Determine dollar sales objective.
2. Define market segments, market potential in each segment, and specific market targets.
3. Determine present predispositions in each segment—levels of awareness, attitudes, and purchasing.
4. Estimate the increases in awareness and attitudes necessary to achieve projected increases in sales.
5. Determine the number of promotional messages required, of various types, to achieve necessary increases in awareness and attitudes.
6. Determine the total cost of delivering the required number of promotional messages.

The fourth and fifth steps require some sophisticated judgments, which can be aided significantly by good market research on the relationship between predispositions and buying behavior. Step 5 also requires the kind of analysis of the specific tasks assigned to each promotional mode that was advocated earlier in this chapter. Costs of promotional effort can be reasonably estimated by the experienced manager.

The objective-and-task approach provides no magic formula, but it does contribute to systematic, logical analysis, in quantitative terms as required for budgeting, of the relationship between communication effort and sales results.

DEVELOPING MESSAGE STRATEGY

Determining the number of sales presentations, advertising impressions, direct-mail pieces, and so on is only part of the problem of planning marketing communication strategy. What will we say? How can those communication devices be used most effectively? How do we propose to differentiate our products and services from those of competitors? The specifics of advertising message strategy and the development of sales presentations will be dealt with in subsequent chapters. Here we will present some brief guidelines for developing message strategy.

Primary versus selective demand

A key strategic issue often present is whether to focus attention on generic demand for the product or service (air freight, data processing, instant photography) or on selective demand for our brand (Emery Air Freight, Honeywell computers, Polaroid). Primary demand stimulation is necessary when the product concept is new and most potential buyers are uninformed. Brand preference is not as important when a marketer is pioneering an entirely new market. At the same time, the marketer who assumes responsibility for developing a market often reaps the benefits of a leadership position when the market matures, though he can also be very vulnerable to the aggressive promotion of brand preference by late-arriving competitors.

This issue of message strategy has its roots in the more basic issues of marketing and communication objectives: Do we want to make the total market grow or do we want to increase our share? Some companies following a high-quality, high-price strategy prefer a limited share of an expanding market in order to avoid price competition and pressures to reduce quality and service. In such cases, promotional effort emphasizes primary (industry) demand.

Product positioning

A company's message strategy determines how its products are viewed vis-à-vis competitors' products. Especially for consumer products, promotional variables are often more important than physical product characteristics in determining how a product is viewed. As stressed in Chapter 3, analysis of buyer perceptions of existing brands can reveal not only the dimensions in which products are perceived but gaps in available product offerings. The subtleties of brand image determine the success of product positioning in the market.

The basic question is, "How do we wish to compete?" and this again goes back to the issue of objectives. The question is as valid for industrial marketers as for consumer products. For example, a manufacturer of an electronic calculating machine with a modest programing capability had to decide whether to sell the product as a minicomputer or as a sophisticated calculating machine. One would be sold primarily in scientific and engineering organizations and the other in business offices, banks, and the like. Selling strategy and advertising approach would be distinctly different, depending on the product positioning chosen. The question of product positioning is really nothing more than one of promotional market segmentation.

Product positioning determines the appeals to be used and the buyer benefits to be stressed. Choices are seldom obvious. Good information about buyer motivations is essential for intelligent design of message strategy. In addition to understanding buyers' needs for the product or service, it is important to know existing levels of awareness and the nature of current attitudes toward the company and its products. In communication terms, the task is to define the meanings we wish potential customers to attach to our product and to work within the structure of existing predispositions to accomplish that positioning in the customer's perception.

PLANNING CAMPAIGN EVALUATION

The planning job is not finished until the evaluation of the communication program has also been planned. The planning of evaluation has three distinct parts:

1. stating campaign objectives in such a way that evaluation is facilitated
2. conducting research on predispositions as necessary to provide bench marks for evaluation
3. providing adequate resources (funds, data, and personnel) to ensure completion of evaluation on time and in a professional manner

The earlier discussion of the problem of setting objectives was intended to explain why objectives should be set in terms specific enough to facilitate measurement of results. On this score, communication objectives (awareness and attitudes) are preferable to sales objectives.

One definition of human intelligence is "the ability to learn from experience." The intelligent manager is one who takes time to learn the lessons provided by past accomplishments and failures. Such learning requires good data and the analytical concepts that can turn data into information.

All evaluation should be forward-looking. The principal use of information about results should be to improve the quality of the next round of decisions. Good evaluation can also ensure objectivity and fairness in the distribution of rewards such as salesmen's bonuses.

In planning campaign evaluation, the manager has several options concerning what to measure. One way to think about these is to think of a sequence of actions and results from the setting of objectives and planning of the campaign through to the hoped-for profit results. This sequence of actions and results is outlined in Table 11-3, along with some suggested questions for evaluation at each stage of the process.

TABLE 11-3
A sequence of communication campaign results

A. *Campaign Planning*
   1. Were objectives clearly stated?
   2. Were predispositions analyzed carefully, by segments?
   3. Was the plan developed explicitly and communicated to the necessary people?
   4. Was each mode tailored to a specific set of tasks?

B. *Message Distribution*
   1. Were the planned number of messages delivered?
      (measures of sales activity and advertising media schedules)

C. *Communication Effects*
   1. How has awareness changed?
   2. How have attitudes changed?
   3. How have company and brand image changed?

D. *Impact on Dealer and Buyer Activity*
   1. Did more dealers stock our products and promote them?
   2. Did buyers initiate more inquiries?
   3. Have consumers shopped for our product, bought it, and used it?
   4. Has word-of-mouth advertising of our products increased?

E. *Impact on Company*
   1. Did sales increase? Were targets reached?
   2. How were costs effected:
      a. product costs associated with volume?
      b. sales costs per call, per order, per dollar of revenue?
      c. advertising costs—per 1000 effective exposures?
      d. sales promotion, display, and other expenses?
   3. How did profit margins and total profits change?

There are five distinct kinds of measures in this model:

1. measures of management activity in terms of thoroughness, care, and effectiveness—how planning was done
2. measures of communication activity such as sales calls and advertising exposures—what was done

3. measures of effects on buyers' mental states—what impact it had
4. measures of buyer activity such as inquiries received, orders, shopping activity, increased dealer stocking, etc.
5. measures of financial impact—on costs, sales, and profits

None of these by itself is adequate to measure the effectiveness of communication, but all together can provide significant clues to strengths and weaknesses in the firm's communication efforts. Each stage in this sequence permits specific measurements, and there are often commercial services available to provide the necessary data. Consumer panels, for example, can provide data on consumer shopping, purchasing, and product usage.

SUMMARY

A "communication" view of promotional activities stresses a systems approach in which each communication mode is viewed as an interdependent part of the total. It focuses on the buyer response desired in terms of changes in awareness, attitudes, and behavior. It also stresses the need for good research data on buyer predispositions as the basis for planning communication strategy and evaluating campaign results.

DEVELOPING EFFECTIVE ADVERTISING

The previous chapter outlined the requirements for effective marketing communication strategy, including analysis of predispositions, selection of target audiences, clear statement of objectives, and planned evaluation. In the present chapter we concentrate on advertising decisions, including setting advertising objectives, developing advertising messages, selecting media, and measuring advertising results. Material on analysis of potential audiences will not be repeated, but the importance of such analysis as the first part of the advertising planning process should not be forgotten. Likewise, the question of advertising budgets has already been dealt with in the section of Chapter 11 entitled "Determining the Level of Effort."

Advertising is perhaps the most exciting and stimulating area of marketing management decision making, reflecting the important role played by creativity and the significance of intangible selling ideas as well as the challenge of dealing with mass media and mass audiences.

FIGURE 12-1
The hierarchy of marketing objectives.

There is some of the thrill of "show biz" in all this, especially when nationally televised programs are the advertising vehicles or when important personalities and celebrities become involved in the firm's promotional activities. This excitement is one of the attractions of advertising management, but there is substantial risk that in this supercharged atmosphere subjective considerations can overwhelm objective, rational decision making.

The good advertising manager is sensitive to this problem and takes care to assess the legitimacy of various opinions offered in evaluation of alternative courses of advertising action. Guided by a clear statement of marketing and advertising objectives, he is able to warn against the dangers of letting personal likes and dislikes interfere with sound business judgments. When the issue is one of taste, as when advertising is potentially offensive or misleading to some people, then a statement of personal opinion has legitimacy and importance. But questions of effectiveness and efficiency cannot be resolved by statements of likes and dislikes, regardless of what level of management utters them. Rather, decisions must be based on careful analysis of what the advertising is intended to do and how well it is likely to do it.

THE IMPORTANCE OF OBJECTIVES

Once again we face the always important question of objectives. Objectives exist in a hierarchy, as shown in Figure 12–1. Objectives at each level must meet the equally important criteria of consistency, reasonableness, and completeness. Advertising decisions cannot be made effectively until several other higher-order marketing decisions have been made, including:

1. clear statement of current marketing objectives in terms of sales volume, market share, and profit contribution
2. definition of market segments
3. statement of product policy and objectives (relative importance of quality, service, etc.; uniqueness from competitive standpoint; emphasis on full line, special features, etc.)
4. selection of channels of distribution and definition of role of resellers in the communication mix (push versus pull strategy)

With these decisions to guide him, the advertising manager must now work with other marketing executives, first to define the role of advertising in the marketing communications mix and second to set specific advertising objectives for the planning period (usually one year).

Defining advertising's role

Chapter 11 developed the idea of the communications mix and stressed that communication planning must consider the unique contribution of each communication mode (advertising, personal selling, sales promotion, packaging, publicity, etc.) as well as interactions, or synergistic effects, among the several modes. In the communication mix, advertising has several unique strengths:

- the ability to reach large numbers of potential customers quickly and economically
- the ability to deliver audiences with particular demographic and socio-economic characteristics
- the ability to deliver the same message consistently in a variety of contexts

Likewise, it has some limitations as a communication mode:

- It is usually more effective at earlier stages of the buyer's decision-making process (awareness and interest) and less effective at later stages (conviction and purchase).
- It is less flexible than personal communication.
- Advertising media carry many messages that compete for audience attention.

The role of advertising in the communications mix obviously must reflect this unique pattern of strengths and weaknesses. In addition, the basic choice between a push strategy and a pull strategy, determined by the nature of product, market, and competition, will define advertising's role.

Stage in the product life cycle is another variable that defines advertising's role. From Chapter 8 it will be recalled that the product life cycle reflects the diffusion process, a social process by which a new product gains market acceptance. Advertising is likely to be especially important early in the product life cycle, when creating awareness is a critical objective and because the early adopters, who are the opinion leaders, rely heavily on the mass media for information. Later adopters, in contrast, tend to rely more heavily on personal and noncommercial sources of information. Thus, the role of advertising in the communications mix changes over time, being relatively more important at earlier stages in the product life cycle and the diffusion process.

Product differentiation

For new products, especially consumer packaged goods, advertising frequently has a major role to play in the implementation of segmentation strategy. The question of product/market positioning involves both message and media decisions.

Advertising message strategy is often the key variable by which the product is defined in the buyer's mind relative to competing brands. Advertising appeals and claims for the product are designed to establish a unique position among competing brands. The economist calls this "product differentiation" whereas the advertising man prefers phrases like "the unique selling proposition," "the product's reason for being," or "product positioning." For products that have only minor physical differences among competing brands, advertising assumes the major responsibility for establishing and maintaining the product in its chosen market segment. Many cosmetic products, health and beauty aids, food items, and household products fall into this category of competition, where brand image is the key competitive variable.

In such cases, actual product characteristics are not unimportant, especially in a regulatory environment that insists that all product claims must be factually justifiable. Different product formulations are required for making toothpastes that prevent decay or make teeth white or clean breath or taste good, and for laundry detergents that make clothes clean or white or bright (three quite different things). But specific product formulations may be easy to create relative to the difficulties of product/market positioning. Actual product differences, while they may exist, are often of small importance in products designed for differential appeal to men versus women or young adults versus middle-aged consumers. Famous brands such as Marlboro cigarettes, Löwenbrau beer, and Johnny Walker scotch whisky reflect effective promotion more than discernible product differences.

Specific advertising objectives

Advertising objectives can be phrased as answers to a series of simple questions:

1. What do we want to say about our product or service? (message strategy)
2. Whom do we want to say it to? (media strategy)
3. What do we want them to do? (behavioral response desired)

Other objectives such as sales volume and market share may be part of the advertising plan and can provide criteria for evaluating advertising performance, but strictly speaking they are inappropriate as advertising objectives because of the usually weak causal relationship between advertising effort and sales results.

Advertising objectives perform three important functions. First, they direct the development of messages and media strategy and the design of advertising tactics. Second, they coordinate decisions in various areas and by various decision makers toward common purposes. Third, they provide standards against which to evaluate advertising accomplishment. In each of these functions they serve to facilitate communication by creating mutual understanding and shared expectations, especially between the advertiser and the various agencies serving his needs. Also, clear statement of advertising objectives can facilitate coordination with other parts of the marketing communications mix, especially personal selling and sales promotion, where the timing of specific actions is crucial. Will the sales force be ready to follow up on leads created by the advertising? Will the distributors be informed of the consumer promotion prior to its announcement in advertising? There is much waste in poorly coordinated communications.

Hierarchy of effects

Advertising objectives, especially those relating to message strategy, must be specific about the behavioral response desired: awareness, attitude change, or buying action. There is also a direct relationship to the measurement question, as explained in the previous chapter.

Awareness is easiest to accomplish and subsequently to measure and attribute to advertising. Awareness objectives often call for greater emphasis on advertising media reach (as opposed to frequency) within defined segments. It is an obviously important objective for new products. Awareness objectives are not confined strictly to awareness of brand name and its existence but also involve developing a correct perception of the product and its attributes. For perceptually complex products, such as a cold remedy that aids sleep and may thus be confused with a sleeping pill, advertising message execution and repetition (media frequency) become very important.

Attitude objectives are concerned with the development of preferences or, more generally, the development of favorable predispositions. This is a more complicated communication problem that requires a longer period and more exposures than the simple creation of awareness. Preferences and "brand image" development tend to be more important for products involving longer buyer decision cycles—such as automobiles, appliances, insurance, and furniture—than for frequently purchased consumer products. Advertising intended to create a favorable image for a company, to support the salesmen, for example, usually has the objective of changing attitudes.

The objective of buying action, when, for example, the aim is to stimulate product trial or inquiries, calls for particular kinds of appeals and inducements. A specific rate of consumer trial is a common advertising objective for many new consumer packaged goods. Sometimes this is a reasonable objective for advertising; sometimes it is not. Direct promotion such as distribution of free samples, special price deals, and in-store demonstrations may be more effective and efficient.

As noted in the previous chapter, it may be easier to change attitudes by stimulating product trial (behavioral change) than to attempt to influence buyer behavior through the intermediate step of attitude change. But eventually attitudes must be consistent with behavior for the behavior change to be permanent. Thus, advertising stressing attitude or brand image objectives aimed at existing customers may be important in order to protect market share.

The nature of advertising objectives determines what is subsequently measured to appraise performance. This planning problem was also discussed in the previous chapter, in the section entitled "Planning Campaign Evaluation" and in the discussion of communication objectives.

Other things being equal, so-called "communication objectives" expressed in terms of awareness levels and attitude shifts are more appropriate than sales objectives in evaluating advertising results. Changes in awareness and attitudes are much more easily attributed to advertising than are changes in sales volume. As the buyer moves along the hierarchy of effects from awareness to buying action, the role of advertising tends to decrease in importance as other variables such as distribution, packaging, display, personal selling, price, and word-of-mouth communication become more important.

CORPORATE ADVERTISING

Corporate advertising is distinct from product advertising. The objective of corporate advertising is to improve awareness of, and develop favorable attitudes toward, a company and its various activities. Company reputation can significantly enhance salesman acceptance and effectiveness with buyers, and it can help sell products. In addition, corporate advertising, like public relations, can improve relationships with various important publics, including shareholders, dealers, suppliers, government officials, employees, and the public at large. Although this chapter focuses on issues of product advertising, the analytical approach applies equally well to corporate advertising—except that sales measures of advertising effectiveness are much less important for corporate advertising.

It appears that a great deal of corporate advertising is wasted because of inadequate planning, lack of clear objectives, and poorly defined advertising need. Much of it seems to be designed to enhance the egos of top management, a tendency revealed by the frequent use of "we" in the copy. One might ask about much corporate advertising, "Who cares?" Is the audience well defined? Are general attitudes in the desired target audiences really important to the company? A hard-nosed approach to the corporate advertising program can produce efficiency in the program. As a general rule there should be a specific purpose for such efforts—for example, to announce a change in corporate name, to correct mistaken impressions about the company's line of business, or to help sell specific products in specific markets. Otherwise, it is likely that the money can be better spent directly for product advertising.

DEVELOPING ADVERTISING MESSAGES

The advertising message is a combination of appeals, images, benefits, facts, and promises. In communication terms, it is the combination of symbols selected by the source to convey his intended meaning. To be effective, the advertising message must do several things:

- It must attract attention.
- It must motivate the receiver.
- It must develop interest to ensure that it is read or listened to completely.
- It must offer need satisfactions to the buyer.
- It must be remembered until buying action can occur.

The advertising message must accomplish these tasks in competition with hundreds of other advertisements, and it must do so in a way that is, at the minimum, inoffensive and hopefully entertaining. As one marketing executive has noted,

To a degree which is literally astounding, advertising . . . exists only on the tolerance, sufferance, and patience of the American consumer.

Advertising technique is to find something that the consumer really wants to do—read or be informed, or take a drive in the country—and then to interpose somewhere in the span of the activity an interruption designed to serve our interests. If we are clever enough, the consumer will (hopefully in good humor) tolerate the interruption and be influenced by it.[1]

[1] Blaine Cook, quoted in *Advertising Age* (July 3, 1967): 1.

There is a school of advertising thought that argues that advertising technique should concentrate on a single selling point and
drive it home with repetition. Such advertising tends to be of the
"hard sell" variety, often in poor taste and offensive in tone and
presentation. It is defended on the basis that people remember it and
it sells the product. In the opinion of many, such advertising is irresponsible and brings about much of the social criticism of advertising
as an institution.

A more recent view, advocated by many newcomers to the field of
advertising, holds that advertising must not only attract attention, be
remembered, and sell the product but also, in itself, be interesting,
entertaining, and in good taste. In other words, the advertising must
have some value in itself for the receiver. This view is more in tune
with the times. Of course, advertising must always be designed to sell
the product, and advertising that draws attention to itself by being
clever and cute often fails in its basic marketing purpose. But there is
no reason why advertising that sells cannot also be interesting and in
good taste. In other words, advertising must both sell and please.

The copy platform

The copy platform is a statement of advertising message objectives
and strategy. It should be developed by the advertiser in consultation
with his advertising agency. The primary purpose of the copy platform is to guide the creative people (at the advertising agency, within
the company, or in other organizations selling creative services) who
must actually develop the advertising. The copy platform should identify
the target audience and the reasons why people will buy the product.
It should define the unique features of the product compared to those
of competitors, its "reason for being."

The copy platform is very important for guiding creative development and evaluating the creative alternatives that are generated. It can
facilitate communication and understanding at all stages of the process.

The value of an idea

How much better is a good selling idea than an "average" idea? What
is the value of such themes as "I'd walk a mile for a Camel" or "We're
number 2, so we try harder" (Avis) or "Does she or doesn't she?"
(Clairol). Nobody knows, of course, but it is recognized by marketing
managers that the quality of the advertising campaign is often the
major ingredient in a marketing success or failure. There are experts
who will argue that a really good advertising idea can increase sales
at least three times over the level to be realized with an average selling
idea. It is fair to generalize that the benefits of really good advertising
substantially exceed the benefits possible from more scientific media

selection and other areas in which quantitative analysis can aid the decision maker.

Recognizing the important value of an advertising idea, one authority has concluded that advertisers typically underspend for the generation of creative alternatives. Assuming that the relative effectiveness of advertising campaigns is normally distributed around an average level of effectiveness, and that the average advertiser spends only 3 to 5 percent of his total media budget on creating the campaign, it can be shown that increasing this level three- to fivefold (that is, up to about 15 percent of budget) would produce more profitable results.[2] To fit the assumptions of this model, however, the alternatives have to be independently generated—that is, by different creative groups, such as several different advertising agencies or at least entirely separate groups within each agency. Implementation of this idea, then, would violate the traditional relationship between an advertiser and his agency, and it has been strongly criticized for this reason. Some advertising agencies are in fact noted for their ability to put several creative groups to work on solving an individual client's problem.

Campaign wear-out

A related question involves campaign "wear-out." When should a successful campaign be replaced by an entirely new one? For a variety of reasons the tendency is to ride a winning horse even after it has tired. It is easier to run the old campaign, especially if it is freshened with new ideas from time to time, than to develop a new one. Also, new campaigns are risky, although advertising research techniques are now good enough to permit careful pretesting and reasonable predictions of success. Nonetheless, it usually takes strong evidence of declining effectiveness from an existing campaign before a new campaign is developed. A more intelligent approach would be to generate new ideas frequently and systematically (say, every year or so) and to compare them with the existing campaign using carefully defined research and selection criteria. One advantage of such an approach is that it can develop a data base against which to evaluate specific creative alternatives, as well as a "pool" of potential candidates.

WORKING WITH AN AGENCY

Most advertisers with budgets of any consequence find it valuable to have the professional services of an advertising agency. These services include

[2] Irwin Gross, "Should the Advertiser Spend More on Creative Advertising?" Proceedings of the 13th Annual Conference, Advertising Research Foundation (November 14, 1967).

- consulting on advertising strategy and related marketing problems
- creating advertising campaigns
- selecting and buying advertising media space and time
- research services of various kinds, including
  —consumer surveys
  —market studies
  —advertising pretesting
  —new-product market tests
  —postcampaign evaluation of advertising

"Creative" versus "full service" agencies

In recent years there has been much argument about the relative merits of the small, specialized "creative boutique" versus the large, full-service or "marketing" advertising agency. A variety of small agencies appeared in the late 1960s and early 1970s, specializing in creative functions. A related development was that of media buying services. From the vantage point of the mid-1970s, it appears that these developments were somewhat faddish. The full-service agencies have continued as the choice of most important advertisers, although the creative function has been reemphasized somewhat relative to other marketing services.

Two observations are relevant in this connection. First, in order to do a good job, the agency must be able to coordinate and combine the several parts of the advertising function, including message development, media selection, and research. While actual research work may very well be conducted by outside research contractors, it should still be managed as part of the total. Similar considerations apply in such related communication areas as packaging, catalogues, sales promotion, salesmen's aids, and display. Some advertising agencies have found it desirable and profitable to offer a special competence in these areas to their clients. This development is a healthy one because it leads to better implementation of the ideal concept of a totally integrated marketing communications mix.

Second, a marketing-oriented advertising agency is no substitute for a well-organized and well-managed marketing capability within the firm. By its very nature as a basic management philosophy and business orientation, marketing (as opposed to selling) is not something somebody else can do for you. Part of the reason for the recent disenchantment (which now seems to have been overstated) with the marketing-oriented agency is that many advertisers realized that they were paying for unnecessary services that merely duplicated their own marketing capabilities.

Working relationships

Within the client organization, an advertising manager or a product manager is most often responsible for the ongoing relationship with the agency, where his counterpart is the account supervisor or account manager. The latter has responsibility for coordinating all of the agency's services as required by that client, including creative, media, production, traffic (i.e., physical flow of work and materials), and research. He represents the client to the agency and vice versa, serving as a vital communication link. He is often "squeezed" from both sides as he tries to explain the client's needs within the agency and subsequently to "sell" the agency's output to the client. His position can be especially sensitive when presenting the results of the creative department's effort, when he must be responsive to the client while defending what the creative people have done. Here is where prior agreement on objectives, advertising strategy, and copy platform becomes extremely important.

Some guidelines for managing this relationship can be offered to the advertiser:

1. Make sure your agency knows everything there is to know about your products, your markets, and your company.
2. Keep the agency completely informed about marketing plans and ideas.
3. Do not interfere in the creative process; never ask for a particular type of advertising or submit specific creative ideas. (As David Ogilvy expressed it, "Why keep a dog and bark yourself?")
4. Insist on good research at all stages of the advertising process, but don't use it as a bludgeon to shut off consideration of new ideas.
5. Request an annual review of advertising performance, agency capability, and possible new campaigns.
6. Challenge the agency to produce its very best ideas for you and, in return, be receptive to new approaches.
7. Protect the agency from the personal whims and fancies of your top management. Keep the advertising review process as simple as possible.

The compensation issue

The traditional way of compensating an advertising agency is with 15 percent of media billings (or 17.65 percent of the true media "price" after deducting the agency commission). The system is implemented by the convention that media actually bill agencies at the published rate less 15 percent. This method reflects the historical fact that the first advertising agencies were sales agents for newspapers and began to develop advertisements as a technique to help sell space. Agencies bill clients for other services (photography, engraving, etc.) purchased from outside suppliers by adding on an additional charge of 15 or 17.65 percent. More recently there has been increased interest in compensation based on a fee for services rendered. Most agencies today offer potential clients an option of commission, fees, or a combination of the two. About three-fourths of total agency income is from commissions, one-fourth from fees.

The commission method has been criticized on several grounds: It encourages the agency to recommend high budgets and high-cost media alternatives; it discourages the development of new campaigns; it has no relationship to results; it has no relationship to the agency's actual costs. It has been defended because it is simple and generally accepted; it avoids the necessity of fee negotiation for every service requested by the client; it avoids price cutting in an industry characterized by very thin profit margins; it provides a predictable income base, allowing the agency to maintain the necessary bundle of services to adequately serve client needs.

The fee method has the merit of asking the client to pay only for the services specifically requested, and this contributes to realistic pricing of those services. It reduces the incentive to overspend. Where adopted, it seems to have improved agency profits (which have been low), and it has contributed to more careful management and control of agency resources. The great disadvantage of the fee method is that it is complicated to administer, requiring frequent negotiation and detailed record keeping. It also has the potential to cause clients to underspend for necessary services, such as research, which the agency might have performed routinely under a commission agreement.

Perhaps the best way to summarize this discussion of advertiser-agency working relationships is to conclude that it should be approached in the same professional manner as any supplier relationship. Mutual obligations should be spelled out in detail and agreed to in writing; the professionalism of the supplier should be respected; the supplier should be expected to earn a fair profit; and disagreements should be resolved quickly and openly. The "solution" of changing agencies should be only an extreme last resort (it is probably somewhat overused) based on a complete evaluation of the entire relationship.

SELECTING ADVERTISING MEDIA

The objective of advertising media strategy is to deliver the maximum number of effective exposures to prospective customers within the constraints of the available budget. The media used contribute to the accomplishment of advertising objectives in three ways:

1. by the quality of the audience they deliver
2. by enhancing the quality of the message itself
3. by their technical or physical characteristics such as frequency of appearance, ability to show motion, and use of color

Specifying target audience

The media selection decision process cannot go forward until the characteristics of the desired audience have been carefully defined. The nature of this problem was discussed in Chapter 11 in the section entitled "Selecting Communication Targets," where it was pointed out that audiences must be defined both by predispositions and by demographics, the latter being more important for the media decision. The definition of market segments is obviously the necessary logical precursor to the definition of target audiences.

The problem of audience definition is implicit in the concept of an "effective exposure," which is a message delivered once to a prospective customer. Stated negatively, the media problem is to minimize the number of wasted exposures, or messages delivered to nonprospects. The very nature of media distribution in both industrial and consumer markets means that not all exposures will be "effective"—that is, delivered to prospective customers. Furthermore, it is never possible to define the characteristics of potential buyers and buying influences with absolute precision. But choices must be made, some audiences with special characteristics sought out, in the interests of advertising efficiency.

Thus, a media plan might include such description of target audiences as the following:

- men between the ages of 18 and 49 with family incomes over $10,000 per year (for power tools)
- all children under 13 years old (for a flavored breakfast cereal)
- doctors in private or clinic-based practices specializing in cardiovascular diseases (for a pharmaceutical product)
- all industrial employees in the Glasgow/Edinburgh industrial area whose attitudes could influence the purchase of industrial tools (for a system of airpowered tools)
- business and professional people who make more than 12 air trips per year (for a national airline)

Without a precise definition of target audience, meaningful evaluation of alternative media is virtually impossible. Lack of such definition is often seen in the use of simple "cost per thousand" media comparisons, without adequate answers to the question, "Cost per thousand *whats?*" Not all audiences are equally valuable.

With a good definition of target audiences in hand, the next problem is to obtain necessary audience data about media alternatives to permit evaluation and intermedia comparisons. The best media are able to do this and have reasonably accurate data on the characteristics or "profile" of the audience reached. However, the advertiser should keep in mind always the fact that such data are usually intended as media-selling tools to convince the advertiser of the high quality of a particular media audience. It is often a good idea to ask for a detailed description of the research plan that produced these data. Such evaluation is often better done by media experts at the advertising agency.

The media selection decision process is in part a mechanical or clerical problem of matching media audience characteristics with desired potential market characteristics, ranking media alternatives on the criterion of cost per effective exposure. But there are also important qualitative differences among media audiences to be considered.

Qualitative value of mass media

The mass media have qualitative characteristics that contribute to message effectiveness in other ways than the composition of the audience delivered. These qualitative characteristics can be grouped into two categories: (1) "technical" or "physical" values relating to the way the medium is produced, distributed, and used by the audience and (2) "image" values that enhance the believability and persuasibility of the message.

In discussing qualitative media value it is necessary to return briefly to the dimension of audience characteristics, this time in qualitative terms rather than strict demographic terms. Behavioral research has found that the different types of mass media—newspapers, magazines, radio, and television—attract quite different types of audiences.[3] An awareness of these general differences among media may help the advertiser to make a first cut across the media selection decision.

In general, laboratory studies have found that aural communication ("through the ear") is somewhat more effective than visual ("through the eye"), especially for audiences with lower intelligence. Thus, radio is somewhat more effective than newspaper, but television, which combines both aural and visual, would be expected to be more effective than either. (These general statements, it should be remembered, make no reference to the economics of media use.) Radio and television are the preferred media of the less educated, while the better educated prefer magazines and newspapers, an obvious reflection of differences in reading skills, among other things. Radio audiences tend to be more suggestible or persuasible, partly because of somewhat lower intellectual ability and partly because radio allows the listener to "fill in" the visual dimensions. There is also evidence that radio listeners see themselves as members of a group engaged in sharing a common experience, a fact evidenced by the popularity of radio station fan clubs, especially among urban teenagers. This sense of sharing with other members of an audience is probably strongest for radio but is characteristic of all media to some degree.

Television tends to be the most real, lifelike, and absorbing of all the media. The "absorbing" quality is especially important for children. Like radio, television also allows active participation in the situation.

[3] Joseph T. Klapper, *The Effects of the Mass Media* (New York: Free Press, 1960).

Use of national television is expensive and therefore mostly for large-budget advertisers.

Magazines have the great merit of catering to special interests and tastes and thus attract a very high degree of reader interest. This characteristic of selectivity has become especially obvious in recent years as various once-great general-appeal magazines like *Collier's*, *Life*, and *The Saturday Evening Post* have disappeared.

Newspapers offer two advantages—timeliness and local-community orientation. They do not permit social-class selectivity or other forms of demographic segmentation, except that young people and teenagers do not read newspapers to the same extent as adults. Newspapers offer great time and place flexibility to the advertiser, especially if the advertising can be placed through local dealers for whom newspaper advertising rates are much less than for the national advertiser—an interesting form of price discrimination.

The ways in which audiences use media are an important determinant of their advertising value. These habits often reflect the technical characteristics of the media. For example, the reader can control the time and duration of his exposure to print media more than broadcast media. The same magazine advertisement may be seen several times by the same reader. Print can be used more flexibly by the reader. Reading is essentially a private activity; television viewing is more likely to be a social occasion involving family or other people; radio listening is now a more personal activity (compared to the pre-TV era, when it often involved the entire family) and is frequently an accompaniment to other activities such as housework and hobbies.

The image or personality of an advertising medium derives from three different characteristics of the medium as perceived by the individual audience members: (1) editorial and programing content; (2) technical characteristics such as size, color, and format; and (3) assumed characteristics of other members of the audience. Compare the different personalities of *The New Yorker* versus *Time*, for example. *The New Yorker* is more concerned with the arts, urban living, and current political opinion as opposed to reporting. The format is tasteful and somewhat subdued and has an emphasis on design that carries over to the advertisements themselves. In terms of audience, it exudes a feeling of urban, cosmopolitan, educated, informed, even snobbish people. *Time*, in contrast, is harder-hitting, emphasizing news and interpreting the forces creating it. It is more concerned with timeliness than "good taste." It seems to appeal to a slightly above-average common man who is busy and involved and wants to be efficiently informed. If *The New Yorker* is better suited to advertisements for Steuben glass, Almaden champagne, and Chanel perfumes—"symbols of good taste"—then *Time* is better suited to Kent cigarettes, Ford cars, and Budweiser beer. Both media may be attractive to airline advertisers, but for different reasons—*The New Yorker* for personal travel, *Time* for business travel. The active, businessman orientation of *Time* is revealed in its large number of advertisements for banks and hotels, whereas *The New Yorker* carries more ads for homemaking and decorative items, travel destinations, and resorts. It is important to recognize that the same person may very well read both, but they get him in quite different moods. The *Time* reader may be more concerned with making a living, the *New Yorker* reader with enjoying it; one with the process of making money, the other with spending it.

Such generalizations are unscientific, of course, and are intended only to suggest the determinants of media "image" and how it influences response to advertising. Technical and professional journals have a specific appeal to the reader that catches him in a particular frame of mind that may be much more important in determining advertising impact and value than details of message execution.

Advertising execution must be tailored to the media situation. Humor, for example, can be effective in some situations and ineffective in others, depending on media "mood."

People come to depend on and trust advertising media, especially print media, in certain ways that reflect editorial policy and content. Advertising in certain magazines may be taken as a virtual "seal of approval" by the magazine itself, especially if the magazine has promoted itself that way to its readers, as with the "*Good Housekeeping* Seal of Approval." Many industrial and technical publications have a similar degree of credibility with their readers.

To summarize, media have significant qualitative differences. Such differences must be considered in message execution as well as in media selection. We will see shortly how quantitative estimates of media cost and value can be combined with such qualitative assessments.

Audience measurement concepts

Media audience measurement concepts can become quite complex but must be understood before much sense can be made of comparisons of media data in developing the media schedule. Remember that an effective exposure is a message delivered once to a prospective customer. Is it better to reach one prospect twice or two prospects once? That depends on the product, predispositions, and marketing strategy, of course, but it is always a question in media strategy—the question of reach versus frequency. *Reach* is defined as "the net unduplicated audience delivered by a media schedule," but this definition is imprecise because "delivered" can mean either vehicle distribution or vehicle exposure. The complexity of the problem stems from the fact that media contribute to advertising message effectiveness in a series of six stages:

1. Vehicle distribution. *Such as the number of copies of a magazine mailed to subscribers and sold on newsstands. Only a portion of the people who see the vehicle will be in the intended audience; there is "wasted coverage" for the advertiser.*
2. Vehicle exposure. *The number of people who actually see the vehicle; likely to be greater than distribtion because of "pass along" readership, although not all distributed copies will in fact be received and read. Furthermore, there are likely to be multiple exposures for each individual. Again, some exposures are "wasted," at this and all subsequent stages.*
3. Advertising exposure. *The number of persons who actually see the advertising, less than the number exposed to the vehicle; there may be multiple advertising exposures to an individual from the same vehicle.*
4. Advertising perception. *The number of people who see the advertising, less than those exposed to it.*
5. Advertising communication. *The number of people who are actually influenced by the advertising.*
6. Sales response. *The number who buy.*[4]

We are leading up to the media evaluation question, but some other concepts must be defined first. The point to be made here is that the unique influence of media is largely confined to the first three stages. After that, message effects become increasingly important. On the question of how to define "reach," one could argue in favor of any of the first three stages, although the third is hardest to defend.

Frequency is the number of repetitions of the advertising message to the average prospect planned as part of the media schedule. It is better thought of as a planned objective rather than an empirically verifiable result, and it is based on a judgment of the value of repetition in accomplishing advertising objectives. Frequency becomes more important as objectives move in the hierarchy of effects from awareness toward sales.

Duplication is the extent to which the same individuals are found in different audiences. The easiest to talk about is paired duplication between two media, although duplication applies to the overlap of all media audiences. Some duplication may be desirable in the media schedule in order to accomplish frequency objectives, but it must be accounted for in appraising media efficiency.

Audience *accumulation* is a measure of the growth in audience due to repeated insertions in a given media, such as consecutive issues of a magazine. Four insertions may be expected to give 50 to 100 percent more exposures than a single insertion.[5]

Waste coverage, the easiest of all audience measurement concepts to define, is the exposure delivered to nonprospective customers.

[4] Audience Concept Committee, *Toward Better Media Comparisons* (New York: Advertising Research Foundation, 1961).

[5] D. B. Lucas and S. H. Britt, *Measuring Advertising Effectiveness* (New York: McGraw-Hill, 1963), p. 362.

A media selection procedure

The following paragraphs describe a reasonably straightforward approach to the media selection decision.[6] Although computer-based mathematical programing models may be much more sophisticated, they all use the same basic logic of matching media audience to customer profile, adjusting for qualitative factors and marketing policy constraints, ranking media alternatives, and then selecting among them until the budget is used up. The more sophisticated models attempt to deal with such complexities as duplication, accumulation, and media quantity discounts in a more complete fashion.

Given a definition of advertising objectives and message strategy, a statement of desired audience, and an advertising budget, the media selection decision proceeds as follows:

1. For a given segmentation variable such as income, develop data on the audience delivered by each media alternative in each segment.

Example:

	Audience Size	
Segment	Alternative A	Alternative B
Under $5,000	1,000,000	500,000
$5,000–7,000	3,000,000	1,000,000
Over $7,500	2,000,000	2,000,000
Total	6,000,000	3,500,000

2. Calculate a "penetration ratio" for each segment, defined as an average of brand sales and product category sales divided by total population percentage in each segment.

Example:

Segment	(1) % of Total Population	(2) % of Product Category Sales	(3) % of Brand Sales
Under $5,000	25	45	50
$5,000–7,000	45	35	25
Over $7,500	30	20	25

Segment	(4) Product Penetration Ratio*	(5) Brand Penetration Ratio*	(6) Average Penetration Ratio*
Under $5,000	1.80	2.00	1.90
$5,000–7,000	0.78	0.56	0.67
Over $7,500	0.67	0.83	0.75

* (4) = (2) ÷ (1); (5) = (3) ÷ (1); (6) = (4) + (5) ÷ 2

[6] Adapted from Philip Kotler, "On Methods: Toward an Explicit Model for Media Selection," *Journal of Advertising Research* 4 (March 1964): 34–41.

Here one of the arbitrary features of this approach is revealed—the equal weighting of product category and brand penetration to calculate the average. If the decision maker believed his brand to be underrepresented in certain segments, he could increase the brand weightings for those segments.

3. Weight the audience data by the penetration ratios reflecting the relative importance of each segment in order to arrive at adjusted audience size.

Example:

Segment	Average Penetration Ratio	Adjusted Audience Size Alternative A	Alternative B
Under $5,000	1.90	1,900,000	900,000
$5,000–7,500	0.67	2,000,000	670,000
Over $7,500	0.75	1,500,000	1,500,000
Total		5,400,000	3,070,000

4. Repeat the calculation for all segmentation variables (such as age and education).
5. Calculate a "scale value" for each segmentation variable for each media alternative by dividing adjusted audience by actual audience.

Example:

$$\text{Income Scale Value} = \frac{5,900,000}{6,000,000} = 0.98 \quad \frac{2,070,000}{3,500,000} = 0.88$$

Alternative A   Alternative B

6. Multiply the scale values for each media alternative (i.e., all values for A, all values for B, etc.) and multiply the result times unadjusted audience size to get a final adjusted audience figure for each alternative.
7. Develop a qualitative index (average value = 1.00) for each media alternative and multiply this times adjusted audience to develop a summary measure of exposure value.
8. For each media alternative divide total cost per insertion by adjusted audience to calculate cost per effective exposure and rank media alternatibes according to the result.
9. Make explicit all decision constraints such as maximum or minimum number of insertions in a single magazine, maximum expenditures in a given mode, and so on, and all technical constraints (e.g., no more than 12 insertions per year in a monthly magazine).
10. Purchase units of the most efficient medium (cost per effective exposure) until a constraint is reached, then shift to the next most efficient medium until a constraint is reached, and so on until the budget is exhausted.

This is an oversimplification of a technically complex problem, but it does outline the major steps involved. Other factors must be considered, including the size of the insertion, the timing of insertions, and correcting audience figures further for duplication. Computers have made such calculations economically possible, allowing the advertiser to consider more alternative combinations of media. A secondary effect has been to stimulate the provision of better audience data from the media themselves.

Needless to say, media selection is a task for the experts. The preceding comments barely scratch the surface of this topic and are intended only to suggest the major strategic considerations involved and the dimensions of the media selection decision.

EVALUATING ADVERTISING EFFECTIVENESS

The advertising planning process is not complete until evaluation has been planned. If it isn't planned, it is unlikely to happen, and the manager loses an opportunity to learn from his experience. There are three parts of the evaluation process—message testing, media evaluation, and overall campaign appraisal. And there is a variety of testing techniques, including buyer surveys, laboratory methods, and use of inquiry and sales measures.

Message testing

Message testing is most commonly done in order to choose among two or more alternative campaign themes or copy approaches. Exposure conditions may be forced (as in a laboratory test) or natural (when actual media are used), and measurement may take place either immediately or some time after exposure. Once again the hierarchy of effects is important since the researcher may wish to measure changes in awareness, attitudes, or buying behavior.

Techniques that ask the respondent whether he likes the advertisement or whether he thinks it would persuade him to buy should be avoided. They put the respondent in the position of being an advertising expert, which he is not, and have low validity.

Recognition measures are one of the most common forms of message testing. The basic technique is to show the respondent a series of magazine advertisements and to ask him which ones he remembers seeing—usually from a single recent issue, which the respondent must first prove he has read. The well-known Starch Readership Service uses recognition measures that are reported as three scores:

1. *Noted*—the percentage of readers who reported seeing the advertisement.
2. *Seen-associated*—those who not only saw the advertisement but associated it with either the company name or the product being advertised.
3. *Read most*—the percentage of respondents who said they read more than half of the advertising copy.

Recognition measures can be used to test alternative messages or for evaluating an advertising campaign. Starch has developed norms for various magazines that can serve as bench marks; many advertisers have developed their own norms based on experience.

Recognition measures are "easy" for the respondent and probably tend to overstate readership. A single advertisement can easily be confused with others, especially if it is only one in a campaign series. Recognition can be influenced by the respondent's interest in the product and his memory ability, as well as by technical features of ads such as size, color, and use of illustrations. (Babies and nudes always get high scores, for example.)

All of this tends to confuse the relationship between recognition measures and the sales effectiveness of the advertisement. Confusion in the reader's mind about whether he saw a particular advertisement or another like it is perhaps the major shortcoming of such measures.

Recall measures are "tougher" for the respondent, who must prove that he has in fact seen the advertisement in question and that he can recall its content. Recall may be "aided" or "unaided," requiring different interviewing technique. Like recognition measures, recall studies depend on surveys of people previously exposed to the advertising, usually under natural conditions. Perhaps the best-known commercial service using recall measures is the Gallup and Robinson Magazine Impact Service. This service calculates three scores for an advertisement:

1. *Proved name registration* (PNR) is a weighted measure of the percentage of respondents who accurately recalled message elements to the extent required to prove that they saw the ad.
2. *Idea registration* is an index of the extent to which specific copy points are recalled by respondents.
3. *Favorable buying attitude* is a measure of the extent to which those who recall the ad credit it with developing favorable attitudes toward the company and the product advertised.

Because recall measures demand so much of the respondent's memory, percentage recall scores tend to be low, in the neighborhood of 5 percent or less. They do eliminate confusion, which is one of the problems of recognition measures. But there is still no clear relationship between advertising recall and sales effectiveness; the respondent may be able to recall the advertising but not be influenced by it.

Attitude measures assess respondents' attitudes toward brands and/or companies before and after exposure to advertising. If field surveys are done, matched samples should be used before and after, rather than the same respondents, in order to avoid bias. In laboratory studies (the laboratory is usually a theater or an auditorium), the same respondents are used. An example of the latter is the Schwerin Standard TV testing service for pretesting TV commercials.

Schwerin invites respondents to preview a television show. Before viewing the show the respondents are asked to select one brand in each of three product categories they would prefer to receive if they win a prize in a drawing to be conducted later. Then they watch a TV show in which there are commercials for a brand in each of the three product categories; afterwards they are again asked to indicate the brand they would prefer if they win the drawing. The measure of advertising message effectiveness is the percentage of respondents shifting preference to the advertised brands. The potential sources of bias in this technique are obvious, but this can be taken into account to some extent as norms are developed from previous experience.

Print advertising campaigns can be assessed by measuring shifts in attitudes over time by means of survey interviewing techniques. Attitude measures are often preferred because they can assess the communication impact of the advertising, not just whether the advertising was seen and remembered, and they are relatively easy to obtain.

Inquiry measures have been used successfully to pretest or evaluate advertising messages designed to get specific action such as requesting a catalogue, asking a salesman to call, or actually sending in an order. Coupons are often used in such advertising, and counting returns is a simple matter. In fact, such measures were used by the early copywriters and represented the beginning of systematic advertising research.[7]

Purchase behavior measures have become more popular owing to the development of new techniques such as CATV (community antenna television), consumer panels, and trailer labs. These make it possible to trace changes in consumer purchase after advertising exposure. CATV permits selective exposure of TV commercials to identified families, whose purchases are recorded in diaries, without their being aware which commercials are part of a test. Trailer labs can be set up in supermarket parking lots and shoppers asked to spend a few minutes viewing TV commercials, for which they are rewarded with coupons to be redeemed in the supermarket. Differential rates of coupon redemptions are measures of advertising impact.

Such techniques overcome one of the traditional problems of using sales measures—establishing a relationship between behavior and advertising exposure—by controlling advertising exposure. CATV permits natural exposure, whereas the trailer labs do not. Both techniques are best used for comparing alternative messages rather than for projecting sales results.

---

[7] For an interesting report of these early efforts, see Claude Hopkins, *Scientific Advertising* (New York: Lord & Thomas, 1923); republished (New York: Moore Publishing, 1952).

Physiological measures have been developed over the years to assess message impact. They are based on a belief that such measures can be more accurate because they are involuntary and therefore eliminate respondent bias. Among the measures that have been tried are galvanic skin response (GSR), salivation, and eye movement (page scanning). The most recently developed physiological technique is a measure of pupil dilation, which is known to be a measure of the subject's interest in a visual subject. Under the commercial name *pupillometrics*, the technique has been used to study product designs (including greeting cards and sterling silver patterns) as well as advertisements. All physiological measures share a common basic weakness: There is no obvious relationship between physiological response, which is a measure of visual interest, and the sales effectiveness of an advertisement. Their apparently objective, scientific nature can be deceptive in this respect.

Each method of message testing has its strengths and weaknesses. Having selected a particular method, the advertiser is well advised to stick with it for a while in order to acquire the backlog of experience necessary to develop norms for his advertising. Given the importance of message effectiveness in determining sales response, however, generation and testing of alternative message approaches is usually a sound investment.

Media evaluation

In the six-stage model of media contribution to advertising results presented earlier, it was said that the direct contribution of media is confined largely to the first three stages of vehicle distribution, vehicle exposure, and advertising exposure. The first and second stages are largely a question of numbers of readers, listeners, or viewers. In the third stage, qualitative questions of message attention value become important and can be assessed with recognition measures. The later stages of advertising perception and communication depend more heavily on message effects, and the measures possible at this stage are of the recall and attitude variety. Assessing media influence on consumer response requires measures of sales or number of inquiries received.

A standard test of media effectiveness is to run the same advertisement in two or more media and to compare the results using similar measures. The comparison of different types of media—say, television and magazines—is very difficult to do but not impossible.[8]

[8] One such test was conducted by Ford Motor involving TV, radio, newspapers, and outdoor advertising in a total of 16 combinations; it took 3 years to complete. See G. H. Brown, "Measuring the Sales Effectiveness of Alternative Media," in *Using Research in Advertising Decisions,* Proceedings of the Seventh Annual Conference, Advertising Research Foundation (1971): 43–47.

It should be remembered that media contribute to advertising effectiveness both through the audience they deliver and by adding to the meaning and impact of the message. These different effects are hard to sort out unless different types of data are collected. A large advertiser may be able to afford research to determine actual audience profile for his advertising as opposed to the general audience delivered by a medium, and he may then understand better the relative importance of audience effects and message effects in the response from a given medium. Another approach would be to survey audience attitudes toward several media alternatives directly, independent of advertising message.

Assessing campaign results

The overall results of an advertising campaign reflect message effectiveness, media effectiveness, budget level, and the interactions among them as well as with other marketing variables. Thus, assessment of campaign results is a distinct and complicated measurement problem. The major issues in this connection were discussed at the end of the previous chapter. It was pointed out that campaign effects can be assessed at five levels: (1) campaign planning, (2) message distribution (vehicle distribution and exposure), (3) communication effects (awareness and attitude measures), (4) impact on dealer and buyer activity, and (5) impact on company sales, costs, and profits.

A combination of measures is strongly preferable to a single measure in evaluating campaign results. For reasons that have been developed in our various discussions of the hierarchy of effects, measures of communication effects should be given emphasis in evaluating the unique contribution of advertising in the overall communications mix.

SUMMARY

Advertising decisions should be made in light of the company's overall corporate, marketing, and.communication strategy and objectives. Message and media decisions require good information about market/audience characteristics and predispositions. Objectives should be defined in terms that permit careful measurement and evaluation. With a rigorous approach management reduces the risk of being overwhelmed by the "show biz" characteristics of advertising. Although advertising is an area of management decision making where management science has a great deal to offer, it should be remembered that qualitative differences in creativity and message quality are the ultimate determinants of campaign effectiveness. Generation and testing of creative alternatives should therefore be an ongoing process. All of this requires a smoothly functioning and professional relationship with the advertising agency, whose performance and compensation should be carefully assessed on an annual basis, not with an eye to changing agencies but in order to develop an increasingly productive business relationship.

SALES FORCE MANAGEMENT

13

For most firms, especially industrial marketers, the sales force is the key element of the marketing communication program. Personal selling is for these firms not only the major item of marketing expense but also the essential ingredient in stimulating demand for the company's products, providing necessary services to distributors and customers, and gathering market information to be sent back to decision centers within the firm. Sales force management is therefore a critical management function in such firms.

Sales force management has two major responsibilities—generating sales volume and developing sales manpower. The latter is essential to the long-term success of the firm in generating sales volume. As in so many management areas, short-term concern (for sales volume now) has a tendency to dominate management attention at all levels of the sales organization unless special steps are taken to attend to the long-term problems (of developing effective sales manpower).

In this chapter we will first look at personal selling as a form of communication and develop some implications of this view for the development of effective salesmen. Then we will consider the nature of the field sales manager's responsibilities and the requirements for effectiveness in this important supervisory echelon. Next, we will analyze the several elements of a company-wide sales management program, including recruitment, selection, training, organization, supervision, evaluation, and compensation of salesmen.

THE NATURE OF SELLING

Selling is the interpersonal communication process of convincing a prospective customer that the benefits to be derived from purchasing and using a product or service are greater than the costs and superior to the benefits offered by competitors. Selling is concerned with identifying, stimulating, directing, and satisfying those needs. The salesman's responsibilities include selecting prospective customers and providing necessary after-sale services to ensure that the product delivers the need satisfactions promised.

That is a marketing management view of the selling function. But, despite its importance to business, selling has not traditionally been recognized as one of society's more honored professions. To illustrate, the *Concise Oxford Dictionary* offers the following definitions of the verb *to sell*:

1. *to make over or dispose of in exchange for money*
2. *to keep stock of for sale or be a dealer in*
3. *betray for money or other reward*
4. *prostitute for money or other consideration, make a matter of corrupt bargaining*
5. *disappoint by not keeping engagement, etc., by failing in some way, or by trickery*
6. *find purchasers*
7. *clear out stock at reduced prices*

Webster's Seventh New Collegiate Dictionary is no more flattering:

1. *to deliver or give up in violation of duty, trust, or loyalty: betray*
2. *a. —to give up (property) to another for money or other valuable consideration for a price*
    —to offer for sale
   b. to give up in return for something else especially foolishly or dishonorably
   c. to exact a price for
3. *a. to deliver into slavery for money*
   b. to give into the power of another
   c. to deliver the personal services of for money
4. *to dispose of or manage for profit instead of in accordance with conscience, justice, or duty*

5. *a. to develop a belief in the trust, value, or desirability of*
   b. to persuade or influence to a course of action or to the acceptance of
     something
6. *to impose upon: cheat*
7. *a. to cause or promote the sale of*
   b. to make or attempt to make sales to
   c. to influence or induce to make a purchase

Only the seventh and last definition begins to capture the nature of selling as a business activity in large, responsible companies. Such negative definitions as those just listed seem to be based on the public's distaste for the practices of itinerant peddlers, petty tradesmen, and unscrupulous pushers who engage in shady practices of various kinds. But even the professional salesman of today often has a tarnished image in the public eye—an unwelcome holdover from the days of the hawkers and peddlers, and a major reason for the low prestige of personal selling as an occupation.[1]

Contrary to the view implied by dictionary definitions, today's salesman is a highly skilled and highly responsible professional, helping to bring together buyers and sellers and focusing all of his company's customer-satisfying resources on the particular needs and wants of his customers. He functions not only as a consultant to his customers concerning their problems but also as a source of market intelligence for his company. He may spend as much time explaining customers' problems to various engineering, production, distribution, and financial managers within his own company, thus securing their services in the best interests of the customers, as he does in the field. The highly trained, professional salesman is the link between the company and its customers, and performs a critical function in the implementation of the customer-oriented marketing concept.

Traditional views of salesmanship

If the dictionaries portray a mythical and outdated view of selling, it is also unfortunately true that another kind of mythology, positive instead of negative, has dominated the professional literature of selling until quite recently. The old "salesmanship" school saw the salesman essentially as a special breed of human being possessing certain unique traits that gave him a persuasive power over others. These views became almost mystical at times and saw the sales interaction as a kind of battle of wits in which the powers of salesmanship were directed at achieving total conquest over the prospect.

The salesmanship school, with its emphasis on the salesman's traits, led to management concern for selecting salesmen with these

---

[1] See John L. Mason, "The Low Prestige of Personal Selling," *Journal of Marketing* 29 (October 1965): 7–10.

special traits. The key to an effective sales force was finding people with the right qualities. Such a view was a major stimulus to the development of psychological testing to identify the personality attributes (especially interests, attitudes, and values) of successful salesmen. The salesmanship school led to overemphasis on selection and underemphasis on training, supervision, and ongoing issues of field sales management. It was based on an assumption that salesmen are born, not made, and it offered a very narrow view of selling, one that assumed that the salesman has all the power and is able to control the sales interview, if only he is clever enough.

Somewhat more sophisticated was the steps-in-the-sale view of selling. This model saw the results of the salesman's actions as a series of mental stages produced in the prospect—attention, interest, desire, and action (or AIDA). It was the salesman's job to move the prospect through these stages smoothly and systematically. Like traditional salesmanship views, the steps-in-the-sale-view saw the salesman as having virtually all the power in the buyer-seller relationship. This model had the benefit of making the salesman somewhat sensitive to what was happening in the buyer's mind.

One more step up the ladder of sophistication and complexity was achieved by the "stimulus-response" view of selling, in which the basic stimulus→organism→response model of psychology was applied to the sales interaction. Each action of the salesman was seen as a stimulus designed to obtain a particular response from the prospect. Again, this view is oriented pretty much to what the salesman does, but it emphasizes more than previous models the importance of understanding the buyer. The original psychological model saw response as uncertain, but this notion didn't survive the transfer to selling very well. Instead, stimulus-response views of selling presented an essentially mechanistic view of the sales interaction—it was up to the salesman to push the right buttons (often referred to in the selling literature as "hot buttons"), to appeal to the right needs, in order to produce the desired responses.

One other view of selling, the so-called "need satisfaction" theory, is really only a variant of the stimulus-response model. The salesman had to find a need and fill it. Need-satisfaction theory emphasized asking questions during the sales interview in order to identify needs and saw the salesman's task as one of building a groundwork of need identification, then moving in efficiently with a presentation and the close.

These various salesmanship views of personal selling might be summarized as follows:

Salesman's Traits + Salesman's Actions + Buyer's Needs = Sales Results

What is missing in this view? Unfortunately, not all buyers with the same needs will respond the same way to salesmen with given traits who engage in specified actions. These salesmanship views are an oversimplification; furthermore, they probably overstate the importance of particular traits possessed by salesmen. They certainly understate the importance of the role played by the prospect in the sales inter-action. From a management viewpoint, they lead to overemphasis on selecting salesmen with the right characteristics and on "programed" behavior on the part of the salesman—for example, in the form of memorized, standardized (or "canned") sales presentations designed to produce desired responses from prospects regardless of who delivers them. Such views have the danger of producing an inflexible response from the salesman in every sales interaction, one not sensitive to the specific situation.

Modern view—interpersonal communication

The modern view of the selling process emphasizes the interaction between buyer and seller; both are seen as active participants in the process, with each influencing the other. In communication terms, both function as sender and receiver; the buyer attempts to influence the salesman just as the salesman attempts to influence the buyer, and each is sensitive to the influence attempts of the other. In other words, the sales interview is seen as a social situation, and the behavior involved should be viewed not as individual behavior but as social behavior.

What is the difference between individual behavior and social behavior? Social behavior is behavior that is rewarded or punished by another person, accepted or rejected by him: There is feedback in the form of communication from the person who is the target of the influence attempt, and this communication is motivated by his goals and perceptions. Social behavior is influenced by how each person in the interaction views the other, thinks and feels about him, and acts toward him.

The predispositions of each actor are a significant influence on his behavior in the interaction. To be effective, the communicator (salesman) must take into account not only the actions of the re-ceiver (prospect) but also his needs, objectives, attitudes, values, beliefs, emotions, and so on. The inferences the salesman draws about predis-positions will determine his own behavior, and the effectiveness of his persuasive attempts will reflect the accuracy and completeness of these inferences. Thus, the salesman needs some special sensitivity in order to be aware of, understand, and respond to the clues that the prospect's behavior (much of it verbal) provides about these underlying pre-dispositions.

Whereas the old salesmanship school assumed that this sensi-tivity was an inborn characteristic, the new communication views assume that it can be learned. This is an issue that is still being debated. Those who lean toward the salesmanship views tend to argue that some potential salesmen seem much more able to develop and learn the necessary sensitivity. While this is certainly true, it is not adequate to support the conclusion that good salesmen are born rather than made through careful training.

Central to the debate is the concept of *empathy* or *empathic ability,* an individual characteristic well known in psychology. Empathy is the ability to sense the reaction one produces in another person; it has often been likened to the sensitivity of a heat-seeking missile, which is able to track another missile by sensing its position and changing course accordingly. Empathy is distinct from sympathy, which is the ability to sense and feel what another person feels and to identify with him. There is strong evidence in the psychological literature that empathic ability is learned rather than inborn. Furthermore, it seems that a person can be highly empathic with certain people and not with others. Thus, it has been found that salesmen are much more effective with prospects who are like themselves, in socioeconomic terms such as income, age, and occupation, and in terms of attitudes on such matters as politics, religion, and beliefs about business and about selling.[2]

One other concept is important in understanding the modern view of selling as a form of communication—the concept of *role expectations.* A role is a social position, and there are two sets of expectations associated with every role—expectations for the behavior of people who occupy that role and expectations for how others should behave toward those who occupy that role. An important source of role expectations is the *stereotype* of the role, which can be thought of as a kind of public consensus concerning role expectations. The dictionary definitions of selling quoted earlier reveal a kind of public stereotype of the social role of salesman. From research we know that both purchasing agents and salesmen are stereotyped as talkative, easygoing, competitive, optimistic, and excitable.[3]

In the sales interaction, communication is effective and the interaction personally pleasant and rewarding for the actors to the extent that they have common role expectations both for themselves and for the other person. Among the sources of role expectations for the salesman are the salesman's own perceptions of how he should perform his role, those he attributes to the prospect (i.e., how he thinks the prospect expects him to behave), the expectations he perceives to be held by his sales manager, and the expectations he perceives to be held by other people in his company with whom he must work, such as technical and production personnel. To the extent that conflicting

[2] Franklin B. Evans, "Selling as a Dyadic Relationship—A New Approach," *American Behavioral Scientist* 6 (May 1963): 76–79.

[3] Wayne K. Kirchner and Marvin D. Dunnette, "How Salesmen and Technical Men Differ in Describing Themselves," *Personnel Journal* 37 (April 1959): 418–419.

expectations for role performance for self or other are held by the salesman and the prospect, the sales interaction is ineffective and a source of tension and frustration. This fact places a premium on the salesman's ability to infer the buyer's expectations.

Finally, as we saw in Chapter 11, the selling company's reputation is an important source of role expectations ("source credibility") for the salesman.

This communication view of the selling process is obviously a much richer and more complicated view of the sales interaction than that offered by the salesmanship views. It tends to stress training and supervision as important management functions while decreasing the emphasis on the selection process. The nature of the training and supervisory implications will be developed later in this chapter.

THE FIELD SALES MANAGER

The first line of field sales management plays a critically important role in the firm's marketing activities and in the development of the field sales organization. People at this level of management typically are called district manager, area manager, or branch manager. They usually report to someone called Regional Manager. At the district level, the manager may have between 3 and 12 or so salesmen reporting to him, along with such staff personnel as an office manager, a credit manager, a sales administration (or order-processing) manager, and so on, depending on the nature of the operation. In larger districts, the salesmen may not report directly to the district manager but to a sales supervisor (or someone with a similar title), who in turn reports to the district manager.

Functions and responsibilities

As noted earlier, the field sales manager has two principal responsibilities—generating sales volume and developing an effective field sales organization. He is also responsible for controlling the costs of running his operation.

In somewhat more analytical terms, the field sales manager has five distinct functions to perform: (1) supervision, (2) developing sales personnel, (3) personal selling, (4) managing the local sales office, and (5) acting as a communication link.[4] Each of these will be discussed briefly.

Supervision is the most important function of the field sales manager because it is through directing and controlling the activities of

[4] K. R. Davis and F. E. Webster, Jr., *Sales Force Management* (New York: Ronald, 1968), pp. 55–64.

his salesmen that the sales manager implements his two responsibilities of generating sales volume and developing sales personnel. The supervisory task is made especially important by the unique nature of the selling job—the fact that the salesman often works alone, without the social support of other salesmen; the fact that he is exposed to frequent failure and rejection in the selling process; and the fact that the results of his activities often are not determined until weeks, months, or even years later. Keeping the salesmen enthusiastic, motivated, and well informed is a difficult and never-ending task.

Development of sales personnel is also an ongoing responsibility, which the field sales manager implements both through formal training activities and through more informal activities such as working with the salesmen in the field, counseling them about specific selling problems, and providing careful guidelines and objectives to direct the salesman and against which they can test themselves and develop their particular interests and abilities. An important part of this responsibility is the goal-setting process in which the manager encourages the salesman to set realistic goals that will help the salesman develop his abilities to the fullest while working toward the company's sales objectives. The trick is to make these goals a challenge but not unrealistic. In his formal training activities, the field sales manager usually needs guidance and specific programs that are designed at the corporate level, and he frequently also needs the benefit of a professional sales training expert on his own staff or at least available in his district from time to time.

The field sales manager's personal selling responsibility is the most controversial. On the one hand, it is often a necessary function because the sales office may be too small to support a full-time manager, and because important customers demand the attention and experience of someone of management rank. In many sales situations, the nature of the commitments that must be made in the name of the selling company is such that management level attention to the account is a necessity. On the other hand, selling activities often conflict with the management responsibilities of the field sales manager. To the extent that his time is devoted to selling, he has less time for developing sales personnel, for supervision, for managing the local office, and for serving as a communication link between the field salesmen and company management. Fulrthermore, the field sales manager's accounts are likely to be the largest and most important accounts in the district. When the manager controls these accounts, other salesmen are deprived of an earning opportunity and a professional challenge. If the salesmen are not capable of dealing with the best accounts, this reveals a basic weakness in the field sales management program.

The nature of the field sales manager's responsibility for managing the local office reflects the number of activities that have been assigned to district offices. Among the functions that may be performed at the local level are order processing, inventory management, customer service, credit and collection, sales training, and payroll administration. Obviously, the greater the number of functions performed locally, the larger the staff required and the more time required to administer the local office. As part of these responsibilities, the field sales manager may also be the representative of the company in the local community, charged with helping the company fulfill its citizenship responsibilities in such areas as charitable contributions, relationships with educational institutions, working to solve community problems such as unemployment and industrial development, and so on.

The field sales manager also serves as a communication link between the local sales organization and higher levels of management. In this connection, he is responsible for interpreting and enforcing company policy, for the implementation of various administrative procedures, and for the more subtle responsibilities of helping the field and management organizations understand one another. He must transfer information about customers, competition, and other market conditions up to the appropriate marketing decision centers. He must make sure that upper levels of sales management have good understanding of salesmen morale, opinions, and attitudes toward such important questions as sales compensation, company credit and service policies, and the reasons for changes in various marketing policies. At the same time, he must explain the reasons for management action to the salesmen and encourage their understanding and support. Like the production foreman, the field sales manager is often "the man in the middle," subject to pressures from both sides and responsible for harmonizing potentially conflicting perceptions and attitudes.

The "supersalesman" problem

It is unfortunately true that a large percentage of field sales managers are promoted to their positions because of their skills as salesmen. Selling prowess may have relatively little to do with management ability. Companies often find it necessary to promote their best salesmen to management positions in order to keep them in the company, perhaps because they want the status of the management title or perhaps because a management position is necessary to increase the man's compensation level because of limits on salesmen's compensation.

The company often loses a good salesman and gains a poor manager as a result. The manager is uncomfortable with his management responsibilities and unable to cope with the new demands on his knowledge, skills, and attitudes. In such circumstances, it is quite natural for him to spend more of his time selling, either to his own accounts or in the company of salesmen, and functioning as a kind of supersalesman. In the short run, this may be the best way for him to keep up the district's sales performance. But over the long run, total organizational effectiveness will suffer as other management responsibilities —especially supervising and developing sales personnel and planning— are ignored.

Abilities required

Ideally, of course, the new sales manager is chosen on the basis of a careful and objective appraisal of his potential capabilities as a manager. But it is too much to expect that these capabilities will be fully developed in a person who is new to the field sales management post. Rather, care must be taken to prepare the new manager for his responsibilities with training and other forms of preparation, as part of his earlier position (say, while he is a salesman), when he first assumes his field sales management responsibilities, and on a continuing basis afterwards.

Every management position requires a blend of skills, knowledge, and attitudes somewhat unique to that position. For the first-line field sales manager, the following abilities seem especially important: human relations and supervisory abilities, administrative ability, planning ability, analytical and decision-making ability, and selling ability.

Each of these abilities can be developed through experience and education. Each has both skill and knowledge components and also requires a particular set of attitudes for maximum effectiveness. To illustrate, supervisory ability requires interpersonal sensitivity as a skill and the ability to get along with others, and it is more effective if based on some sound knowledge of motivation, communication, and human perception. Furthermore, an effective supervisor must have a set of attitudes that includes respect for those supervised as well as strong identification with management and the responsibilities inherent in the supervisory post.

In this list of required abilities, selling ability is intentionally placed at the end. A field sales manager should have some selling experience because this will help earn the respect of his salesmen and will also ensure that he has full understanding of the problems his men are facing in the field. But in his actual management activities, the four other abilities will be more important determinants of his effectiveness.

THE SALES MANAGEMENT PROGRAM

The sales management program consists of the policies and strategic decisions guiding the sales organization at a given time. A sales plan, including the sales volume objective and other more specific objectives such as the development of particular markets and specific classes of customers, is an integral part of the sales program. In addition, the sales management program consists of policies and procedures relating to the recruitment, selection, training, organization, supervision, evaluation, and compensation of salesmen and their field sales managers. In the remainder of this chapter, we will briefly sketch the major management considerations in each of these areas.

Recruitment

Growth and turnover require the continual replenishment of the sales force. Programs for recruiting new salesmen should guide decision making at the local level and coordinate activities among districts and regions. A key input to the recruitment process is a good description of the selling job, one that makes a realistic appraisal of the requirements of the job and of the kind of person who can fill that job and be happy doing it. A frequent error is to overspecify the requirements for effectiveness in the job, requirements that are unrealistically high given the nature of the work and the level of compensation. Such over-specification can often be observed in newspaper advertisements that list desired characteristics in applicants—several years of experience, technical university degrees, and the like—followed by a very modest salary figure. The result can be to attract people who are overqualified for the job and will not be challenged by it or to scare away applicants who might be well qualified. Of course, the reverse error is also to be avoided—understating the job requirements and thereby attracting a large number of unqualified applicants.

A certain amount of centralized planning and decision making for sales force recruitment is likely to be required in any medium- to large-size sales organization. Local managers are often unable to plan and coordinate a recruitment program effectively, especially when colleges and universities provide a major source of sales manpower. Likewise, decision making at the local level is likely to produce a large amount of unevenness in programs and in results among districts. Finally, it is likely to be unreasonable to constrain recruitment to a given locality, because this limits the supply of qualified applicants. For the large national or multinational company, which is likely to transfer people frequently, it may in fact be preferable not to hire locally.

Selection

Recruitment policies should be designed to provide a stream of job applicants of adequate quality to ensure that qualified people can be found for all available positions. The selection process is the information gathering, information evaluation, and decision making required to screen applicants and choose among them.

The selection process must start with a clear specification of the characteristics desired in a salesman. These provide the criteria against which applicants are evaluated. Their consistent use among all involved in the selection process is an important determinant of the quality of decision making.

The selection process typically makes use of information from three sources: an application form, personal interviews, and psychological tests. None of these is likely to be adequate by itself, but each can make an important contribution. The application blank, despite its simplicity, can be an extremely useful device for making the selection process as efficient as possible. Careful use of the selection blank can help eliminate, early in the process, those who are clearly unqualified by reason of age, lack of experience, or lack of education, for example. It can also provide clues for important areas to be explored in the personal interviews, such as the reasons for frequent job changes, explanations of gaps in the employment record, or possible health problems.

The personal interview can be conducted either by individuals or by a group. Group interviews provide the advantage of multiple impressions and viewpoints based on the same information, but they can be somewhat overwhelming. In the interview, the objective should be to learn as much as possible about the applicant's interest in and qualification for the job. Other objectives, such as learning how the applicant performs under stress, are usually not appropriate and can lead to a kind of game playing that is neither necessary nor desirable. Group interviews have also been known to bring out some unpleasant tendencies in the interviewers, each of whom tries to impress his colleagues with the tough and clever questions he asks the applicants. Above all else, the interview should be guided by a clear set of decision criteria and information collection objectives to determine the applicant's job interests, abilities, and aspirations. Such specific guidelines can help avoid the natural tendency of the interviewer to prefer people with whom he personally establishes a good rapport. Whether or not the interviewer likes the applicant is of some importance, but it should not be the sole determinant of the outcome of the interview.

Use of psychological tests is one of sales management's most complicated and controversial problems. Attempts to make management decision making more scientific, as well as the desire to find an objective basis for selection, have encouraged heavy use of psychological testing, and there is no doubt that a good deal of such testing has been misdirected and misused. There are some irresponsible consultants and testing firms operating in this area as well, often making questionable claims about test accuracy, reliability, and validity.

Psychological tests are of four major types: intelligence tests, aptitude tests, interest tests, and personality tests. Intelligence tests attempt to measure an individual's overall ability to cope with intellectual tasks. Most frequently, they measure a combination of verbal and mathematical ability. In sales force management, they have probably been the most successfully used of the four types of tests, although serving primarily as an indication of a person's ability to benefit from a sales training program rather than as indicators of potential job success. They may serve as a rough screening device in the sales force selection process, but they do not have a major role to play because intellectual ability is not often the major determinant of sales success. Other information sources such as the interview and the scholastic record are probably adequate to identify any important deficiencies in intellectual ability.

Aptitude tests attempt to measure special abilities such as mechanical, clerical, musical, or artistic ability. In selling, they have not proved to have a large correlation with on-the-job performance, although some, such as the Canfield test "How Perfect Is Your Sales Sense?" consisting of fifty questions describing typical selling situations, have been fairly widely used, apparently with helpful results. On balance, however, sales aptitude tests have a checkered record of success, especially for higher-level sales jobs where there is low uniformity in the task and job performance is more difficult to measure.

Interest tests operate on the assumption that people in particular occupations tend to exhibit similar interests, often in areas that are not directly related to the occupation itself. For example, people in the same occupations often tend to have the same interests in sports, music, literature, social relationships, and so on. Some of the most popular tests, such as the Strong Vocational Interest Blank, have been used so widely that the data base on which the analysis can be based is very large indeed; this should improve both the reliability and the validity of such tests. The Strong test asks for the expression of likes and dislikes for a variety of activities, school subjects, and peculiarities of people, occupations, and amusements. The applicant's test profile is then compared with that of thousands of other people who have supposedly been successful in the selling profession. One of the major weaknesses of the interest tests is that they are easily "faked" by correct guessing of the answers that would be expected of a person applying for the job in question.

Personality tests attempt to measure the emotional, social, and motivational aspects of behavior. These dimensions can be especially important in determining the salesman's attitudes toward his work, his ability to persevere, and his ability to accept supervision and to form productive and supportive relationships with his manager and other salesmen. To some extent, emotional factors such as "ego drive" mentioned earlier can also determine the drive and ambition of the salesman and the rewards he will derive from the selling experience.

It is unfortunately true, however, that personality tests are among the most unreliable of all psychological tests. A major reason for this is that psychological theory relating to the area of personality is very weak and incomplete compared with other areas of psychology. There are many competing theories of personality development and structure, and the various personality characteristics supposedly measured by such tests are not easily defined. For example, some of the most popular personality tests claim to measure such traits as ascendancy, objectivity, dominance, introversion, neuroticism, deference, ardor, intraception, succorance, and so on, concepts about which there is substantial difference of opinion with respect to both what the characteristic actually is and what relevance it has for performance of the selling task. So, despite the potential relevance of personality measures for selecting salesmen, personality tests are likely to be least useful in the task.

The key issue in the use of a psychological test is whether it will predict reasonably well an applicant's success in the selling job. Because all selling jobs are not alike, measures of predictability should be developed for each company. Developing such measures ideally would require the company to give all applicants the test (or series of tests) to be validated and then to hire applicants irrespective of results on the test. When a sufficient number of candidates had been tested and their sales performance measured carefully over a reasonable period of time (probably a minimum of two years and hopefully longer), then discriminant analysis or other statistical techniques could be used to determine whether there was a useful correlation between test scores and sales performance. More commonly, however, companies rely on measures of correlation developed by the seller of the test based on experience with several companies. In such cases, the correlation data have meaning only if they have been developed for salesmen in specific selling tasks similar to those of the company in question.

Despite the difficulties involved in using psychological tests, the majority of firms employing salesmen in reasonably large numbers rely on them to some degree. The test should be viewed as only one of several sources of information to be used in the selection process and should not be the determining factor. As a general guideline, it is better to use test results as a basis for rejecting applicants rather than for selection. In other words, psychological tests should be used to screen out applicants, to eliminate them from further consideration because of evidence of lack of basic interest, aptitude, or ability. To use psychological tests as the basis for acceptance, requiring all applicants to fit a particular profile or set of interests and aptitudes, would result in hiring salesmen who were highly similar on the measured characteristics. This is an unwise pattern to follow, given the inherent weaknesses in psychological testing. As pointed out in our discussion of the differences between the traditional salesmanship school and the modern communication views of selling, there is more to the sales interaction than the salesman's characteristics and activities.

Training

There is a trade-off between selection and training in the sense that the more careful the selection process the less waste there will be in the training process. If the company plans to spend little time and money training salesmen, then those involved in the selection process must be much more careful to choose people with necessary experience and skills. Conversely, if the company uses relatively "easy" selection criteria, then more effort must be put into training those who are hired.

Under the communication view of the selling process, training must focus on listening and interactive skills as well as the traditional skills of selling. A new salesman needs training in all three areas of knowledge, attitudes, and skills. In the knowledge realm, knowledge of products, company, and markets are all of obvious importance, although there is sometimes a tendency to overstate the importance of product knowledge, especially in industrial companies selling technical products. Seldom, for example, is it necessary for the salesman to be able to actually make the product or take it apart and reassemble it, yet many sales training programs have required the new salesman to spend months or even years actually working in the factory learning such knowledge. (Of course, detailed product knowledge is important when the salesman also has a field service and repair function to perform). More important is knowledge concerning how to apply the product to specific customer problems.

Company knowledge involves knowing company organization, procedures, policies, and so on, especially as these relate to responding to customer needs and requests. The salesman must know how to place an order correctly and how to resolve such related questions as delivery, credit, and service. He must know how to bring all of the company's resources to bear on solving customer problems, and he must not "overpromise" in his relationships with customers.

The development of attitudes is a sensitive area and is better done by guideline and example rather than by dictating rules. In the matter of planning daily activities and organizing the call schedule, it is important that the salesman develop the habit of putting in a full workday and going about his activities in a carefully planned, efficient, and thorough manner. This training is best done by showing the salesman how careful planning can increase his effectiveness.

Skills in selling techniques can be developed in a variety of ways. Modern thought favors training by professional sales training personnel rather than the traditional "mother hen" approach of assigning a senior salesman to work with a trainee. There are three weaknesses in the mother hen approach. First, senior salesmen are often unable to articulate the reasons for their own effectiveness and follow a "watch what I do and do what I do" approach that leaves much doubt in the trainee's mind about what he should be watching and doing. Second, salesmen are not necessarily good teachers and usually lack the necessary training knowledge and skills. Third, many of the salesman's practices and habits may be unsuited to the new trainee and may even be bad examples. There is little uniformity or quality control in sales training through the mother hen approach.

Modern sales training practices focus on developing selling skills by exposing salesmen to a body of conceptual knowledge about the selling process and then providing simulated real-world experience through the use of role playing, videotape playback, and so on. These approaches get heavy trainee involvement in the training process and give him experience in the actual selling situation as well as some insight into the characteristics of his own behavior. Heightened sensitivity results from asking sales trainees to assume buying roles and by having them watch videotapes of their sales presentations.

In addition to the actual sales presentation, salesmen need to be trained on other parts of the sales call, including approaching the customer and identifying sales prospects, as well as techniques for overcoming prospect objections, actually asking for the order ("closing"), and follow-up procedures.

In evaluating any sales training program, it is important to consider who is actually doing the training and how the trainer was trained for his responsibilities. In addition to formal sales training activities involving professional training personnel, continuing training activities in the field should also be evaluated. The field sales manager should be prepared for and evaluated on this responsibility. Like other areas of company activity, the sales training program should be guided by carefully stated and communicated objectives. These goals should relate not only to the preparation of new salesmen for their responsibilities but also to the continual development and updating of experienced salesmen in such areas as new products, new company policies, and the latest selling techniques. Finally, programs for identification and development of management potential in the sales organization should also be carefully planned and periodically evaluated.

Organization

There are three broad categories of field sales organization: geographic, product, and customer organization. In practice, most sales organizations have a geographic structure within one of the other two—product or customer specialized organization, the choice of which is determined by customer and product characteristics and requirements. Two central issues in sales force organization are the levels and functions of field sales management and the relationship between line and staff activities.

The role played by the field sales manager is often poorly understood. This level of management is sometimes regarded as an expense to be avoided as long as possible. In such cases, salesmen report directly to the national sales manager, who usually has inadequate time to plan, supervise, and control the activities of his salesmen. As a result, they function relatively independently, without adequate guidance and with little relationship to the company's overall marketing program. Furthermore, they develop their abilities only to the extent that they are self-motivated to do so, which is seldom indeed.

Among well-managed companies, the field sales manager's dual responsibility for sales volume and sales organization development is well understood, and he is given adequate time and support to do his job effectively. He is regarded as an asset rather than an expense. As a general guideline, the field sales manager should have between 6 and 10 salesmen reporting to him. All of their activities should be directed by him, and all communications to them should go through him. He should be guided in his salesman relationships by clearly stated goals and policies that coordinate activities at the field sales management level.

For maximum effectiveness, the field sales manager needs appropriate staff support for such functions as sales force compensation, training, evaluation, and control. The flow of information and communications with the sales force should be coordinated centrally, especially where product managers are competing for the salesmen's time in the field. In most firms, a centrally managed market research function can provide more accurate and more complete market information to the local managers than they would be able to develop on their own. Likewise, advertising and sales promotion activities are usually more effectively and efficiently managed when they are planned and implemented by central staff, even when they must be specifically tailored to local market situations. The greater expertise of the staff specialist is often a more important consideration than the economic questions of avoiding duplication of effort, securing quantity discounts for purchase of media and promotional materials, and so on. Seldom is the field sales manager expert in such fields as advertising, market research, sales training, or sales force compensation.

Supervision

Earlier comments about the role of the field sales manager emphasized his supervisory responsibilities. At this stage we wish to emphasize, as part of the sales management program, some general guidelines for thinking about the supervisory task and some of the most important considerations in designing programs for ensuring that the field sales manager performs the supervisory task effectively.

Supervision is at once both the direction and control of salesmen and the continual development of their abilities. Salesmen will accept the field sales manager's attempts at directing and controlling their efforts only if they perceive that this will help them accomplish their own personal objectives. The essential ability of the leader is to make other people want to follow him in pursuit of their own interests. From this observation flows the logical conclusion that it is essential that the sales manager know his men, their needs, attitudes, aspirations, and perceptions, and that he know them both as individuals and as a group, since the salesmen influence one another in important ways, especially in the formation of attitudes and perceptions.

Just as it is useful to train salesmen, through both conceptual knowledge and exposure to actual selling situations, to interpret and respond to customer needs, so in sales manager training it is important that conceptual knowledge about motivation and supervision be developed as the basis for understanding salesmen's motives and behavior. Likewise, supervisory practices must be tailored to the needs of the individual salesman just as selling approaches must be tailored to individual customers. The skilled supervisor knows how to use the three basic forms of influence—use of authority, use of knowledge, and use of persuasion—flexibly and combines them in a supervisory blend best suited to the needs of the situation. He issues orders and applies sanctions (authority), explains the reasons for policy and the need for action (persuasion), and helps the salesman plan his activities and work with specific customers (knowledge) in such a manner that the proper degree of dependence-independence is developed in his relationship with each salesman, again depending on the latter's needs.

Evaluation

Evaluation is necessary for three reasons—to measure performance against planned sales and marketing objectives, to distribute rewards for performance, and to guide the development of the individual salesman. By definition, evaluation involves the use of targets for performance, criteria against which to compare actual accomplishment. Among the most important criteria are sales quotas (both for sales volume and for specific activities such as new-account development), expense control, and personal-development objectives. A continuous flow of current, complete, and accurate information about sales force performance and sales volume accomplishment is necessary to keep the sales organization "in control" and directed toward coordinating objectives.

It is important that all evaluation be forward-looking and oriented toward the future and improved performance, rather than backward-looking and oriented toward finding fault and placing blame. Some backward-looking is necessary, of course, to determine equitable distribution of the rewards of goal attainment. But the basic orientation should be forward, positive, and concerned with the development of the business and the individual.

In evaluating sales force performance, it is often tempting to compare salesmen and sales districts with one another, ranking them on such measures as sales as a percentage of quota, total sales volume, and so on. Such comparisons can stimulate the basic competitive sense of the salesmen and managers involved, but there is danger that such comparisons can be overdone and can become quite negative in character. Many variables—including accuracy of the forecasting and quota-setting process, differences in competitive activity, quality of supervision, and product and pricing strategies—determine a given salesman's performance; such variables affect his current performance compared with that of another salesman. When comparisons are made, the standards used should be the most equitable and objective that are available.

In some cases, it makes more sense to evaluate salesmen on the basis of effort rather than sales results. This is especially true where there is a long time lag between effort and actual sales results and where many factors beyond the control of the salesman determine the final outcome. Measures of activity include number of calls, number of new accounts, calls per day, and the care with which selling activity has been planned and reported.

When poor performance is indicated by evaluation measures, it is important to develop a thorough understanding of the reasons for poor performance and to avoid the tendency to jump to the conclusion that the salesman is to blame for failure to accomplish preset objectives. Especially important is consideration of the quality of the supervision he has been given, the extent to which he has been properly trained, and changes in competitive conditions in the markets he serves. In any discussion of individual performance, the sales manager must be thoroughly prepared to understand these variables because the salesman will bring up many factors to explain why he has failed to reach his quota.

Compensation

The sales compensation program must be designed with several requirements in mind. The objectives of a compensation program should be:

1. to attract and retain qualified salesmen
2. to reward effort and accomplishment fairly
3. to stimulate the highest possible level of effective selling activity
4. to attain particular selling objectives such as development of new accounts and introduction of new products
5. to encourage the most complete response to customer needs through provision of service and complete performance of the salesman's responsibilities
6. to control selling expense

The typical sales compensation plan has both fixed and variable components, although a few companies use either a straight salary or a fully variable commission system. In "mixed" plans, it is common to have the major portion paid by salary (roughly 65 to 90 percent of total), with the variable portion being primarily commission payments as a percentage of sales volume (perhaps 10 to 30 percent of total compensation), and some smaller portion (say, 5 to 10 percent) paid in the form of a bonus tied to specific accomplishments other than the salesman's individual sales volume, such as total district sales or company profitability.

When the salesman operates pretty much as an independent agent and is not expected to perform any functions other than selling, these conditions favor the use of variable compensation; under such circumstances the salesman is responsible only for selling and is paid only if he produces sales results. Sales agents, brokers, and other agent middlemen are often compensated on this basis.

For most companies, however, straight commission plans are not consistent with other objectives and with the nature of the salesman's responsibilities. A fixed salary compensation is the best arrangement in the following cases: when the salesman's efforts do not produce immediate sales results; when he is responsible for non-selling activities; or when he shares responsibility for sales results with other people, such as applications engineers.

Related to the question of whether to use fixed or variable compensation is the question of whether to reward effort or results. Once again, the main points of analysis are whether the salesman is responsible for more than sales volume and whether there is a clear and direct relationship between effort now and results now. When this relationship is weak, effort is a more important measure of effectiveness and should be more carefully measured and rewarded. When results reflect effort by many people over extended periods rather than the salesman's immediate efforts, rewarding results can result in windfall compensation for the salesman as well as long periods when income is inadequate for the salesman's personal needs. As a general rule, the more variable the sales patterns (seasonal and cyclical) are, the more desirable a heavy fixed compensation element is.

There has been much pointless debate on the question of whether money or something else is the most important motivator of salesmen. It is probably fair to generalize that salesmen as an occupational group are somewhat more interested in monetary rewards than many other occupations, but that certainly doesn't mean money is their only interest. Given the nature of the salesman's work, his isolation from other company employees, and the frequent absence of immediate rewards in the sales interaction, salesmen probably have an above-average need for intangible rewards such as the pat on the back for a job well done and words of encouragement from an understanding manager. Recognition for unique accomplishments in the form of certificates, plaques, and prizes of various kinds can also be effective because they appeal to the salesman's basic competitive instinct. In any sales contest it should be possible for many if not all salesmen to win prizes and recognition if they accomplish a stated objective. To make one salesman compete with all the rest for one or a few prizes is not entirely healthy.

A compensation plan is so basically important and sensitive a device in the sales management program that it should be designed with special care. Sound research on salesmen activities, interests, and effectiveness, on market conditions, and on company marketing programs and objectives should be the starting point for the redesign of a compensation program. This is one area in which an outside specialist can be especially helpful.

As a general guideline, there are seven stages in the development of the compensation plan:

1. *Defining the sales job. Determining what it is salesmen should do and be paid for.*
2. *Establishing compensation objectives. In relationship to the nature of the selling job and the company's marketing objectives.*
3. *Determining the level of pay. Determining how much the salesman should be paid, as indicated by the nature of the work, competitive labor market conditions, years of experience, and so on.*
4. *Determining the compensation method. The relative proportions of fixed and variable compensation, as determined by the nature of the salesman's responsibilities.*
5. *Testing the compensation plan. First with paper-and-pencil to determine financial and economic consequences of different assumptions about sales volume, sales force size, etc., and then in the field to determine the reactions of salesmen and their managers.*
6. *Implementing the plan. Explaining the reasons for changes and dealing with questions and objections on this sensitive question; it is absolutely essential that salesmen be involved in the design of the compensation plan and that they be informed about changes long before they become effective.*
7. *Administering the plan. Including all the procedural detail necessary to make a plan work smoothly and to keep it up-to-date with changing market conditions; careful attention to administrative requirements should be part of the planning of the compensation program.*[5]

Integrating sales program elements

As in other areas of marketing programing, the development of an effective sales program requires careful consideration of interactions among program elements and their skillful blending to achieve a

---

[5] F. E. Webster, Jr., "Rationalizing Salesmen's Compensation Plans," *Journal of Marketing* 30 (January 1966): 55–58.

synergistic result. So far we have considered primarily the elements of the program having to do with the administration of the sales organization. To integrate the sales program into the marketing program and blend the two together in an ongoing program for effective implementation of marketing strategy, the following steps are required:

1. Determine the role of personal selling in the marketing mix, as explained in Chapter 11.
2. Analyze customer buying patterns as the basis for developing key account strategies and training salesmen to develop effective sales presentations.
3. Measure the market as carefully as possible and allocate selling effort accordingly, using quotas and other standards of sales performance.
4. Build an effective sales organization.
5. Administer the ongoing sales organization.
6. Evaluate and control the sales management program's effectiveness.

The logical relationship among these elements, suggested in Figure 13–1, is self-explanatory.

THE CAREER PATH CONCEPT

A major problem in most sales organizations is to plan the development of sales force management talent. As explained earlier, there is a tendency to use sales management positions as rewards for successful selling accomplishments. A related problem is how to motivate and reward the senior salesman who has reached the top of the pay scale or has lost interest in his selling assignment.

To cope with these problems, some forward-looking companies have adopted the "career path" concept in their sales organizations. There are several essential features to this approach. First, salesmen are systematically evaluated and counseled by their managers at frequent time intervals, quarterly, semiannually, or at least annually. In these sessions, past performance on a variety of indicators is discussed, such as total sales, number of new accounts, lost business, information reporting, performance against quota, and so on. In addition, the salesman's personal development and objectives are discussed—his use of company training aids, attendance at outside seminars, studies of particular products or markets, and so on. These counseling sessions should follow a "management by objectives" format in which the salesman is encouraged to set specific objectives both for his own development and for business accomplishment. Then these objectives become the basis for evaluation at the next session.

A second feature of this career path concept is a clear distinction between selling and management potential. Soon after the salesman has settled into his job—say, at the end of two years—an initial evaluation is made of the extent to which he may have interest and ability

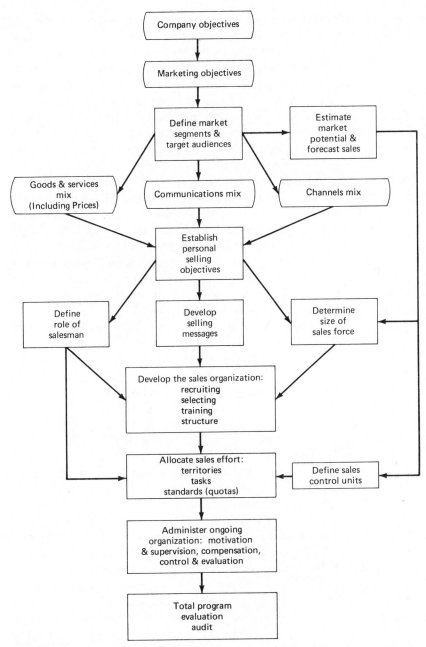

FIGURE 13-1
The sales management program.

in the management area. If the potential is there, the company can begin to test this interest and to develop the necessary abilities through special projects such as market analyses, working with more junior salesmen, and so on. By the end of another two to three years at the most, the salesman is moved into a position of management responsibility such as a sales supervisory post reporting to the district manager.

A third feature of the career path concept is a clear recognition of the value and importance of the professional salesman. The career path for the professional salesman includes promotion through the position of sales representative to account management responsibilities. The account manager is responsible for one or a few major large accounts; he performs a variety of consulting and service functions, perhaps at several levels of the customer's organization, up to and including top management, as well as the more traditional responsibility for sales volume with that account. Higher compensation levels for account managers are an important part of the total scheme of the career path, making it possible to retain and reward senior salespeople fairly and avoiding the necessity of putting them into management posts for which they do not have adequate interest and ability.

A fourth feature of the career path concept is an "up or out" rule at lower levels of the sales organization. The major reason for this rule is to avoid blocking the career path for junior people and thus to reduce turnover among qualified younger people. Through the sales representative and sales supervisor ranks, it is required that the man be promotable to higher-level account manager or district manager posts. If he has neither professional sales career potential nor management potential, then he must be removed from the organization. As hard-nosed as this rule sounds, it clearly makes good sense for the long-term health and viability of the organization.

A final feature of these plans in many cases is the provision of at least two levels of performance and compensation within each job. Thus, the progression through the organization might be as depicted in Figure 13–2: from sales trainee through two levels of sales representative to two levels of sales supervisor and two or more levels of account manager. The responsibilities of levels I and II would be substantially the same, but the level designation would indicate a higher level of accomplishment and a higher level of compensation.

Obviously, initial judgments as to a salesman's long-term interest and potential for professional management or professional selling responsibilities might be in error. Initial supervisory experience, for example, might convince the young man that he is more interested in and better qualified for major selling responsibilities. Thus, at the sales supervisor levels it is possible to transfer into account manager responsibilities, and vice versa. At higher levels of the organization, however, this is no longer possible. Thus, it would not normally be permitted for an account representative at level II to move into a supervisory post, nor for a district manager to move into an account representative position.

There are a number of advantages to the career path approach. Perhaps most important, it ensures the orderly development of manage-

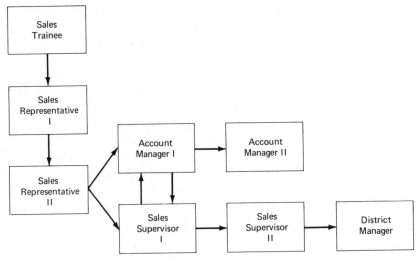

FIGURE 13-2
An illustration of the sales career path concept.

ment capabilities within the organization. It also ensures that the individual salesman's personal development is carefully planned and monitored. Bottlenecks created by unpromotable people in the lower levels of the management hierarchy are avoided. Furthermore, the development of the individual salesman is managed in a more systematic fashion and becomes somewhat independent of the interests and characteristics of his manager at a given time. This avoids the serious problem created when district managers are changing fairly rapidly while the salesman is left behind to shift for himself in terms of personal development. Finally, it makes the firm more likely to keep its most qualified young people, those who can see clearly a career path of enlarged opportunities. In the absence of such programs, the best people, those with the most ability and ambition, are the ones who will be most quickly discouraged by lack of personal development, lack of opportunities, and the obvious existence of people at lower management levels who cannot be promoted further.[6]

SUMMARY

Sales force management is an important management function that has often received inadequate attention in the total marketing mix.

[6] For a more complete description of the sales career path concept based on the experiences of several large companies, see A. E. Pearson, "Sales Power Through Planned Careers," *Harvard Business Review* 44 (January–February 1966): 105–116.

The development of effective sales manpower, although a long-term affair that can easily be undervalued because it doesn't produce immediate sales results, is as important as long-term product development strategy in determining the success of the business in the marketplace. Guided by a communication view of the selling process, with its emphasis on an active role for the buyer in the sales interaction, the development of sales manpower should be carefully planned and should make use of training techniques that emphasize behavioral concepts, active involvement of the trainee, and feedback on actual selling situation performance. The sales management program must be developed and monitored at the highest levels of the organization, with special attention devoted to the development of management competence at the field sales manager level.

MULTINATIONAL MARKETING

A large portion of the world's economic activity is managed by companies doing business in several countries. The larger the firm, the more likely it is to have multinational operations; but size is not a prerequisite for successful multinational marketing. Because of the relatively small size of their home markets, European manufacturers seldom confine their marketing within national borders. With about one-third of the world's gross national product, the United States is a very attractive market for consumer and industrial goods from other parts of the world. At the same time, the U.S. market has spawned many of the world's largest corporations now doing business on a multinational basis—familiar names like General Motors, Ford Motor, IBM, Eastman Kodak, E. I. Du Pont de Nemours, General Electric, ITT, Union Carbide, Caterpillar Tractor, and Colgate-Palmolive.

HOW IS IT DIFFERENT?

Is multinational marketing really different from plain old domestic marketing? Yes and no. It is different in that it is more complex and there is a greater degree of uncertainty as a result. Predictions of response to marketing strategy and tactics are likely to be more difficult for several reasons:

1. Doing business in several countries and many different languages means that the important cultural base can no longer be taken for granted as it is in domestic marketing.
2. Detailed and accurate market information is usually harder to come by when the company moves outside of its home markets.
3. Physical distances complicate channels of communication and systems of managerial control.
4. Monetary matters now become a problem for specific managerial decision making; getting paid for a transaction is often not a routine affair.
5. The nature of relationships with dealers and salesmen is likely to be quite different than it is in home markets.

Further complexities result from such political, institutional, and governmental factors as tariffs, trade barriers and quotas of various kinds, and the current state of national and international politics. So multinational marketing is, in its specific details, a unique and complicated problem because of two sets of factors: (1) the different market structures encountered in each country and (2) the nation-to-nation political-economic interface across borders.

But marketing principles remain the same regardless of market context. Notice that the major sources of complexity and uncertainty in multinational marketing are primarily cultural, social, and governmental, and that these factors are likely to be unique to each national market setting. The only way for a manager to develop a really sound and useful understanding of these factors is to actually work and live in the situation. The more experience he accumulates in many different market settings, the more quickly he should be able to learn when placed in a new one.

Multinational marketing calls for the same analytical, conceptual, and planning approaches as do other forms of marketing. As a management profession and body of knowledge, multinational marketing is not significantly different from domestic marketing. So the training of a multinational marketing manager should likewise concentrate on the basic concepts and analytical disciplines of marketing. These concepts and analytical approaches provide the intellectual tools with which the marketing manager will be able to learn from his accumulated multinational experience.

With the growing importance of multinational operations, however, a marketing manager's education and training is incomplete without some attention to the international dimension.[1] In business

---

[1] Some authorities make a distinction between *inter*national marketing, meaning an exchange of goods between countries and *multi*national marketing, meaning marketing in more than one country. Although I prefer the latter meaning, I shall use the two words more or less synonymously.

schools and management development programs, this exposure can be achieved in part through the use of case studies calling for the application of analytical skills in a variety of different national and international settings. In company operations, it can be achieved by keeping all members of the management team informed of the company's multinational activities and problems as part of their training and by exposing the most qualified to multinational assignments.

The purpose of these introductory comments is to "demystify" the subject of multinational marketing so that in this chapter we can concentrate on the central issues in managing multinational marketing operations: how to tailor marketing strategies to local conditions and how to achieve coordination among marketing activities in several nations while preserving local autonomy and the ability to respond to the unique opportunities and requirements of each market.

STAGES IN EVOLUTION OF MULTINATIONAL MARKETING

A fairly typical evolution of multinational marketing begins with export marketing and ends with a multinational corporate strategy encompassing production and marketing operations throughout the world. Several different views of this evolutionary process have been developed. We will consider two: the notion of an international-trade life cycle and the so-called EPRG framework.

The international-trade life cycle

According to this view,[2] international trade progresses through a series of stages, from initial export from a single country through to a final stage, in which import competition reappears in the original country. These four stages are:

1. Home country exports new products.
2. Foreign production is begun by home country companies on foreign soil and by foreign companies.
3. Foreign production becomes competitive in other export markets.
4. Import competition appears from foreign producers exporting into the home country.

The electronics industry in the United States, for example, has witnessed this cycle of events as technology, for both industrial and consumer products, has successively been developed in the United States and exported, then produced abroad—usually to exploit favor-

[2] Developed by L. T. Wells, Jr., "A Product Life Cycle for International Trade," *Journal of Marketing* 32 (July 1968): 1–6.

able local labor conditions or develop a favorable local market situation —then exported into other foreign markets from foreign production, and then copied by foreign competitors who become importers into the United States, where, more often than not, they compete on a price basis.

This cycle can begin either because the home country producer aggressively seeks new foreign markets or because overseas buyers or sales agents seek out the company and its products. Referring back to the product life cycle concept developed in Chapter 8, it will be recalled that this concept describes a sequence of stages in the develop-ment of a market for a product. Obviously, the product life cycle begins anew when a product enters a new market, in this case a foreign one. Therefore, one way to extend a product's overall life cycle is to introduce it into a series of foreign markets, thus achieving the greater profitability that usually accompanies products in the introductory and growth stages of the product life cycle. This is a major reason why manufacturers begin to seek out export markets where they encounter little or no competition. Such markets offer a kind of "technological monopoly," as the home market did when the product was new there. Many companies have become aware of such opportunities only when they have been approached by potential customers or agents in foreign markets.

The international-trade life cycle concept has the product life cycle concept imbedded in it both as a force leading to export marketing and as the basic conceptual model for the international-trade life cycle itself. In the latter role, the model is applied to the case where the "product" is not a single manufacturer's product but rather a class of products such as bicycles, automobiles, or color televisions, and the decision maker is not a single firm but an entire industry. As an analytical concept, the international-trade life cycle provides a means for understanding some of the forces shaping world markets over time.

The EPRG framework

According to this view,[3] companies pass through four stages, labeled ethnocentrism, polycentrism, regiocentrism, and geocentrism, represent-ing increasing degrees of internationalization. Marketing strategies are modified accordingly.

In the *ethnocentric* stage, the company is oriented toward its home market and export markets receive secondary consideration. Foreign markets are viewed mainly as a means of disposing of excess produc-

---

[3] Developed originally by Howard Perlmutter and applied to the development of marketing strategy by Y. Wind, S. P. Douglas, and H. V. Perlmutter in "Guide-lines for Developing International Marketing Strategies," *Journal of Marketing* 37 (April 1973): 14–23.

tion. It is essentially a selling-oriented, rather than marketing-oriented, viewpoint. Business is conducted through an export department composed mostly of home country nationals. There is very little about the ethnocentric firm that is "international" in any real sense. Ethnocentric marketing relies heavily on sales agents; if company marketing personnel are used in foreign markets, they are more likely to be home country, as opposed to host country, nationals. Market research in foreign markets is likely to be minimal or nonexistent, and marketing decisions for foreign markets are likely to be copies of domestic marketing decisions modified only slightly to reflect local conditions. For example, advertisements may be merely translations of advertising used in the home market.

As the business grows into a *polycentric* stage, it establishes subsidiary companies in foreign markets. It is this stage that characterizes the operations of most multinational companies. In the polycentric stage, subsidiaries operate relatively independently and develop their own marketing plans and programs. Most marketing personnel are nationals of the host country, and product, pricing, distribution, and promotional variables are all influenced mainly by local market conditions and traditional practice. Product lines may be highly specialized to each market. The polycentric stage may result from the acquisition of strong local companies or from a conscious decision to minimize home country influence when establishing operations *de novo* in foreign countries.

A *regiocentric* stage comes as the firm attempts to achieve regional coordination and to break from the confines of national boundaries, nationalistic traditions, and suboptimal decision-making units. The regions might be largely defined by continents, with some variations such as combining North Africa and Southern Europe into a single region. Product lines and marketing policies are then developed and coordinated on a regional basis.

Ultimately, the firm (in this ideal conceptualization) will move from regiocentricism to a *geocentric* orientation, which is global or worldwide. With this orientation, the firm would be influenced only minimally by nationalistic considerations. It would follow the policy of "the best man for the job, irrespective of nationality," for example, and would be guided by worldwide corporate and marketing strategies. Given the strong worldwide trend toward nationalism, geocentrism is still an ideal concept for most companies. Even regiocentrism (which is really only an interim stage between polycentrism and geocentrism) is hard to achieve when such regional concepts as the European Economic Community, the Latin American Free Trade Area, and the European Free Trade Area are having difficulty moving beyond traditional definitions of national trading positions and prerogatives.

The popularity of the polycentric orientation will be better understood after we have examined the decisions required in developing multinational marketing operations and the problems involved in balancing local autonomy with an overall marketing strategy and planning system.

DEVELOPING MULTINATIONAL MARKETING OPERATIONS

In developing its foreign operations, a company has a series of decisions to make, including which markets to enter, how to enter them, the marketing mix to use in each country, and how to organize its multinational marketing operations. This section will develop the principal considerations in the first three decision areas; the fourth will be developed in the next section, which discusses the relationships between local decision-making autonomy and multinational strategic planning in a centralized marketing department.

Selecting markets

The factors to consider in selecting foreign markets to enter are similar for both domestic and international market entry decisions and include market potential, rate of growth, availability of distribution, consumer preferences and buying habits, the state of competition, and the business environment. The problem is still one of matching company resources to available market opportunities. Appraisal of foreign markets is often more difficult, however, because the analyst is limited by his domestic marketing experience and cultural bias and is unable to understand subtle but major differences in shopping habits, product usage patterns, and tastes. Such factors are especially important in appraising markets for food products, personal-hygiene products, and household items. To illustrate the surprises in store for the analyst who assumes that one country is like another, the following examples have been reported in various studies:

- *Germans and Frenchmen actually eat more spaghetti than Italians.*
- *The average Frenchman uses twice as many cosmetics and beauty aids as does his wife.*
- *Wholesalers in France will not promote a product aggressively whereas German wholesalers will. German wholesalers are quite powerful and well-organized, offering efficient access to small retailers. Italian wholesalers are said to be aggressive but not well organized.*[4]

   Stage of economic development and rate of economic growth are important factors in appraising national market potentials and fore-

---

[4] P. Kotler, *Marketing Management: Analysis, Planning, and Control,* rev. ed. (Englewood Cliffs, N.J.: Prentice-Hall, 1972), pp. 848–849.

casting sales. Consumer incomes determine spending power, but stage of economic development is not always correlated with demand for a firm's products. For purposes of discussion, we can define four stages of economic development:

Subsistence economies—the country exists almost entirely on simple agriculture, and there is little economic activity with few people in the market economy.

Raw-material exporting economies—countries exporting oil, metals, rubber, and other raw materials, industries that provide some employment but concentrate wealth in the hands of a few, with ownership often in the hands of foreigners.

Developing economies—countries enjoying some industrial expansion and economic growth, with improving standards of living and a developing middle class relying to some extent on imports.

Industrial economies—more-or-less self-supporting economies, growing at modest rates, with the highest standards of living, and a strong middle class, and heavily involved in foreign trade both as importer and exporter.

In the subsistence economies consumer demand is almost nonexistent, and industrial demand is limited primarily to agricultural products and areas where the government has money to spend, such as health-related products. The raw-material exporting economy may have a small but very wealthy upper class that is an attractive market for luxury products and consumer durables. More important, such economies offer major markets for mining and construction equipment and various other goods and services (such as petroleum and rubber products, shipping, and passenger air travel) needed to support the mining and extractive industries and their personnel. The increased economic activity involved in exploiting natural resources also helps support other parts of the economy such as agriculture, and there may be growing demand for farm tools, implements, tractors, and fertilizers.

The developing economies often represent major market opportunities, even better than the industrial economies, for products that appeal to consumers who have some discretionary income for the first time. Examples of such products are certain small appliances, including radios and small kitchen appliances, bicycles and motor scooters, and the least expensive makes of automobiles. But for most manufacturers it remains true that the industrial countries with their disproportionately high purchasing power are the major market opportunities.

Several statistical techniques such as regression analysis, time-series analysis, and development of multiple factor indexes are available to help the international marketer appraise alternative markets for entry. These techniques can be used to forecast market growth for particular products. Such analysis can also help in determining the combination of conditions that are most favorable to a given firm by investigating the pattern of past successes and failures and matching this against new opportunities.[5]

Of course, political and governmental factors cannot be overlooked in appraising national markets, including the stability of the local political situation (as the necessary basis for stable economic growth) and the current state of home-country–host-country relations. The impact of this dimension in defining market opportunities can be seen currently in the tremendous increase in American firms seeking markets in the Soviet Union and other Eastern European countries as a result of the recent dramatic change in political relationships. To a lesser extent but for similar reasons, Mainland China is also becoming an attractive market, albeit with limited purchasing power, for some American firms, and even more so for Japanese firms. Likewise, developments within international trade associations such as the European Economic Community concerning tariffs and quotas can rapidly change the pattern of opportunities facing the multinational marketer.

Method of entry

Marketing considerations must be integrated with financial, legal, and manufacturing considerations in selecting the method by which the firm will do business in a foreign market. The choices are as follows:

1. *Export*—selling products manufactured elsewhere, usually through a local agent. A variety of agents is usually available, or the company may elect to deal directly with foreign customers. In the latter case, a company manager or salesman will probably visit these customers from time to time.
2. *Joint venture*—doing business through a local business under some form of contractual agreement such as:
   a. *Licensing* a local producer to manufacture and sell the company's products. The license may cover a manufacturing process, product design, trademark, patent, or something else of value. The licensor thus has few start-up costs in entering a market while the licensee gains a valued product, name, or production expertise.
   b. *Contract manufacturing* establishes local production but the firm remains responsible for marketing, a strategy followed by Sears-Roebuck, for example.
   c. *Management contracting* is a method for transferring the company's management knowhow, which may be the critical resource, into a new market through a local company which retains responsibility for both manufacturing and marketing, a method used by Hilton Hotels, for example.
   d. *Joint-ownership* means becoming a partner in a local business either established or new. It has the merit of combining the firm's business knowhow with the local partner's knowledge of local conditions.

[5] R. J. Moyer, "International Market Analysis," *Journal of Marketing Research* 5 (November 1968): 353–360.

It is becoming more popular as governments develop stronger regulations against foreign ownership.
3. *Direct investment*—either acquiring a local business or setting up an entirely new operation completely owned by the firm (or at least it owns a controlling interest). With direct investment come all the problems, profit opportunities, and responsibilities of complete control. Some governments are encouraging foreign direct investment as a means of stimulating economic growth whereas others are discouraging it because it puts control of productive resources in the hands of foreign nationals.[6]

There are therefore many ways in which a firm can enter foreign markets. Truly multinational marketing comes about as the firm goes beyond simple export and an occasional joint venture and establishes direct investments in several countries, either in the form of subsidiaries manufacturing and marketing locally or sales subsidiaries controlled from headquarters. Under these circumstances, the need for a multinational marketing strategy emerges.

Marketing mix: strategic options

The firm doing business multinationally has a choice of five different strategic alternatives in its approach to different markets, according to a view put forth by W. J. Keegan. In this framework, marketing strategies are divided into two parts—the product and services mix and the communications mix. Keegan's five strategic alternatives are:

1. Straight extension. *Offering the same product with the same communications in all markets. This strategy assumes that the product benefits realized by customers are the same in all markets. Coca-Cola has been offered as an example of a straight extension strategy.*
2. Communications adaptation. *Offering the same product with different communications, a strategy which recognizes that the same product may offer different benefits in different markets, or that different markets have unique communication requirements due to tastes, taboos, etc. An example of communications adaptation is the small garden or lawn tractor sold in the U.S. which is sold as a farm implement in developing countries.*
3. Product adaptation. *Offering different products in different markets but with essentially the same communications. This strategic option recognizes different tastes or usage requirements but implies that product benefits remain the same. For example, Hershey has developed a chocolate bar for the Canadian market that is somewhat more bitter than its U.S. product.*
4. Dual adaptation. *Modifying both products and communications to fit local market requirements. For example, a given brand of automobile must be modified to meet local regulations in each country for such things as headlights and exhaust controls as well as to meet local*

[6] Kotler, op. cit., pp. 855–861.

driving and road conditions. Likewise, communications may be quite different; a car may be offered as a luxury product in one market (e.g., Volvo in Switzerland) and as a practical vehicle in another market (e.g., Volvo in the U.S.).

5. Product invention. *Developing an entirely new product to meet local requirements, a strategy also requiring new communications. Examples include development of a hand-powered washing machine for underdeveloped countries and development of very simple utilitarian automobiles for Asian markets.*[7]

In appraising these five strategic options, the marketing decision maker must begin his analysis by considering the structure of each market, especially buyer preferences, habits, and needs, and the conditions under which the product will be used, as part of a total product use and consumption system involving other products and services, social structures, and so on. Next the product itself must be analyzed in terms of benefits to be delivered and strengths and weaknesses compared to competing and substitute products. Finally, the costs of modifying products and communications must be compared with the benefits that might accrue from a more precise meeting of local requirements. Or, stated the other way around, the cost economies of standardized marketing must be compared with the reduced marketing effectiveness that may result from a failure to adjust marketing strategy to local conditions.

A straight extension strategy offers certain cost savings as well as the chance to exploit a strong marketing idea, such as the youthful image and styling of "Levis" jeans and the Avis Rent-A-Car "We try harder" campaign. But usually there is also some decrease in marketing effectiveness, although the straight extension strategy may still be the most profitable option. Changing products to meet local use conditions or communications to meet local tastes and needs involves increased marketing costs that are, hopefully, more than offset by increased revenues due to improved competitive effectiveness. The route to improved profitability is determined by both the nature of the product and of the market served. Each situation requires its own cost-benefit analysis.

MULTINATIONAL STRATEGY VERSUS LOCAL AUTONOMY

The overriding issue in the management of multinational marketing activities is that of how to balance the benefits of a true multinational marketing strategy against the strengths of local decision-making

---

[7] W. J. Keegan, "Five Strategies for Multinational Marketing," *European Business*, no. 24 (January 1970): 35–40.

autonomy. Both are desirable, but they often conflict. Most multinational companies have tried to maintain local autonomy through independent local subsidiaries while installing some kind of multinational superstructure to achieve necessary consistency and coordination.

Marketing in ITT-Europe

ITT-Europe, for example, consists of about 120 separate companies in a broad range of industrial and consumer products and services. One of ITT-Europe's goals is to increase profits by 12 to 15 percent per year. In 1972, ITT-Europe generated almost half of ITT's worldwide sales of $9 billion.

Before 1968, there was no marketing department. Most local companies had sales managers and/or product managers, but few had marketing managers. In 1969, a marketing group was formed at corporate headquarters in Brussels with the major objective of encouraging the development of marketing competence in the subsidiary companies in order to ensure continued growth in sales and profits. In the words of Hans Bryers, the Dutch-born marketing director of ITT-Europe who was responsible for this development,

We began by evaluating the marketing competence in subsidiary companies. Then we developed a "fire brigade" of experts to solve specific problems for the local companies. The fire brigade gets called in to put out a fire and while we are there we install a sprinkler system.

At ITT-Europe a complex reporting system monitors local company performance on a monthly basis; the corporate marketing director reviews these reports carefully to identify possible problems as they are developing. Mr. Bryers has found that the best barometer for this purpose is "order intake by month by product for each company compared to budget and trend." The local marketing director reports to the managing director of the subsidiary, who in turn reports to a group general manager who reports to the president of ITT-Europe. There is also a group marketing director to whom the company marketing director reports on a "dotted line" basis. Bryers has explained:

When we identify a problem, a hole developing in sales, we go to the Marketing Director and say "You have a problem, let's do something about it." Sometimes, we have to take the initiative in going into a company. We like to think of ourselves as consultants from headquarters who give advice but because we represent top management of ITT-Europe, that advice carries considerable weight.

The ITT-Europe headquarters marketing organization is prepared to offer guidance in all areas of marketing management, including market research, new-product planning, market planning, advertising and sales promotion, field selling, distribution and warehousing, sales administration, and customer service. The ITT-Europe example is an illustration of one company's attempt to develop coordinated multinational marketing activities while preserving local autonomy.

Benefits of local autonomy

Arguments in favor of preserving strong local management and decision-making autonomy are undoubtedly familiar to the reader, so this review can be brief. For multinational marketing they include:

1. the need to conform to local, legal, and governmental constraints such as product standards, pricing restrictions, and the like
2. the incentive value to local management of freedom of action
3. the knowledge of local markets, buyer behavior, and competitive conditions, permitting more sensitive and better-informed decisions
4. the flexibility to respond to changing local conditions

Arguments in favor of strong local marketing management often take the form of arguments against a standardized international marketing strategy, usually based on the uniqueness of the local market conditions. These are well presented by Professor Buzzell in the summary shown in Table 14–1.

Advantages of multinational standardization

But Buzzell has also identified some important benefits to be derived from standardization of multinational marketing strategies. In his article he cites the following benefits:

1. *Significant cost savings from standardized development and production of packages, advertising, and other promotional materials.*
2. *Economies of scale from more efficient utilization of production and distribution facilities—centralizing orders for more standardized products in fewer locations.*
3. *A consistent marketing approach and brand image, especially important in European markets where consumers frequently cross national borders.*
4. *Improved planning and control throughout company operations.*
5. *Better exploitation of good ideas, for new products, new distribution schemes, and new promotional approaches.*[8]

SSIH—need for multinational strategy

The factors can be illustrated by the problems facing Société Suisse pour l'Industrie Horlogère (SSIH), the Swiss holding company that manufactures and distributes Omega, Tissot, and some other watch

    [8] Robert D. Buzzell, "Can You Standardize Multinational Marketing?" *Harvard Business Review* 46 (November–December 1968): 102–113.

brands throughout the world, as they attempted to develop a marketing program for two new Omega electronic watches to be introduced to the public in 1974. The Omega brand was known throughout the world as a standard of watchmaking excellence. Two products, the Omega Megasonic 720 (a "tuning fork" watch) and the Omega Megaquartz 2400 (a quartz crystal watch), represented tremendous investments in product research and development.

Competition in the electronic watch industry was developing at a very fast rate, and the new Omega products needed rapid and wide-scale market acceptance if SSIH was to recover its investment in product development. The situation was complicated by the fact that distribution was achieved both through independent importing and sales agents in most markets (including several of the most important, such as Switzerland and the United States) and through sales sub-sidiaries in a few other large markets (such as the United Kingdom). Some degree of standardization in the marketing program was clearly called for by several considerations:

- The need to generate large sales volumes to recover major product development expenditure.
- The need for consistent and continued development of the Omega brand image for quality and technological leadership.
- The desire for consistency in the marketing and selling approach and the consumer benefits to be stressed.
- The possibility of obtaining economies in the development of display and promotional materials.
- The need for proper balancing of electronic and mechanical watches in the product mix to ensure efficient utilization of manufacturing capability (which had to be programed two to three years in advance).

One of the more important underlying problems in the SSIH situation was the need to develop retailer and consumer understanding of the new electronic watches. It was quite certain that the Megasonic 720 and Megaquartz 2400 watches would have a relatively short product life cycle and would be replaced by another generation of electronic watch technology in a few years as leaders in the Omega line. If consumer and retailer preference and acceptance were not developed now, the next generation of Omega watches could not be a profitable development. So failure by some national distribution organizations to aggressively market the new Omega Megasonic 720 and Megaquartz 2400, and to contribute to the development of the Omega brand image throughout the world, could have serious long-term consequences for SSIH. A carefully planned and implemented multinational marketing strategy was called for, but as an aid to local marketing, not as a substitute for it.

Clearly, the question of local autonomy versus multinational strategy is not an either/or question but one of finding the right

TABLE 14-1
Obstacles to standardization in international marketing

Factors Limiting Standardization	Elements of	
	Product Design	Pricing
Market characteristics		
Physical environment	Climate Product use conditions	
Stage of economic and industrial development	Income levels Labor costs in relation to capital costs	Income levels
Cultural factors	"Custom and tradition" Attitudes toward foreign goods	Attitudes toward bargaining
Industry conditions		
Stage of product life cycle in each market	Extent of product differentiation	Elasticity of demand
Competition	Quality levels	Local costs Prices of substitutes
Marketing institutions		
Distributive system	Availability of outlets	Prevailing margins
Advertising media and agencies		
Legal restrictions	Product standards	Tariffs & taxes
	Patent laws	Antitrust laws
	Tariffs & taxes	Resale price maintenance

balance in each company's unique marketing situation. At the moment there does seem to be a slight trend toward more rather than less standardization as companies try to exploit the opportunities for cost reduction and greater consistency that are present in multinational operations while trying to preserve local autonomy in large degree. At

Marketing Program		
Distribution	Sales Force	Advertising & Promotion; Branding & Packaging
Customer mobility	Dispersion of customers	Access to media Climate
Consumer shopping patterns	Wage levels, availability of manpower	Needs for convenience rather than economy Purchase quantities
Consumer shopping patterns	Attitudes toward selling	Language, literacy Symbolism
Availability of outlets Desirability of private brands	Need for missionary sales effort	Awareness, experience with products
Competitors' control of outlets	Competitors' sales forces	Competitive expenditures, messages
Number and variety of outlets available	Number, size, dispersion of outlets	Extent of self-service
Ability to "force" distribution	Effectiveness of advertising, need for substitutes	Media availability, costs, overlaps
Restrictions on product lines	General employment restrictions	Specific restrictions on messages, costs
Resale price maintenance	Specific restrictions on selling	Trademark laws

Source: Robert D. Buzzell, "Can You Standardize Multinational Marketing?" Harvard Business Review 46 (November–December 1968): 102–113, at 108–109. Reproduced with permission.

the same time, however, it remains true that most large multinational companies do not have a true multinational marketing strategy. Rather, they have developed planning and coordinating mechanisms for achieving some consistency and cost economies among a large number of national marketing strategies.

MULTINATIONAL MARKETING PLANNING

Installing such planning and coordinating mechanisms is far from easy. In fact, the marketing planning problem illustrates well the basic assertion made at the beginning of this chapter, that multinational marketing differs from domestic marketing in complexity but not in principle. The benefits of marketing planning and a general approach to planning were developed in Chapter 6, and need not be reiterated here. Instead we will look only at the factors complicating the multinational marketing planning process and then develop some guidelines that experienced managers have found useful in the task.

Sources of complexity

Multinational marketing planning is made difficult by a combination of economic, physical, psychological, and cultural considerations, which can be summarized briefly under several headings:

Market information availability
Market information, the essential basis of all marketing planning, is usually harder to obtain in foreign markets, partly because the marketer is less familiar with data sources and partly because, using the American market as a reference point, there is simply less information available. Syndicated market information sources are usually found only in the more developed countries. In addition, especially in industrial markets, there is the fact that companies in other countries, especially European firms, are reluctant to divulge information about sales volume and other aspects of their operations. Therefore, the possibilities of gathering market information through industrial trade associations and other cooperative ventures are limited.

Cost of market information
Market information that might be economically gathered by the parent company in its domestic operations may be prohibitively expensive for local subsidiaries because of their smaller scale of operations. At the same time, it is impossible for the parent company, perhaps thousands of miles away, to generate the necessary data because it must ultimately be collected from local sources.

Language
Even if the company has adopted a standard language (usually English, but sometimes French, German, or Spanish) for its multinational dealings, this language competence is likely to exist only at top levels of the local subsidiary managements. Thus, the information-gathering process becomes exceptionally difficult when the planner gets

down to the level of salesmen, dealers, and customers who are likely to be fluent only in the host country language.

Local autonomy
By now a familiar issue to you, local autonomy is desirable, and the planning process must enhance the strength and contribution of local management, not detract from it. Local management is more interested in participating in the planning process to the extent that they perceive it as helping them and enhancing their effectiveness.

Accounting system differences
Especially where the multinational company has grown through acquisition of local companies but also where it has established local operations, local accounting conventions and legal requirements can lead to a large degree of noncomparability among the internal records of subsidiary companies. This is a major source of complexity in the marketing planning and coordination process. Frequently the only solution is to keep multiple sets of books—perhaps one for local management, one for headquarters, and one for the government.

Physical distances
This dimension underlies many of the problems of communication that accompany attempts at multinational marketing planning, leading to high costs for travel and information collection, long delays in securing desired data, and distortion and noise in the communication process.

Differences in product life cycle
As the number of local subsidiaries and markets served increases, the range of product life cycle stages from introduction to decline reaches its maximum. There are important differences in the nature of competition, types of markets served, profit margins, sales volume, and the marketing problems facing management. Performance data, market share, types of customers, availability of information, and many other factors will differ significantly as a result, making data comparisons much more difficult.

Availability of marketing personnel
Outside the United States and to some extent the United Kingdom, trained marketing personnel—especially in such sophisticated areas as marketing planning and management science—are very hard to find. Here again size is a problem, since the smaller the local subsidiary, the less likely it is to have well-trained marketing personnel. The operation of an effective marketing planning system and implementation of the results of such a system both depend heavily on the availability of qualified marketing personnel.

Differences in market structure

Here is an obvious reason why it is hard to plan marketing operations at a multinational level. Some market segments that are critically important in certain national markets may be unimportant or completely nonexistent in others. For example, a Swedish manufacturer of electrical equipment whose major market throughout the world was in the railroad industry has found a profitable business in Venezuela despite the fact that there are very few railroads in Venezuela. This means that a marketing planning system for the company using commonly available data on the railroad market as the basis for forecasting and goal setting must be substantially revised in the case of the Venezuelan market and others like it. Differences in market structure include not only major variations in the importance of market segments but also differences in distribution structures, competition, and purchasing patterns.

Given these complicating factors (and others could also be named), the manager can easily reach the conclusion that meaningful marketing planning at the multinational level is virtually impossible. Multinational marketing planning is indeed a frustrating experience, but some system is absolutely necessary in order to avoid chaos in multinational operations.

The necessity of multinational marketing planning

Each multinational company is likely to find a somewhat different set of complicating factors and potential benefits in planning its activities, but some combination of the following factors is likely to make marketing planning a necessary and beneficial activity:

1. As in all planning systems, there are the benefits of securing coordinated action toward common objectives—a rationale developed in Chapter 6.
2. In multinational operations there is the added benefit of contributing to a feeling of identity and common purpose with the larger corporate structure and other subsidiary companies. There is no doubt that managers of subsidiary companies within a multinational corporate structure find support and security in a planning system.
3. A planning system can contribute to the sharing of marketing ideas among subsidiary companies—for example, ideas about new market segments, selling ideas, and advertising approaches. Among the most important ideas to be shared are those defining entirely new market opportunities, but before they can be shared they must be defined, evaluated, and communicated by a reporting and planning system. Such sharing is unlikely to occur spontaneously.
4. Centralized planning activity can aid in market information collection and analysis by suggesting what data are likely to be of greatest value and by providing plans for gathering such data and frameworks for analyzing it.

5. The process of planning has the important benefit of creating a shared consensus concerning the opportunities and problems facing the company and of approaches for solving problems and exploiting opportunities.

Going back to our earlier discussion of the benefits of standardized marketing strategy while at the same time preserving local autonomy, it is clear that local autonomy can be preserved only to the extent that it is informed and coordinated by a strong centralized planning system. The question is really not *whether* to plan multinational operations but *how* to plan them.

Guidelines for implementation of multinational marketing planning

The following comments are based primarily on conversations with marketing managers in a variety of multinational companies, mostly Europeans but also from North and South American and Australian companies, concerning the planning activities in their companies. Once again, a list of considerations is presented in the interest of efficiency:

1. Planning must be regarded as a line function, not a staff function. The planning department cannot do the planning; it can only design and manage a system that facilitates planning by operating executives.
2. Top management support for and involvement in the planning process must be apparent from the outset. Two of top management's most important functions are specifying corporate objectives to guide activities at all levels and supporting all requests for information made by line and staff executives. All requests for information should come through line management.

The major problems involved in the implementation of a multinational planning system are problems of communication. International marketing executives define these communication problems in the following terms:

3. All information requested from the local manager should, ideally, be valuable to him as well as to corporate management and planners. The local manager should be able to see his own self-interest in every planning request.
4. Whenever possible, information should be gathered by means of personal contact rather than through the mail.
5. The local manager should know how every piece of information collected will be used. Results of the planning process should be fed back to him, hopefully in a form that is more useful than the data he originally provided.
6. Information once requested should be insisted upon because it should not be requested unless it is absolutely necessary to the planning process

and because this will demonstrate to the local manager the importance of his role in the process.

It is important to specify the role of corporate management *vis-à-vis* local management in the planning process. Following the earlier guideline that planning is a line function not a staff function:

7. The primary objective of the planning system should be to encourage and support the best possible planning at the local level, informed by corporate objectives.
8. A key role for headquarters staff is to determine corporate organizational support for the planning function, including coordination of marketing plans with plans in other decision areas such as finance, production, and purchasing.
9. Headquarters must facilitate an exchange of ideas but avoid an overly aggressive role, which can foreclose a free exchange of ideas and opinions (especially about problem definitions and alternative courses of action), since this would impinge on the decision-making latitude of local management.

Ideally, it is possible to achieve some degree of centralization of information, as necessary for coordination without an undesirable degree of standardization, by "searching for mutually acceptable, harmonized decisions."[9] The planning process should be viewed as a mutual responsibility producing joint benefits for corporate headquarters and the local subsidiary. The key objective should be to develop a shared viewpoint, a consensus concerning objectives and short-term targets for market development, profitability, product line development, and various elements of marketing strategy such as promotion, distribution, and pricing. In this manner it is possible to secure coordination while preserving local autonomy, a valuable asset in the multinational company. Without a shared viewpoint, coordination and cooperation can be exceptionally difficult.

SUMMARY

As the firm extends its operations across national borders, it encounters marketing problems similar to those found in domestic markets and amenable to the same decision-making approaches. But multinational marketing is a more uncertain and more complicated undertaking because of two sets of factors: (1) the different market structures and buyer behavior patterns encountered in each country and (2) the economic and political complexities of the nation-to-

---

[9] R. J. Aylmer, "Who Makes Marketing Decisions in the Multinational Firm?" *Journal of Marketing* 34 (October 1970): 25–30.

nation interface. The uniqueness of the local operating environment and the communication inefficiencies introduced by physical distance and cultural differences mean that a strong local management with decision-making autonomy is necessary. Yet there is still need for a planning and coordinating mechanism to ensure that overall corporate objectives are met and that the multinational operation stays in control.

SOCIAL ASPECTS OF MARKETING DECISIONS

Two new dimensions are being added to the traditional concerns of marketing management. First, there is heightened awareness of the need to ensure that marketing decisions are consistent with the overall public welfare as well as with the best interests of the individual consumer. Second, there is growing recognition that knowledge and skills in marketing management are as necessary and helpful in the efficient and effective operation of nonprofit organizations as they are to business firms. Both of these trends emphasize "social" aspects of marketing—the concept of socially responsible marketing action and the concept of marketing as a social process not confined to the particular interests of business organizations. One result has been a reshaping of the so-called marketing concept as a business philosophy.

Many of the forces creating evolutionary change in the marketing concept can be summarized under the label "consumerism." *Consumerism* has been defined simply as "a social movement seeking to augment the rights and power of buyers in relation to sellers."[1] In addition to the traditional concerns of consumer movements throughout the twentieth century for protecting the consumer from unsafe and unhealthy products, deceptive business practices and other abuses, the new consumerism reflects some basic shifts in consumer attitudes toward products, consumption, and the environment. It is also distinct from earlier movements in the massive political and governmental response at local, state, and federal levels and the resulting structural changes, which are likely to be quite permanent. As a result of these attitudinal and structural changes, today's marketing decision maker faces a new, dynamic market environment within which the effectiveness of his decisions is determined.

THE AFFLUENT SOCIETY

Most of the various criticisms of marketing and business practice subsumed under the heading "consumerism" are, of course, limited pretty much to the "affluent" societies. Most people would accept a definition of affluence as occurring where the average consumer has discretionary income to spend beyond the necessities of food, shelter, clothing, health care, transportation, education, and modest recreation. Certainly, the countries of North America and Western Europe fit this definition, as do such highly developed nations as Australia and New Zealand. Most experts usually exclude Japan and the Soviet Union from the list of affluent nations, although Japan is fast approaching affluence.

The socialist countries of Eastern Europe call for somewhat more complicated judgments because centrally planned decisions about the mix of industrial and consumer goods result in a different pattern of consumer goods than one would expect to find in a capitalist country with the same gross national product (GNP). Also, the relationship between per capita GNP and per capita income differs between socialist and capitalist countries because of the relatively greater portion of state-provided goods and services in the former.

The forces of consumerism are closely correlated with degree of affluence and have been heard most loudly in North America and Western Europe. But if we include public concern for environmental quality under the consumerism umbrella, then it clearly includes Japan, Brazil, the Soviet Union, and other socialist countries where production processes have caused substantial environmental pollution and deterioration. Likewise, the resource-rich African nations, although developing

---

[1] Philip A. Kotler, "What Consumerism Means for Marketers," *Harvard Business Review* 50, no. 3 (May–June 1972): 48–57.

slowly and far from affluence, are not unconcerned about environmental questions. Nonetheless, environmental pollution is most serious in the developed nations because virtually all pollution comes from production and consumption.

THE ISSUES OF CONSUMERISM

In the affluent countries, there are twelve more or less distinctive major themes that summarize the bulk of consumerist complaints about the way business serves the consumer's interest. These are as follows:

1. The consumer's decision process has become exceedingly difficult owing to increased product complexity and numbers of products, and marketer-provided information has become increasingly inadequate.
2. Deterioration of environmental quality has been hastened by marketing practices that encourage unnecessary and undesirable consumption and by excessive packaging and outdoor advertising.
3. Many marketing practices are deceptive and misleading, especially for disadvantaged consumers (the poor, the uneducated, the elderly, the very young).
4. Business, and especially marketing, practices are responsible for the materialistic values of society, values that are inadequate for individual or national purposes.
5. Advertiser "control" of the mass media (in varying degrees of directness) is responsible for poor media quality, especially by catering to the lowest common denominator of public taste, and results in exploitation of some consumers—especially children.
6. Major firms in many industries overspend for promotional activities, increasing prices paid by consumers.
7. Retailing institutions are often incapable of providing necessary installation and postsale services, and consumers seldom have effective recourse to the manufacturer.
8. Overemphasis on private goods and services has caused inadequacies in public goods and services.
9. Marketing communications often cause people to buy things they do not need.
10. Product quality is often inadequate, especially with respect to safety, durability, and ease of repair.
11. Proliferation of goods and services, often based on trivial differences, is unnecessarily wasteful of scarce natural resources.
12. Poverty is an embarrassment to the affluent society.

Not all of these charges are heard with equal seriousness in all affluent countries, but they are usually heard to some degree. Some point to marketing practices (packaging, product development, and advertising), whereas others represent more basic structural problems in industrial societies (market concentration, materialistic values, and resource depletion). By and large, however, the consumerists are not antibusiness but probusiness responsibility. They are more likely to ask for improved management and system performance than for change in the system itself.

CAUSATIVE FORCES

Four sets of factors, somewhat interacting, can be defined as the principal forces behind the development of the new consumerism of the 1960s and 1970s. These are (1) increasing consumer education and income, (2) product proliferation and complexity, (3) increased public awareness of the problems of environmental deterioration, and (4) changing social values relating to consumption and the quality of life.

Consumer education and income

At the heart of consumerism is a better-educated and more affluent consumer. Education is closely related to occupation, and together they have a major influence on income. The better-educated consumer is first of all likely to have higher expectations concerning the performance of the business system and its impact on him personally. Second, he is more likely to be aware of the social issues relating to the conduct of business affairs, issues such as environmental quality, market concentration, and deceptive business practices. Finally, the educated consumer is much more aware of the courses of action available to him, privately and publicly, for seeking redress for his grievances against specific businesses and the business system at large. A college graduate is much more likely to put pen to paper and write to a company president; he is more comfortable expressing himself in writing and in public.

Consumer incomes have been increasing at a healthy if not spectacular rate in most of the developed nations, permitting a rather steady increase in the quantity of goods and services consumed. In the United States, the total value of goods and services (in constant dollars) more than doubled (104 percent) in the 1950–1970 period, representing not only larger quantities of goods and services but a much larger variety as well. Since the American population increased only 35 percent during this period, the net result was an increase of somewhat over 50 percent in per capita consumption of goods and services.

Even at that, however, economic performance may not have lived up to expectations for a sizable portion of the population, both those who remain below the poverty level and those who are economically well off but are frustrated by inability to achieve the ever-higher standard of living to which they, rightly or wrongly, aspire.

A recent report by the Council on Trends and Perspective of the Chamber of Commerce of the United States offered this thought-provoking comment:

... *Despite material progress, the great majority of Americans suffer from insecurity and frustration based on an illusion of affluence spread by educational institutions and the mass communications media, especially television.*

The fact is that only 54 percent of American families can afford what is now perceived, by today's criteria, as a "low, moderate" life standard. . . . So, paradoxically, personal insecurity grows as we become affluent. The source of insecurity is the widening gap between the "taught norm" of emerging life styles and the economically supportable level of living. Our aspirations have outpaced our means of satisfying them.[2]

But the better-educated consumer is not likely to accept his frustrations and adjust to them, especially when they can be directed at specific problems that he encounters in the marketplace, not only at the moment of sale but over the period during which he expects the product to yield up a stream of benefits. He is more likely to speak out. Howard Harder, chairman of the board of CPC International, has put it this way:

Consumerism is not, as some would like to think, a novel form of recreation for an affluent and spoiled society which, bored with guilt over its prosperity and good fortune, now petulantly turns on its benefactors. . . . We are dealing with a new consumer who is no longer merely the family purchasing agent, but a whole person, with a whole new concept of value in the marketplace.[3]

Product proliferation and complexity

To respond to an increasingly affluent consumer, industry has turned out an ever-expanding stream of new and more sophisticated products. Almost two-thirds of all American households own their own homes, in which it is more than likely that they also have wall-to-wall carpeting, fine furniture, an automatic washing machine, a clothes dryer, a color television set and a black-and-white one as well, a refrigerator, a kitchen range, a variety of radios, a tape recorder, and a phonograph, as well as several small electric appliances—can opener, toothbrush, food blender, carving knife, toaster, clocks, and hair dryer. In the

[2] Chamber of Commerce of the U.S., Council on Trends and Perspective, *Business and the Consumer—A Program for the Seventies* (unpublished report, undated), p. 24.

[3] Howard C. Harder, *The Consumer Movement: A New Dimension in International Marketing*, an address before the 8th International Congress on Food Distribution of the Association Internationale de la Distribution des Produits Alimentaires, Vienna, Austria (June 8, 1972), p. 2.

garage, there are more likely to be two cars than one, one of which is two years old or less and probably has air conditioning. Many of these products represent quite new and sophisticated technology and engineering, and many of them are exceptionally complex, such as color television and the newer automobiles with the difficult combination of high compression, high horsepower, and low emissions of combustion by-products.

It is estimated, roughly, that the average supermarket in the United States stocks about 8000 items, an increase of over 30 percent in the decade of the 1960s. Although retailing in the rest of the world is generally on a smaller scale, the Western European consumer faces a shopping situation that approaches the American in complexity of available choices. Many modern packages, usually designed to meet government requirements to provide information on volume of contents, unit pricing, and ingredients, read like a chemist's laboratory manual. Food items are supposedly made more attractive to the consumer by the addition of preservatives, coloratives, flavor enhancers, vitamins, and other artificial and natural ingredients. Emphasis on taste and convenience must at times lead to compromises with nutritional values. In the worst cases, subsequent medical evidence reveals unexpected consequences from the ingestion of the results of sophisticated food chemistry—cancer, high blood pressure, and dietary deficiency. It is not easy to be a consumer under these conditions.

The eloquent E. B. Weiss has described the consumer's predicament:

Technology has brought unparalleled abundance and opportunity to the consumer. It has also exposed him to new complexities and hazards. It has made his choices more difficult. He cannot be chemist, mechanic, electrician, nutritionist and a walking computer (very necessary when shopping for fractionated-ounce food packages). Faced with an almost infinite product differentiation (plus contrived product virtues that are purely semantic), considerable price differentiation, the added complexities of trading stamps, the subleties of cents-off deals, and other complications, the shopper is expected to choose wisely under circumstances that baffle professional shoppers.[4]

The paradox of consumerism is that the loudest criticisms of marketing seem to be caused by the success of business in serving the consumer, in catering to his every whim and fancy. Products are proliferated and technology is advanced first and foremost to serve the consumer's needs. As Chapter 1 spelled out, that is what the marketing concept is all about—bending supply to the will of demand. The result has been to deliver to the average consumer in many of the developed countries the highest standard of living ever seen on the

---

[4] E. B. Weiss, "Marketers Fiddle While Consumers Burn," *Harvard Business Review* 46, no. 4 (July–August 1968): 49.

face of the earth. And many consumers seem to be unhappy about it—at least, about some aspects of it.

Peter Drucker, one of the "fathers" of the marketing concept as a business philosophy, has called consumerism "the shame of the marketing concept" and has said that consumerism is evidence that business never really adopted the marketing concept and never really became consumer-oriented.[5] He is wrong; consumerism is rather good evidence of the success of the marketing concept and reveals a basic weakness in the concept itself, which we will discuss in a moment.

Philip Kotler has correctly noted that affluence creates its own discontent:

The very achievement of the affluent society ironically brings about, eventually if not immediately, a relative decline of interest in privately produced goods and services. Though people still respond to fashion changes, new product features, and highly touted promotions and product claims, they are increasingly preoccupied with concerns other than goods and wealth acquisition.[6]

Thus, the very materialistic success of American civilization may defuse its interest in further material acquisition.[7]

Consumerism is the public asking both for refinement in marketing practice—to make it more informative, more responsive, and more efficient—and for a new concern with factors other than privately consumed goods and services that determine the quality of life. Often the concern for quality of life translates itself into demand for more public goods and services such as better highways, crime-free cities, more education, better airports, and so on, and for improved environmental quality.

Environmental deterioration

Although environmental pollution is not new,[8] there is a new level of public awareness and concern about environmental quality. Greater awareness has been stimulated by various action groups in communities and regions most seriously affected by pollution; by the efforts of state, national, and international conservation groups such as Friends of the Earth, the Sierra Club, and the Audubon Society; and by pub-

---

[5] Peter Drucker, "The Shame of Marketing," *Marketing/Communications* (August 1969): 60.

[6] Philip A. Kotler, *Marketing Management: Analysis, Planning and Control,* 2d ed. (Englewood Cliffs, N.J.: Prentice-Hall, 1972), p. 10.

[7] Ibid., p. 805.

[8] In the mid-1860s, for example, royal commissions were gathering evidence and searching for solutions to serious problems of air and water pollution created by British chemical producers. Especially serious were gas emission and alkali pollution of rivers. See L. F. Haber, *The Chemical Industry During the Nineteenth Century* (Oxford: Clarendon, 1958), pp. 204–210.

licity about these efforts. Legislative and political figures in local and administrative posts have responded to the resulting pressure, as has the business community.

The rich pollute the earth; pollution is a particularly serious problem for the affluent society. This fact calls into question the commonly held viewpoint that economic growth is the key to improvement of the human condition. Public awareness of these issues has been stimulated by the publication of the first results of the Club of Rome's study of "the predicament of mankind"[9] and other treatises relating to economic growth, population growth, resource depletion, and pollution, and a general decline in the quality of life.[10] One result of these publications and the public understanding that has developed partly as a result is the creation of a kind of "negative feedback loop" that begins to correct the basic problematic trends. For example, the birth rate in the United States declined below the "replacement rate" in late 1972, at least partly owing to developing awareness of the problems of population growth. It is an encouraging sign that individuals can develop a sense of personal responsibility for problems facing society at large. The congressional defeat of the supersonic transport (SST) program, the result of a rather massive organization of public opinion by conservation groups, suggests an abandonment of unanimous belief in the so-called "technological imperative" that "whatever can be will be."

Evolving social values

Evolving social values are the least distinctive of the four sets of factors that have contributed to consumerism, for they probably result to large degree from the operation of the other three—increasing education and income, product proliferation, and consumer awareness of the problems of the environment. Social values are so deep and pervasive that they are hard to define and measure, except for major shifts over long periods of time, and the available evidence is not always terribly convincing. Measures of changing values among college students, for example, while showing some dramatic shifts, leave unanswered the questions of how permanent such changes will be. The sharp ideals of youth are known to lose their clarity in the workaday world of middle age. Children become more like their parents, not vice versa.

Nonetheless, there is enough evidence of evolving social values relating to products and consumption to support the argument. There is an evolving social consensus in the United States (bringing it closer

---

[9] Dennis H. Meadows et al., *The Limits to Growth* (New York: Universe Books, 1972).

[10] Among the most important works are E. J. Mishan, *Growth: The Price We Pay* (London: Staples, 1969), and Barry Commoner, *The Closing Circle: Nature, Man & Technology* (New York: Knopf, 1971).

to Europe, some would say) that "quality of life" involves more than GNP and the acquisition of material goods. But the phrase "quality of life" has never been satisfactorily defined except in the negative sense of "less emphasis on materialism," "less crime and urban blight," and so on. It is not really a rejection of the standard of living but a redefinition of what is "good" so as to emphasize more public goods and services and the amenities of life like privacy and quiet.

The roles played by various products in individual life styles change over time as a reflection of continuously evolving social norms and values. The way a European views his automobile is very different from the American, and Americans today view their cars very differently from the commonly held views of the 1920s. Today's American regards his automobile in much more utilitarian terms and takes it much more for granted. (The relative aggressiveness of European drivers reflects a much higher degree of ego involvement in the automobile.)

The social process involved seems to work as follows: As societies become more affluent, products become more accepted and taken for granted. The importance of product "image" and its relationship to individual self-concept becomes relatively less. The social-demonstration aspects of products become less important as the general level of material well-being increases. As product image becomes less important, the intrinsic and utilitarian values of the product become more important—durability, safety, economy, ease of repair, reliability, and so on. People seem to buy products more for themselves and less for others. Perhaps affluent consumers are simply more socially secure in their consumer role. The better-educated and better-informed consumer is more concerned with nutrition, safety, durability, and so on and less concerned about what other people think.

At the same time, the sophisticated consumer is likely to be more "socially responsible." He is likely to be more concerned about the effects of his individual consumption on the environment and on other people. In other words, the affluent society moves toward a "socioecological" view of products, in which products are viewed in terms of the entire stream of costs and benefits for all consumers, voluntary and involuntary, over the entire life cycle of the product from raw material to junk pile recycling. The socially responsible consumer is likely to demand a very different mix of goods and services than his less sophisticated predecessor.

MANAGEMENT RESPONSE TO CONSUMERISM

The "ideal"

Ideally, consumerism represents a wonderful opportunity for the forward-looking, aggressive firm. Consumerism challenges marketers to be more informative, more effective, and more responsible. It adds a new dimension, a social one, to the challenge to the marketer and the ideal against which he measures his own performance. It suggests new ways of competing for the consumer's preference—through better products (safer, more nutritious, less polluting, more durable and reliable, easier to repair, and so on), better services (better-trained dealer servicemen, regional customer service centers, and direct channels of communication to the company), better customer information (advertising, personal selling, packaging, and labeling), and the need to develop many entirely new products to conserve natural resources, permit recycling when possible, stop pollution, and serve the needs of the sophisticated, socially responsible consumer.

That some aspects of consumerism can be costly to marketers is undeniable—the need to provide more consumer information, to eliminate some products, to absorb more of the "social costs" (especially the costs of pollution) involved in the production, consumption, and disposal of many products. But each of these "costs" also involves a profit opportunity for those smart enough to see it. Some modest fortunes have already been made by owners of firms designing and manufacturing equipment to reduce pollution in various production processes, for example. The highly creative advertising done by Volvo in the United States ("Most cars are built to last a lifetime—theirs, not yours") and by Fiat in Europe ("The cities can no longer afford the automobile") has responded directly to the socially responsible consumer. The markets they are going after may not be "mass" markets, but they are large enough to permit very profitable segmentation strategies, and they are growing. Whirlpool's inauguration of the now-famous "Cool Line"—direct, toll-free telephone service to the company for customer product and service complaints—has given its promotional program an important point of difference. A variety of new products such as radial tires (new to the United States but not Europe), lead-free gasolines, recycled paper products, trash collection service that promises recycling, and the Wankel engine are responsive to the new consumer values.

Actual response

Unfortunately, such positive business responses to the new marketing environment have been the exception rather than the rule and piecemeal rather than part of a planned program of response. The typical firm seems to regard consumerism as something that does not concern it. One common argument, "We have always been consumer-oriented," is based on the mistaken assumption that nothing has changed. Consumerism is too often viewed as a threat to specific businesses and to the free-enterprise system, as something to be fought rather than responded to positively. The research on which these conclusions are based was conducted in the summer of 1972,[11] and hopefully the business community will continually move toward the positive response of which it is capable.

Only 31.5 percent of the industrial-products firms responding to the survey saw consumerism as something that influences them. The others failed to realize that the consumer-goods markets, which all industrial firms ultimately serve, to a varying degree to be sure, will inevitably translate the consumerism pressures they feel into demands on their industrial suppliers. As one of the "enlightened ones" noted: "We recognize that even though the vast majority of our products are sold to other manufacturers, these companies in turn sell their products (with our components) to the consumer." Of all firms (both industrial and consumer goods) responding, the kinds of positive actions reported were as follows (with many companies reporting multiple positive responses):

	Percentage of all Survey Respondents (n = 157)
Improved customer service	19.2%
Created new "consumer affairs" position	18.6
Modified products	14.7
More careful review of advertising claims	12.2
More informative packaging and labeling	7.1
Corporate advertising to tell "our side of the story"	5.1
Made packaging recyclable or easier to use	3.2
Incorporated ecological appeals into advertising	3.2
Joined consumer organizations	3.2

Improved customer service goes to the heart of some of the most serious issues of consumerism concerning product reliability, durability and quality, dealer service, and the alleged "impersonality" of business. It helps companies do something they have wanted to do all along— live up to the product claims made in their advertising and to the expectations created. Creating a customer affairs position in the organization is an important move if it is accompanied by the development of a complete program for improving organizational response to consumerism in a planned and integrated fashion. Otherwise, it is a shortsighted public-relations ploy to intercept customer complaints before they reach important company officials who might be in a position to do something. The "flak catcher" creates only a transparent illusion of responsiveness.

It is discouraging that the advertising response has been one of defensiveness and caution. Instead of trying to make advertising more informative and helpful to the consumer, the typical company has

[11] Frederick E. Webster, Jr., "Does Business Misunderstand Consumerism?," *Harvard Business Review* 51 (September–October 1973): 89–97.

responded by being more cautious in the claims made for its products. This reaction suggests that U.S. Federal Trade Commission decisions and policies relating to claim substantiation and "corrective" advertising for ads judged to be deceptive may have had the undesirable effect of driving advertisers into a defensive corner where advertising can no longer perform its role of informing the consumer.

The companies who reported corporate advertising responses likewise typically adopted a defensive posture, in this case one of "telling our side of the story." The motives often seemed to be deeply imbedded in a paranoid view of the world, directing company advertising "against those who want to destroy the credibility of business with its customers and threaten the free-enterprise system."

Such limited vision is not likely to be capable of identifying new profit opportunities in a changing market environment.

A positive approach

It is not possible to suggest a step-by-step approach for responding to consumerism in all company and market situations, but some general guidelines for positive response can be defined. First, the overriding objective guiding all company action should be to create a satisfied customer in a manner consistent with the public welfare. As we shall see, a new marketing concept is developing that recognizes the importance of adding a societal dimension to the definition of customer satisfaction. Second, it must be recognized that there are two dimensions to customer satisfaction—an informed customer and a product that works. Third, programs for auditing company performance in the product area and for improving it should recognize all five interacting ways of ensuring a product that works:

1. anticipating customer mistakes (through customer-market research, if necessary) and designing them out of the product
2. developing the highest practicable standards of production quality control
3. informing the consumer about proper product use and care
4. establishing warranty and guarantee programs that are clear, fast, complete, and honest
5. maintaining a completely effective service program, including quality control provisions and backstopping the dealer organization with company-provided service where necessary

Fourth, it should be recognized that an informed customer, the other part of the customer satisfaction equation, requires both accurate and complete information and a set of realistic expectations about product performances. This has three rather obvious implications: Advertising should be informative and truthful in all respects, even for those most likely to be misled; communications should not "overpromise"; and customers should be educated with respect to the responsibility for, and proper methods of, product use and care. To see this concept in action, look at the customer service information—and strict requirements—for Mercedes-Benz automobiles.

Fifth, corporate advertising should not be overemphasized. Consumers are more concerned about products and their performance than about companies as such. Companies become more important to the consumer when products and dealers fail to perform as expected. Corporate advertising and attempts to improve company image are ineffective ways of dealing with basic problems of product quality, service, and customer information.

Sixth and last, effective response requires an integrated, planned program for making the entire business responsive to the changing consumer. Top-management direction and involvement are essential and can be aided by a high-level consumer affairs position.

A REVISED MARKETING CONCEPT

From this discussion of the issues of consumerism, the changing consumer, and the dimensions of effective company response to a changed marketing environment, the need for a revised concept of marketing becomes clear. The new consumer in the affluent society is increasingly desirous of a new dimension of social responsibility in his consumption activities, and this calls for a new kind of "socially responsible" marketing.

What social responsibility is not

Many words have been wasted in debates about social responsibility. More often than not, when two experts (usually economists) argue about whether business should be more socially responsible, they are using fundamentally different definitions of the term *social responsibility*. Very briefly, the major questions about the social responsibility of business might be summarized as follows:

Is the only responsibility of business to make a profit?
Those who answer yes argue that the only people with a legitimate claim on the business are the owners. The argument of the "invisible hand" of the (perfect) market mechanism ensuring the maximum public welfare is always used. This view seems to overlook the fact that most businesses of major consequence are corporations and that corporations are social creations. Furthermore, it makes the questionable assumption that the owners are only interested in profits and would not agree to the use of their share of the firm's resources for socially desirable purposes.

Does social responsibility conflict with profitability?
The "profits should be the sole concern" school assumes that there is
such a conflict. A slight softening of the argument occurs when it is
observed that sometimes social responsibility can be a substitute for
more government regulation, which has the potential to reduce profitability. The purists in the profit school note correctly, however, that
to be consistent it is necessary to admit a legitimate role for government in defining the rules of the profit-seeking game, thus relieving
the executive of the burden of defining socially responsible action.

What are the characteristics of the socially responsible firm?
Here is where the greatest misconceptions exist. The common definition
of social responsibility by the corporation involves the use of business
resources (facilities, money, and personnel) for nonbusiness and non-
profit-seeking purposes. Included in the typical list of socially responsible acts would be

* grants to educational institutions
* allowing employees to participate in political campaigns and civic responsibilities, sometimes on company time
* donating money or the use of facilities to support community projects
  such as recreation, cultural, and educational programs
* participating in government-sponsored programs for hiring and training
  minority group members
* donating products to worthy causes

Of course, each of these actions could be justified partly, but not
exclusively, in terms of long-run profitability as it is enhanced by a
better labor supply, better relationships with the host community, better
government relationships, and so on.

In my opinion, social responsibility is not simply the distribution
of the company's resources and wealth for socially desirable ends. It
is not generosity and gifts. Rather, it is using the power and resources
of the corporation to achieve socially desirable results, using the corporation as an entity, as part of its daily efforts, in a socially responsible
fashion. Profit is a measure of how well the corporation serves the
society from which it ultimately draws all its resources. And, as
society evolves the consensus definition of the common welfare and
the common good, the corporation should be rewarded with profits
for different accomplishments.

Under the old marketing concept, profits were the reward for
creating a satisfied customer. Marketing was responsible for organizing
all of the firm's resources toward that objective. But the emphasis
was on the satisfaction of the individual customer, and that is the
major weakness of the marketing concept. Until recently, the major
responsibility of the modern corporation has been viewed by most as
providing a stream of products and services valued by society to

create an ever-higher standard of living. As we argued in Chapter 1, that was the social rationale for the marketing concept as a management philosophy. Of course, that is a marketing man's viewpoint. Those who identify with the financial function of the business would argue that the major objective must be to maximize the return on shareholders' wealth, but the marketing man would reject that as confusing means with ends. From a social standpoint, business exists ultimately to serve the interests of the public as consumers, not as investors, and the former almost always outnumber the latter.

The new consumerism, with its questioning of product proliferation and the decline in environmental quality, emphasizes an important fact: Satisfaction of individual customer desires does not necessarily create a truly satisfied consumer.

Within each of us there exists a conflict between satisfaction here and now and satisfaction over the longer run. Each cigarette can deliver enormous temporary satisfaction but only at the cost of chronic cough and eventual ill-health. It is easier at the moment to simply toss the beer can out of the car window, but eventually we tire of looking at the blighted highways and the ever-mounting pile of junk at the town dump. We enjoy the performance of the high-compression engine using high-octane gasoline and then complain loudly about air pollution. Unfortunately, there are many areas in which consumers behave one way out of desire for convenience and immediate satisfaction and talk another way when expressing themselves in public and taking the longer-term view.

The optimistic fallacy

The old marketing concept contained an optimistic fallacy in the assumption that the individual consumer's need satisfaction was always consistent with the long-term public welfare. Increased concern for the environment and an evolving definition of "the good life" have brought that fallacy to our attention and made us realize that the two are often inconsistent. The socioecological product concept stresses the unintended public consequences (before, during, and after) of private consumption. A new marketing concept must factor the needs, desires, and general welfare of the public at large into the equation and be concerned with the satisfaction of consumers in the aggregate as well as the individual consumer.

The new marketing concept

Tentatively, because this area is so dynamic, the following definition of the revised marketing concept can be proposed: The purpose of the business is to earn a profit by creating satisfied consumers with an offering of products and services consistent with the public welfare. This is simply a restatement of the old marketing concept with the very important addition of recognition of management responsibility for defining and responding to the best possible concept of the public welfare.

The new marketing concept recognizes the public's stake in the private relationship between a customer and the company. It also recognizes the marketing manager's legitimate responsibility not only for responding to the needs and wants that the customer brings to the firm but also for helping to shape and refine those needs to make them more consistent with the general welfare and the consumer's own long-term welfare. Thus, a moral dimension is added explicitly to the marketing manager's responsibilities, one of judging what is in the best interests of the individual consumer and of the public at large. A truly professional manager should be willing to accept that responsibility. For most, the alternative of having government define what is in the consumer's best interest is even less attractive. As least in the free-enterprise system, the consumer still has relatively free choice in the marketplace and can decide which management definition of his self-interest he wishes to accept. One of the awesome responsibilities of economic decision makers in the communist countries is to decide on such questions where the range of discretion for the individual citizen is much smaller and the consequences for the decision maker of being wrong are much more serious.

It is important to note that a revised marketing concept may challenge the basic strategic notion of segmentation. In an important sense, segmentation strategies have pitted the interests of some consumers against others. If a sufficiently large segment could be found to make a product profitable, that product would be offered regardless of the consequences for the rest of the population. A good example of this is the snowmobile, a product that has found a very large and growing market, whose owners are generally ecstatic over the thrills obtained from product use, and the consequences of which influence negatively—with noise and damage—an even larger number of people.

On the other hand, the socially responsible consumer, as defined earlier, probably still represents a relatively small segment of most markets and must be approached selectively, so segmentation may become even more important in the future. In general, the socially responsible consumer has been found to be more cosmopolitan, less dogmatic, less conservative, less status-conscious, and less personally competent than the less socially concerned consumer. These social-psychological variables are more sensitive discriminators than the easier-to-measure demographic variables, which means that attempts to segment markets on this basis are likely to be very difficult indeed.[12]

---

[12] W. T. Anderson, Jr., and W. H. Cunningham, "The Socially Conscious Consumer," *Journal of Marketing* 36, no. 3 (July 1972): 23–31.

Under the revised marketing concept, the purpose of the business is to provide a stream of socially desirable as well as individually desired products and services. That should not be particularly surprising; after all, how else can business make its contribution to the definition of the quality of life, if that is our ultimate objective? As was shown in Chapter 1, the purpose of every business is to transform resources obtained from the environment into goods and services valued by people. All that has changed is to add a new dimension of accountability to the individual citizen, not just to the person who buys the product.

This new view of marketing also suggests a new view of corporate social responsibility, not as the redistribution of profits earned in the marketplace after the shareholders are satisfied but as a responsibility for generating true social value in the marketplace. In the last analysis, that is what consumerism is all about—a strengthening of the role of business in a free-enterprise society. This is a more "wholistic" view of business purpose than one that defines customer satisfaction, shareholder interest, and social responsibility in very distinct terms.

NONBUSINESS MARKETING

The revised marketing concept is quite consistent with the increased emphasis on marketing in nonbusiness organizations because of its broadened definition of marketing managment responsibilities. In fact, one of the forces leading to a broadened definition of the marketing concept is the increased importance of marketing in nonprofit organizations, which for the sake of brevity we can refer to as NPOs. Marketing in NPOs has also been described as "social marketing," but this term is easy to confuse with the notion of socially responsible marketing, which has also been labeled societal marketing.

Marketing in NPOs is distinctive from business marketing only in that profit seeking is not the motivation. But this is a very tenuous distinction indeed. Many NPOs actually do occasionally earn a "surplus" in a given year, when revenues exceed budget forecasts or when costs are lower relative to revenues than expected, but this is never called profit. Like a business, every NPO is organized to offer some product or service to some "market," although the latter may be called a clientele or a public or an audience. One of the challenges of management in fund-raising organizations is to define the product that is offered to donors in return for their donations.

In NPO marketing, the purpose of the organization can still be viewed as to create a satisfied customer by offering goods and services consistent with the public interest. In common with business marketing, NPO marketing has four characteristics—the characteristics of all marketing that distinguish it from other areas of human activity:

An organization Marketing is not an individual undertaking, although it may be undertaken on behalf of an individual such as a political candidate, an inventor, or a celebrity. Rather, it is a management competence, and management by definition involves organizations and "getting things done through people." Some would say that business firms provide the model for other forms of organization in the modern world because the corporation in particular has demonstrated the highest degree of effectiveness and flexibility in dealing with complex social problems. Of course, there may be exceptions to the definition of marketing as necessarily involving an organization—as in the case of the individual craftsman selling his wares—but virtually all marketing involves a formal organization of some kind. (In fact, the craftsman may become a corporation for tax purposes, complete with accountant, lawyer, and board of directors!)

Economic resources Marketing is essentially concerned with allocating scarce economic resources most efficiently and effectively in pursuit of organizational objectives. In NPO marketing, choices must be made about products and services to be offered, prices to be charged, channels of distribution to be used, promotional and communications media to be used, and so on. In NPO marketing, the budget constraint normally replaces the profit target as the focus of management attention, but the effects in decision making tend to be similar. In both business and NPO marketing, segmentation strategies are the key to efficient utilization of scarce productive and promotional resources.

A professional approach Although it was not always so, marketing is today a profession that requires specialized training and practice. It has professional associations in many countries (most of them modeled after the American Marketing Association). These associations often have a code of ethics to which members must subscribe as a condition of membership. Certification to practice marketing may exist in several forms, although not as tightly enforced as in other professions such as medicine, accounting, and law. Candidates for marketing jobs usually must present some evidence that they are entitled to call themselves experts in this specialized field. Marketing decision making increasingly requires a kind of professional knowledge based on theoretical concepts in the social sciences and the analysis of data carefully gathered according to well-defined standards of quality.

A minimum requirement for calling an activity marketing would seem to be that the practitioner is aware that such a body of knowledge and competence exists and attempts to make use of it in his decision making. Just as few parents scrubbing a child's injured knee would claim to be practicing medicine, so many of the people who occasionally sell something cannot be said to be engaged in marketing.

A *market*   Of course, marketing requires a market, which should be defined as an aggregate of individuals rather than a single individual. NPO may differ from business marketing, however, in that the "market" in which it is operating may not have a price-setting mechanism in the same sense as the economist's market. In NPO marketing, a market consists of a collection of individuals from which the organization must elicit a response (awareness of a problem, changing attitudes, new practices, purchase of services, and so on) in order to achieve its organizational purpose.

SUMMARY

Modern marketing management represents an exciting professional challenge, as the definition of marketing effectiveness and marketing responsibility changes and as marketing competence becomes more important to nonbusiness organizations. The forces labeled "consumerism" are a healthy set of demands for a more effective response by business to a changing definition of the common good and the public welfare. Increased marketing effectiveness in nonprofit organizations can help improve the quality of public goods and services and correct for imbalance in the mix between private consumption and publicly provided need satisfactions. In all of this there are some magnificent opportunities for increased managerial satisfaction, increased marketing professionalism, and increased business profitability, as well as enhanced performance by organizations in the public sector. Perhaps the major value of the revised marketing concept is that it destroys some artificial distinctions and apparent conflict between business social responsibility, shareholder interest, customer satisfaction, and the overall public welfare. Under the new marketing concept, profit is seen as the reward to the business for generating true economic and social value in the marketplace through the provision of a desired stream of products and services consistent with the public welfare.

SUGGESTED READINGS

Chapter 1: *Marketing Management and Corporate Strategy*

H. Igor Ansoff, "Toward a Strategic Theory of the Firm," in H. Igor Ansoff, ed., *Business Strategy* (Harmondsworth, Middlesex, England: Penguin Books, 1971), pp. 11–40.

K. R. Davis, *Marketing Management: Text and Cases*, 3d ed. (New York: Ronald, 1972).

Philip A. Kotler, *Marketing Management: Analysis, Planning, and Control*, rev. ed. (Englewood Cliffs, N.J.: Prentice-Hall, 1972).

Theodore Levitt, "Marketing Myopia," *Harvard Business Review* 38 (July–August 1960): 45–56.

Chapter 2: *Buyer Behavior*

P. D. Bennett and H. H. Kassarjian, *Consumer Behavior* (Englewood Cliffs, N.J.: Prentice-Hall, 1972).

Gordon T. Brand, *The Industrial Buying Decision* (London: Cassell/Associated Business Programmes, 1972).

D. F. Cox, ed., *Risk Taking and Information Handling in Consumer Behavior* (Boston: Harvard Business School, Division of Research, 1967).

J. F. Engel, D. T. Kollat, and R. D. Blackwell, *Consumer Behavior* (New York: Holt, Rinehart & Winston, 1968).

F. E. Webster, Jr., and Y. Wind, *Organizational Buying Behavior* (Englewood Cliffs, N.J.: Prentice-Hall, 1972), or "A General Model for Understanding Organizational Buying Behavior," *Journal of Marketing* 36 (April 1972): 12–19.

Chapter 3: *Market Segmentation Strategy*

N. L. Barnett, "Beyond Market Segmentation," *Harvard Business Review* 47 (January–February 1969): 152–166.

R. E. Frank, W. F. Massy, and Y. Wind, *Market Segmentation* (Englewood Cliffs, N.J.: Prentice-Hall, 1972).

D. Yankelovich, "New Criteria for Market Segmentation," *Harvard Business Review* 42 (March–April 1964): 83–90.

Chapter 4: Marketing Research

S. Banks, *Experimentation in Marketing* (New York: McGraw-Hill, 1965).

H. W. Boyd, Jr., and R. Westfall, *Marketing Research: Text and Cases*, 3d ed. (Homewood, Ill.: Irwin, 1971).

P. E. Green and D. S. Tull, *Research for Marketing Decisions*, 2d ed. (Englewood Cliffs, N.J.: Prentice-Hall, 1970).

K. P. Uhl and B. Schoner, *Marketing Research: Information Systems and Decision Making* (New York: Wiley, 1969).

Chapter 5: Management Science and Information Systems in Marketing

R. D. Buzzell, D. F. Cox, and R. V. Brown, *Marketing Research and Information Systems: Text and Cases* (New York: McGraw-Hill, 1969).

D. F. Cox and R. E. Good, "How to Build a Marketing Information System," *Harvard Business Review* 45 (May–June 1967): 145–154.

D. B. Montgomery and G. L. Urban, *Management Science in Marketing* (Englewood Cliffs, N.J.: Prentice-Hall, 1969).

S. V. Smith, R. H. Brien, and J. E. Stafford, eds., *Readings in Marketing Information Systems* (Boston: Houghton Mifflin, 1968).

Chapter 6: Marketing Planning and Forecasting

B. Charles Ames, "Marketing Planning for Industrial Products," *Harvard Business Review* 46 (September–October 1968): 100–111.

J. C. Chambers, S. K. Mullick, and D. D. Smith, "How to Choose the Right Forecasting Technique," *Harvard Business Review* 49 (July–August 1971): 45–74.

T. C. Coram and R. W. Hill, eds., *New Ideas in Industrial Marketing* (London: Staples, 1970).

D. W. Ewing, ed., *Long-Range Planning for Management*, 3d ed. (New York: Harper & Row, 1972).

Chapter 7: Managing Creativity in Marketing

W. J. J. Gordon, *Synectics* (New York: Harper & Row, 1961).

J. W. Haefele, *Creativity and Innovation* (New York: Reinhold, 1962).

A. F. Osborn, *Applied Imagination*, 3d ed. (New York: Scribner, 1963).

G. A. Steiner, ed., *The Creative Organization* (Chicago: University of Chicago Press, 1965).

Chapter 8: Product Policy and New Products

Theodore Levitt, "Exploit the Product Life Cycle," *Harvard Business Review* 43 (November–December 1965): 81–94.

D. Luck and T. Nowak, "Product Management—Vision Unfulfilled," *Harvard Business Review* 43 (May–June 1965): 143–154.

E. Pessemier, *New Product Decisions: An Analytical Approach* (New York: McGraw-Hill, 1966).

E. M. Rogers and F. F. Shoemaker, *Communication of Innovations: A Cross-Cultural Approach* (New York: Free Press, 1971).

F. E. Webster, Jr., "New Product Adoption in Industrial Markets: A Framework for Analysis," *Journal of Marketing* 33 (July 1969): 35–39.

Chapter 9: Pricing Decisions

Gilbert Burck, "The Myths and Realities of Corporate Pricing," *Fortune* 85 (April 1972): 85–89, 125–126.

A. D. H. Kaplan, Joel B. Dirlam, and Robert F. Lanzilotti, *Pricing in Big Business* (Washington, D.C.: Brookings, 1958).

Robert A. Lynn, *Price Policies and Marketing Management* (Homewood, Ill.: Irwin, 1967).

Alfred N. Oxenfeldt, "Multi-Stage Approach to Pricing," *Harvard Business Review* 38 (July–August 1960): 125–133.

Chapter 10: Distributor and Physical-Distribution Management

L. P. Bucklin, ed., *Vertical Market Structures* (Glenview, Ill.: Scott, Foresman, 1970).

J. L. Heskett, R. M. Ivie, and N. A. Glaskowsky, Jr., *Business Logistics: Management of Physical Supply and Distribution* (New York: Ronald, 1964).

R. Little, "The Marketing Channel: Who Should Lead this Extra-Corporate Organization," *Journal of Marketing* 34 (January 1970): 31–38.

J. F. Magee, *Physical Distribution Systems* (New York: McGraw-Hill, 1967).

W. M. Stewart, "Physical Distribution: Key to Improved Volume and Profits," *Journal of Marketing* 29 (January 1965): 65–70.

Chapter 11: Marketing Communication Strategy

T. Levitt, "Communication and Industrial Selling," *Journal of Marketing* 31 (April 1967): 15–21.

K. S. Palda, "The Hypothesis of a Hierarchy of Effects: A Partial Evaluation," *Journal of Marketing Research* 3 (February 1966): 13–24.

M. L. Ray, "A Decision Sequence Analysis of Developments in Marketing Communication," *Journal of Marketing* 37 (January 1973): 29–38.

F. E. Webster, Jr., *Marketing Communication: Modern Promotional Strategy* (New York: Ronald, 1971).

Chapter 12: Developing Effective Advertising

L. Bogart, *Strategy in Advertising* (New York: Harcourt Brace Jovanovich, 1968).

D. Gensch, "Media Factors: A Review Article," *Journal of Marketing Research* 7 (May 1970): 216–225.

J. C. Maloney, "Is Advertising Believability Really Important?" *Journal of Marketing* 27 (October 1963): 1–8.

R. E. Quandt, "Estimating the Effectiveness of Advertising: Some Pitfalls in Econometric Methods," *Journal of Marketing Research* 1 (May 1964): 51–60.

I. S. White, "The Functions of Advertising in Our Culture," *Journal of Marketing* 24 (July 1959): 8–14.

Chapter 13: Sales Force Management

K. R. Davis and F. E. Webster, Jr., *Sales Force Management: Text and Cases* (New York: Ronald, 1968).

D. B. Montgomery and F. E. Webster, Jr., "Application of Operations Research to Personal Selling Strategy," *Journal of Marketing* 32 (January 1968): 50–57.

A. E. Pearson, "Sales Power Through Planned Careers," *Harvard Business Review* 44 (January–February 1966): 105–116.

F. E. Webster, Jr., "Interpersonal Communication and Salesman Effectiveness," *Journal of Marketing* 32 (July 1968): 7–13.

Chapter 14: Multinational Marketing

R. D. Buzzell, "Can You Standardize Multinational Marketing?" *Harvard Business Review* 46 (November–December 1968): 102–113.

J. Fayerweather, *International Marketing*, 2d ed. (Englewood Cliffs, N.J.: Prentice-Hall, 1972).

J. K. Sweeney, "A Small Company Enters the European Market," *Harvard Business Review* 48 (September–October 1970): 126–132.

H. B. Thorelli, ed., *International Marketing Strategy* (Harmondsworth, Middlesex, England: Penguin Books, 1973).

L. T. Wells, Jr., "A Product Life Cycle for International Trade," *Journal of Marketing* 32 (July 1968): 1–6.

Chapter 15: Social Aspects of Marketing Decisions

P. Kotler, "What Consumerism Means for Marketers," *Harvard Business Review* 50 (May–June 1972): 48–57.

P. Kotler and S. Levy, "Broadening the Concept of Marketing," *Journal of Marketing* 33 (January 1969): 10–15.

F. E. Webster, Jr., "Does Business Misunderstand Consumerism?," *Harvard Business Review* 51 (September–October 1973): 89–97.

F. E. Webster, Jr., *Social Aspects of Marketing* (Englewood Cliffs, N.J.: Prentice-Hall, 1974).

INDEX